IBM WebSphere Application Server v7.0 Security

Secure your WebSphere applications with Java EE and JAAS security standards

Omar Siliceo

[PACKT] enterprise 88
PUBLISHING   professional expertise distilled

BIRMINGHAM - MUMBAI

IBM WebSphere Application Server v7.0 Security

First published: February 2011

Production Reference: 1180211

Published by Packt Publishing Ltd.
32 Lincoln Road
Olton
Birmingham, B27 6PA, UK.

ISBN 978-1-849681-48-3

www.packtpub.com

Cover Image by David Guettirrez (bilbaorocker@yahoo.co.uk)

Credits

Author
Omar Siliceo

Reviewers
Domenico Cantatore
Ty Lim
Jose Mariano Ruiz Martin

Development Editor
Susmita Panda

Technical Editors
Neha Damle
Erika Fernandes
Gaurav Datar

Indexer
Monica Ajmera Mehta

Editorial Team Leader
Vinodhan Nair

Project Team Leader
Priya Mukherji

Project Coordinator
Sneha Harkut

Proofreaders
Aaron Nash
Steve Maguire

Graphics
Geetanjali Sawant

Production Coordinator
Alwin Roy

Cover Work
Alwin Roy

About the Author

Omar Siliceo, a professional Systems Engineer with a Master of Science degree in Electrical Engineering, started his IT career in the year 1991 as a Research Specialist, performing the roles of systems specialist, Internet and Unix systems administrator, and Internet systems consultant, when he was invited to join the Computer Center group at Vanderbilt University. In 1994, he joined the information technology team as a consultant, performing systems integration at the King Faisal Specialist Hospital and Research Centre in Saudi Arabia. After returning to the United States of America in 1997, he launched his IT consulting practice, creating partnerships with companies such as CTG and Ajilon. During the period from 1997-2004 he spent most of it (1997-2002) working with IBM in finding e-commerce solutions for customers such as Macy's, the NBA Store and Blair, and event Cybercast Infrastructure Administration for customers such as The Wimbledon Championships and The Masters Golf Tournament. It was during this period that he became exposed to early WebSphere technologies, including but not limited to WebSphere Application Server, WebSphere Commerce Suite, WebSphere Portal, and WebSphere Everyplace Suite.

In his last year with IBM, he focused on providing design, programming consultation, and problem solving to Fortune 500 software vendors and software integrators who were IBM's business partners. Between 2002 and 2004, he served as a consultant to The World Bank Group and Blue Cross Blue Shield of Florida. His role was the administration of WebSphere environments including some special projects such as the rollout of the latest version of their WebSphere environments. In 2004, he interrupted his consulting practice when he was invited to join the IT engineering team at Cummins, Inc. He served as Senior Web Technologies Engineer and later on as the Web Deployment team manager. As Senior Engineer, he architected the infrastructure environment for WebSphere 5.1, defining standards for platform creation, WAS deployment, and integration with existing enterprise technologies and services. In 2008, he resumed his consulting practice, supporting WebSphere Application Server, WebSphere Portal, and WebSphere Edge Components efforts and initiatives with Bank of America (2008), Blue Cross Blue Shield of Florida (2008 2009), and The World Bank Group, where he is currently Senior WebSphere Suite consultant.

First and foremost, I would like to thank the Lord for providing this unique, challenging, and rewarding opportunity as well as the resources to complete this fun project. Secondly, I would also like to thank my wife, Melissa, for her love, support, and encouragement throughout this undertaking. In addition, I wish to extend my gratitude to my sons, Tano and Chago, for allowing me to give up time that otherwise I would have spent with them.

Furthermore, I would like to express my appreciation to Packt for having reached out to me to propose this project. In particular, I thank my editorial team and their management for all the support provided in order to make this project a reality. I also would like to thank the technical team of experts who painstakingly reviewed each of the chapters for their corrections, observations, and most welcomed suggestions to improve the quality of this work.

Finally, I want to thank the folks at The World Bank Group, in particular Srini, Balaji, Suresh, and Ajay, for their encouragement during this project. I think they promised to buy a copy each.

About the Reviewers

Domenico Cantatore is a senior IT Specialist working for IBM Software Group in Dublin.

His areas of expertise include infrastructure architecture design, implementation, problem determination and performance, analysis, and tuning on WebSphere and Tivoli® products. These products include WebSphere Application Server, WebSphere Portal Server, WebSphere Process Server, WebSphere Commerce Server, WebSphere MQ, WebSphere Message Broker, and ITCAM. He has 10 years of experience in IT and various industry certifications.

Ty Lim has worked for various software startup companies, consulting firms, and was working in the Healthcare IT field for the last eight years. He now works in the telecommunications industry.

Ty Lim has been in the IT industry for more than 15 years. He started out using WebSphere Application Server back in 2003 and has been utilizing the technology ever since. He has a background in JAVA programming, Unix/Linux Systems administration and he keeps up to date with the latest open source technology. He holds a degree in Computer Science from the University of the Pacific, and is currently pursuing his Masters Degree in Information Systems at Boston University. He has interests in application server technology, open source technology, network security, and Java programming.

I would like to thank my parents (Lina and Roland) for giving me what I needed growing up so that I could achieve what I needed to accomplish thus far in my career. (A good home, a great education, and a drive to keep going.) I love you guys so much. 'Thank you' does not quite show the magnitude of what I owe you.

To Mike and Penny, both of you have shown me a lot over the last several years. Thank you so much for being my friends. Both of you have achieved what I have always sought. I hope this rolling stone can someday put up roots somewhere. Give a big hug to my god daughter Sophia for me. Tell her, her god father loves her very much.

To my sister Eileen and my brother-in-law Nguyen. Both of you have been an inspiration to me over the last several years. I wish both of you complete happiness.

To my colleagues in New York and New Jersey (BrianK, GeorgeT, TomB, DonN, JonL, JohnW, MikeR, GregM, MarkD, JohnH, VinceH), guys you're the best in the business. I can't be more prouder to call both a colleague and a friend. Keep up the great work.

To Jenny, thank you for being my friend all these years, I cherish our friendship very much.

To my friends and colleagues in CA and overseas, I hope to see all of you soon (or someday). All of you have been my inspiration for working my way back home.

To Geri, I just wanted you to know, that your happiness has always meant very much to me. I hope you find happiness wherever you go.

Jose Mariano Ruiz Martin is a Computing Science Engineer and senior specialist at Technologies of Information. He has worked at some of the most important Spanish companies including Telefónica Spain, Vodafone Spain, Caja Madrid, and Mapfre as systems engineer and technical leader.

After finishing his degree in Computing Science and completing a Master's in Computer Networking and Communications, he has specialized in systems engineering, obtaining several certifications such as Sun Certified Security Administrator, Sun Certified System Administrator for Solaris 9, BEA Certified WebLogic 9 Administrator, BEA Certified WebLogic 8.1 Administrator, and Cisco Certified Network Associate. Besides this he has been a professor at several courses on Information Systems Administration.

He is now working at IBM Spain on electronic commerce infrastructures and SOA/BPM technologies as IT specialist on the IBM's WebSphere platform.

I would like to dedicate this book to all those who do not resign themselves to be mere spectators in life, and work resolutely to achieve their own goals; with a special mention to my father, who is still the best example for both my brother and me, and has resisted all the difficulties he has had to face.

www.PacktPub.com

Support files, eBooks, discount offers and more

You might want to visit www.PacktPub.com for support files and downloads related to your book.

Did you know that Packt offers eBook versions of every book published, with PDF and ePub files available? You can upgrade to the eBook version at www.PacktPub.com and as a print book customer, you are entitled to a discount on the eBook copy. Get in touch with us at service@packtpub.com for more details.

At www.PacktPub.com, you can also read a collection of free technical articles, sign up for a range of free newsletters and receive exclusive discounts and offers on Packt books and eBooks.

PACKTLIB®

http://PacktLib.PacktPub.com

Do you need instant solutions to your IT questions? PacktLib is Packt's online digital book library. Here, you can access, read and search across Packt's entire library of books.

Why Subscribe?

- Fully searchable across every book published by Packt
- Copy & paste, print and bookmark content
- On demand and accessible via web browser

Free Access for Packt account holders

If you have an account with Packt at www.PacktPub.com, you can use this to access PacktLib today and view nine entirely free books. Simply use your login credentials for immediate access.

Instant Updates on New Packt Books

Get notified! Find out when new books are published by following @PacktEnterprise on Twitter, or the Packt Enterprise Facebook page.

Table of Contents

Preface

IBM WebSphere Application Server Network Deployment is IBM's flagship J2EE application server platform. It implements the J2EE technology stack. This stack enables the WebSphere Application Server platform to execute the user's Java enterprise applications that perform business functions. There are several roles who use this platform such as architects, developers, and administrators, to mention a few. Within the administrator role, in turn, there are several functions such as installation, performance, security, and so on.

This book starts with an in-depth analysis of the global and administrative security features of WebSphere Application Server v7.0, followed by comprehensive coverage of user registries for user authentication and authorization information. Moving on you will build on the concepts introduced and get hands-on with a mini project. In the next chapter, you work with the different front-end architectures of WAS along with the Secure Socket Layer protocol, which offer transport layer security through data encryption.

You can learn user authentication and data encryption, which demonstrate how a clear text channel can be made safer, by using SSL transport to encrypt its data. This book will show you how to enable an enterprise application hosted in a WebSphere Application Server environment to interact with other applications, resources, and services available in a corporate infrastructure. Platform hardening, tuning parameters for tightening security, and troubleshooting are some of the aspects of WebSphere Application Server v7.0 security that are explored in the book. Every chapter builds strong security foundations, by demonstrating concepts and practicing them through the use of dynamic, web-based mini projects.

What this book covers

Chapter 1, A Threefold View of WebSphere Application Server Security, uses a novel approach to compare ways in which WebSphere security elements are perceived, usually according to the role of the individual working with the technology. These ways or views help you understand the foundations of WebSphere security, providing multiple angles from where to analyze this set of technologies and communicate in their language with different functional teams within your organization.

Chapter 2, Securing the Administrative Interface, walks you through the necessary steps to secure access to the WebSphere graphical interface, known as the **ISC** (**Integrated Solutions Console**). As a prerequisite to securing the ISC, you must first enable the WebSphere Application Server platform security, known as global security. During these processes, the chapter succinctly describes relevant security topics (for example, user registries) and highlights what parameters are required in order to perform each step.

Chapter 3, Configuring User Authentication and Access, provides concise technical background on the security topics related to setting up user authentication (validation of presented user credentials) and user access — determining if an authenticated user has rights to access to the requests made. The chapter describes some important concepts such as WebSphere Security Domains (a new feature in version 7 of WAS), user registries (reviewed in more depth), as well as a review of popular user registries available to be used in a WebSphere environment. The chapter ends by binding all these concepts using a mini project that walks you through protecting application servers.

Chapter 4, Front-End Communication Security, describes and compares popular infrastructure architectures used to design front-end of a WebSphere environment. The chapter goes on explaining a major security used to secure communication channels, SSL, and describes several related aspects such as SSL certificates and CA (certificate authority). At the end, the chapter walks you through the process, in the way of a mini project, used to secure the front-end of a WebSphere environment from the HTTP server (IHS) to the actual Application Server.

Chapter 5, Securing Web Applications, briefly introduces concepts related to securing Java Web Applications (or more succinctly Web Applications). The chapter then uses an in-depth mini project where you will be walked through in the various stages to design, code, package, deploy, and configure a simple Web Application that offers access to employees of a fictional corporation. Each type of employee will have access only to sections of the Web Application. Therefore, you will configure WebSphere in order to implement this secure functionality.

Chapter 6, Securing Enterprise Java Beans Applications, introduces concepts related to **Enterprise Java Beans (EJB)** technologies such as declarative and programmatic security. The chapter then uses the mini-project approach to walk you through the stages needed to design, code, package, deploy, and configure a simple EJB application. The mini-project in this chapter reuses modules from the previous chapter to implement a very simple portal application that will offer a better user experience to the employees of our fictional corporation.

Chapter 7, Securing Back-end Communication, focuses on two major concepts: authentication and data encryption. Authentication is reviewed from the point of view of trust between two infrastructure components, for example, WebSphere and a back-end database. The chapter expands on the major topics by providing in detail two examples of their use. It explores how encryption is used in the communication between WebSphere and a popular type of user registry, LDAP. The chapter also examines the use of authentication during the exchanges between WebSphere and databases using the JDBC protocol.

Chapter 8, Secure Enterprise Infrastructure Architectures, describes areas that will enable an enterprise application hosted in a WebSphere environment interact with possibly other applications, resources, and services available in a corporation infrastructure. It covers central concepts such as LTPA and SSO. The chapter ends by showing you how to fine-tune authorization at the HTTP Server level as well as at the WebSphere level.

Chapter 9, WebSphere Default Installation Hardening, deals with engineering the default WebSphere installation by changing its default parameters in order to harden the product's security side and customizing the files that hold the WebSphere environment security certificates and signers. The chapter focuses on two major aspects. While it points out what characteristics in the OS to review and modify, on the other hand, it discusses securing files related to certificates — key and trust stores — and files that hold passwords.

Chapter 10, Platform Hardening, looks at aspects of the platform where WebSphere is hosted that can be modified to increase the environment security. The chapter breaks down the OS into areas relevant to the WebSphere platform: generic operating system characteristics (for example, user accounts), file system features (for example, file permissions), and network system configuration.

Chapter 11, Security Tuning and Troubleshooting, overviews three major areas that can be improved by tuning key parameters as well as a couple of troubleshooting areas. The tuning section overviews general security, CSIv2 connectivity, and user directories and user permissions. Finally, the troubleshooting section reviews general security configuration exceptions and run time security exceptions.

What you need for this book

The following is a list of software that you will need to download for this book:

- IBM WebSphere Application Server Network Deployment version 7.0 (this is the specific software for which the book is written)
- Software used to write example code and to package examples so they can be installed (deployed) into WebSphere
- IBM Application Server Toolkit for WebSphere Application Server version 6.1
- IBM Rational Application Developer Assembly and Deployment Features for WebSphere Software V7.5 for Multiplatforms
- Eclipse Java EE IDE for Web Developers version 3.5.2 (Open source available at www.eclipse.org)

Who this book is for

If you are a system administrator or an IT professional who wants to learn about the security side of the IBM WebSphere Application Server v7.0, this book will walk you through the key aspects of security and show you how to implement them. You do not need any previous experience in WebSphere Application Server, but some understanding of Java EE technologies will be helpful. In addition, Java EE application developers and architects who want to understand how the security of a WebSphere environment affects Java EE enterprise applications will find this book useful.

Conventions

In this book, you will find a number of styles of text that distinguish between different kinds of information. Here are some examples of these styles, and an explanation of their meaning.

Code words in text are shown as follows: "Start the wsadmin interface."

A block of code is set as follows:

```
LoadModule ibm_ssl_module modules/mod_ibm_ssl.so
Listen [Server_IP]:8444
<VirtualHost [Server_IP]:8444>
SSLEnable
SSLServerCert ihs1.wasmaster
```

```
SSLProtocolDisable SSLv2
</VirtualHost>
KeyFile /opt/IBM/HTTPServer/ihsserverkey.kdb
SSLDisable
```

When we wish to draw your attention to a particular part of a code block, the relevant lines or items are set in bold:

```
getParamAndForward(request, response);
```

Any command-line input or output is written as follows:

```
AdminTask.createSecurityDomain('-securityDomainName secappsvr01.
yourcompany.com -securityDomainDescription "Security domain for
SecureAppServer01" ')
```

New terms and **important words** are shown in bold. Words that you see on the screen, in menus or dialog boxes for example, appear in the text like this: "From the list of links located at the bottom, on the right-hand side of the window, click the **Open WebSphere Bindings** link"

Warnings or important notes appear in a box like this.

Tips and tricks appear like this.

Reader feedback

Feedback from our readers is always welcome. Let us know what you think about this book—what you liked or may have disliked. Reader feedback is important for us to develop titles that you really get the most out of.

To send us general feedback, simply send an e-mail to feedback@packtpub.com, and mention the book title via the subject of your message.

If there is a book that you need and would like to see us publish, please send us a note in the **SUGGEST A TITLE** form on www.packtpub.com or e-mail suggest@packtpub.com.

If there is a topic that you have expertise in and you are interested in either writing or contributing to a book, see our author guide on www.packtpub.com/authors.

Customer support

Now that you are the proud owner of a Packt book, we have a number of things to help you to get the most from your purchase.

> **Downloading the example code for this book**
>
> You can download the example code files for all Packt books you have purchased from your account at http://www.PacktPub.com. If you purchased this book elsewhere, you can visit http://www.PacktPub.com/support and register to have the files e-mailed directly to you.

Errata

Although we have taken every care to ensure the accuracy of our content, mistakes do happen. If you find a mistake in one of our books—maybe a mistake in the text or the code—we would be grateful if you would report this to us. By doing so, you can save other readers from frustration and help us improve subsequent versions of this book. If you find any errata, please report them by visiting http://www.packtpub.com/support, selecting your book, clicking on the errata submission form link, and entering the details of your errata. Once your errata are verified, your submission will be accepted and the errata will be uploaded on our website, or added to any list of existing errata, under the Errata section of that title. Any existing errata can be viewed by selecting your title from http://www.packtpub.com/support.

Piracy

Piracy of copyright material on the Internet is an ongoing problem across all media. At Packt, we take the protection of our copyright and licenses very seriously. If you come across any illegal copies of our works, in any form, on the Internet, please provide us with the location address or website name immediately so that we can pursue a remedy.

Please contact us at copyright@packtpub.com with a link to the suspected pirated material.

We appreciate your help in protecting our authors, and our ability to bring you valuable content.

Questions

You can contact us at questions@packtpub.com if you are having a problem with any aspect of the book, and we will do our best to address it.

1
A Threefold View of WebSphere Application Server Security

Imagine yourself at an athletic event. Hey! No, no-you are at the right place. Yes, this is a technical book. Just bear with me for a minute. Well, now that the little misunderstanding is out of the way let's go back to the beginning. The home crowd is really excited about the performance of its team. However, that superb performance has not been yet reflected on the scoreboard. When finally that performance pays off with the long-waited score, 'it' happens! The score gets called off. It is not at all unlikely that a controversial call would be made, or worse yet, not made! Or so we think. There is a group of players and fans of the team that just scored that 'see' the play as a masterpiece of athletic execution. Then there is another group, that of players and coaches of the visiting team who clearly see a violation to the rules just before the score. And there is a third group, the referees. Well, who knows what they see! The fact is that for the same action, there may be several perceptions of the same set of events. Albert Einstein and other scientists provided a great example of multi-perception with the wave-particle duality concept. In a similar fashion, a WebSphere based environment could be analyzed in a number of forms. None of the forms or views is absolutely correct or incorrect. Each view, however, helps to focus on the appropriate set of components and their relationships for a given situation or need.

WebSphere Application Server technology is a long and complex subject. This chapter provides three WAS ND environment views, emphasizing security, which will help the reader connect individual security tasks to the big picture. One view aids the WebSphere administrator to relate isolated security tasks to the overall middleware infrastructure (for example, messaging systems, directory services, and back-end databases to name a few). This is useful in possible interactions with teams responsible for such technologies. On the other hand, a second view helps the administrator to link specific security configuration tasks to a particular Enterprise Application (for example, EJB applications, Service Integration Bus, and many more) set of components. This view will help the administrator to relate to possible development team needs. The chapter also includes a third view, one that focuses on the J2EE technology stack as it relates to security. This view could help blend the former two views. So, in a nutshell, the three major parts that make up this first chapter are:

- The Enterprise Application Server infrastructure architecture view
- The WebSphere Application Server architecture view
- The WebSphere technology stack view

Enterprise Application-server infrastructure architecture view

This chapter starts with the Application Server infrastructure architecture view. The actual order of each of these major chapter sub-sections is really unimportant. However, since it needs to be a beginning, the *infrastructure architecture* view is thus selected.

A possibly more formal name for what it is desired to convey in this section would be the *Enterprise J2EE Application server infrastructure architecture*. In this way, the scope of technologies that make up the application-centric architecture is well defined as that pertaining to J2EE applications. Nevertheless, this type of architecture is not exclusive to a WebSphere Application Server Network Deployment environment. Well, it's not in a way. If the architecture does not mention specific implementations of a function, it is a generic view of the architecture. On the other hand, if the architecture view defines or includes specific branded technologies of a function (for example, IHS for a web server function), then it is a specialized architecture. The point is that other J2EE application server products not related to the WebSphere umbrella may use the same generic type of infrastructure architecture.

Therefore, this view has to do with J2EE application servers and the enterprise infrastructure components needed to sustain such application servers in a way that they can host a variety of enterprise applications (also known as J2EE applications). The following diagram provides an example of a basic WebSphere Application Server infrastructure architecture topology:

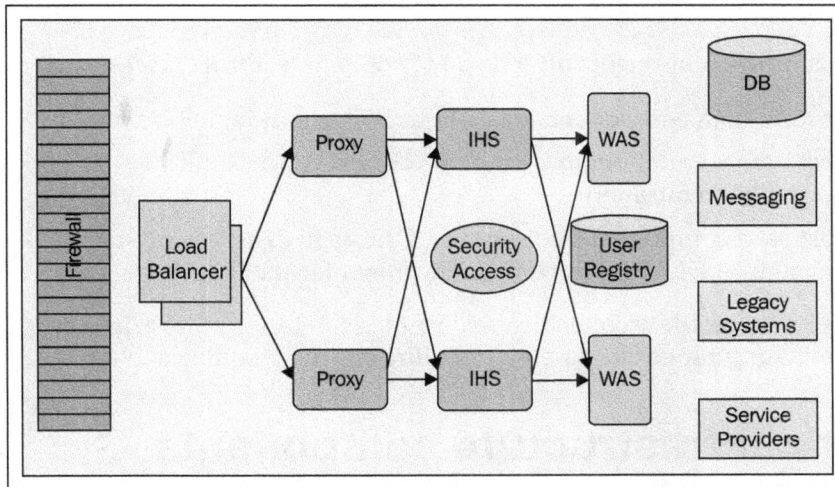

[The use of multiple user registries is new in version 7.0]

Simple infrastructure architecture characteristics

The architecture is basic since it only shows the minimum infrastructure components needed by a WebSphere Application Server infrastructure to become functional. In this diagram, the infrastructure elements are presented as they relate to each other *functionally*. In other words, the diagram is generic enough that it only shows and identifies the components by their main function. For instance, the infrastructure diagram includes, among others, proxy and messaging servers. Nothing in the diagram implies the mapping of a given functional component to a specific physical element such as an OS server or a specialized appliance.

Branded infrastructure elements

The infrastructure architecture presented in the diagram depicts a WebSphere clustered environment. The only technologies identified by their brand are the IBM HTTP Server (**IHS**) web server component (represented by the two rectangles (light blue) labeled **IHS**) and the **WebSphere Application Server (WAS)** nodes (represented by the rectangles (green) labeled **WAS**).

These two simple components offer a variety of architectural choices, such as:

- Hosting both components in a single OS host under a WAS node
- Host each component in their own OS host in the same sub-network (normally an intranet)
- Host each component in different OS hosts in different sub-network (normally a DMZ for the IHS and intranet for the WAS)

The choice for a specific architecture will be made in terms of a variety of requirements for your environment, including security requirements.

Generic infrastructure components

The infrastructure diagram also includes a number of components that are only identified by their function but no information is provided as to the specific technology/product implementing the function. For instance, there are four shapes (light yellow) labeled **DB**, **Messaging**, **Legacy Systems**, and **Service Providers**. In your environment, there may be choices to make in terms of the specific component. Take for instance, the DB component. Identifying what DB server or servers will be part of the architecture is dependent on the type of database employed by the enterprise application being hosted. Some corporations limit the number of database types to less than a handful. Nevertheless, the objective of the WebSphere Administrator responsible for the environment is to identify which type of databases will be interfacing with the WAS environment. Once that fact is determined, the appropriate brand/product could be added to the architecture diagram.

Other technologies/components that need to be identified in a similar way are the user registry (represented by the shape (light purple) labeled **User Registry**), the security access component (represented in the diagram by the oval (yellow) labeled **Security Access**). A common type of user registry used in WebSphere environments is an LDAP server. Furthermore, a popular security access product is SiteMinder (formerly by Netegrity, now offered by CA).

The remaining group of elements in the architecture has the function to front-end the IHS/WAS environment in order to provide high availability and added security. Proxy servers may be used or not, depending on whether the IHS function can be brought to the DMZ in its own OS host. Specialized appliances offered by companies such as CISCO or F5 normally implement load balancers. However, some software products can be used to implement this function. An example to the latter is the IBM WebSphere Edge suite. In general, most corporations already own and use firewalls and load balancers; so for the WebSphere administrator, it is just a matter of integrating them to the WebSphere infrastructure.

Using the infrastructure architecture view

Some of the benefits of picturing your WebSphere environment using the infrastructure architecture view come from realizing the following important points:

- Identify the technology or technology choices to be used to implement a specific function. For instance, what type of user registry to use.

- An immediate result of the previous point is identifying the corporate group the WebSphere administrator would be working with in order to integrate (that is, configure) said technology and WebSphere.

- Once the initial architecture has been laid out, the WebSphere administrator will be responsible to identify the type of security involved to secure the interactions between the various infrastructure architecture components. For instance, what type of communication will take place between the IHS and the Security Access component, if any. What is the best way to secure the communication channel? How is the IHS component authenticated to the Security Access component?

WebSphere architecture view

The next view to be presented is that of the WebSphere Application Server *product architecture*. In a nutshell, the WebSphere Application Server product is an implementation of the J2EE set of specifications with some added functionality only found in this IBM product. Therefore, as opposed to the previous section, this view is unique to WebSphere.

Consequently, this section briefly presents the salient components of the J2EE technologies and their relation to each other from the functional and architectural point of view. Furthermore, emphasis will be placed on aspects that affect or may be affected by security considerations.

WebSphere Application Server simplified architecture

The following diagram depicts a simplified version of the WebSphere Application Server architecture. It presents the application server in the context of a WebSphere node. The application server is the implementation of a JVM. The JVM is made up of various components and at the same time, the JVM interacts with several external components that make up the WebSphere node. So, the diagram presents two major components of a WebSphere environment. On the one hand, the JVM is represented by the parallelogram (purple) labeled **Application Server**. On the other hand, a larger parallelogram (teal) labeled node represents the **WebSphere node**.

Keep in mind that the simplification to the architecture has been done to concentrate on how it relates to application hosting in a secure environment.

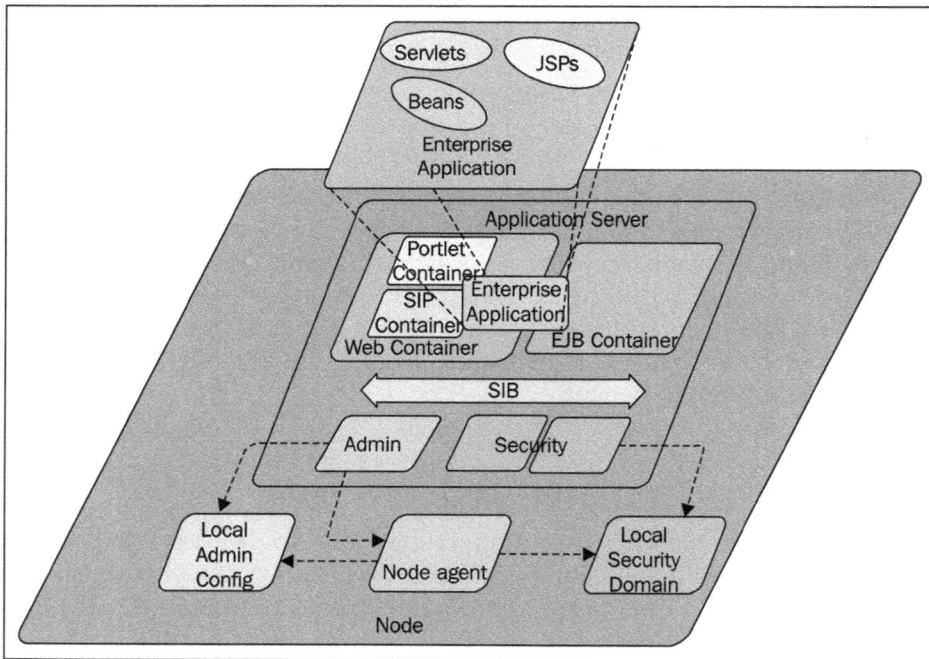

[✎ The concept of **local security domains** is new in version 7.0.]

WebSphere node component

The node component of this simplified architecture occupies itself with administrative and thus security aspects between the WebSphere environment and the infrastructure. In the previous diagram, three components can be observed. The first component is the node agent; represented by the small parallelogram labeled **Node agent**. Notice that the node agent in itself is implemented by a specialized JVM, containing the components required to efficiently perform administrative tasks, which will include security related tasks. The node agent will interact with WebSphere environment administrative components externals to the node (and not included in the diagram). The chief among those external WebSphere components is the Deployment Manager. One of the responsibilities of the node agent as it pertains to the node and thus, to the application server JVM, is to maintain updated and valid copies of the node configuration repository. Such a repository may include information dealing with security domain information, either inherited from the WebSphere cell global security or customized for the node, represented by the parallelogram (black) labeled **Local Security Domain**.

WebSphere JVM component

The second major component of this simplified architecture is the implementation of a JVM. It is represented in the diagram by a large parallelogram (purple) labeled **Application Server**. A WebSphere JVM is made of, among other components, several containers such as the Web and EJB containers. Containers, on top of hosting instantiations of Java classes such as servlets and beans, that is, offering the runtime environment for those classes to execute, deal with security aspects of the execution. For instance, a Web Container may, given the appropriate settings, oversee that hosted resources only execute if the principal making the request has the required proof that entitles such principal of receiving the result of said request.

In addition to containers, a WebSphere JVM may also instantiate a service integration bus (SIB) if a hosted application makes use of the JVM messaging engine. In the diagram, the arrow (brown) labeled **SIB** represents the bus. Finally, the other JVM components included in this simplified architecture are the administrative component and the JVM security mechanism. This mechanism will interact with the containers to ensure that security is propagated to the classes executing in the said containers.

From this discussion, it can be extrapolated that each vendor has certain leniency as to the actual implementation of Sun's JVM. IBM is not an exception to this practice. If you wish to find out more about the particulars of the IBM JVM implementation for WebSphere please refer to the Information Center article "Specifications and API" (`http://publib.boulder.ibm.com/infocenter/wasinfo/v7r0/index.jsp?topic=/com.ibm.websphere.nd.doc/info/ae/ae/rovr_specs.html`). In that article you will find out which Java specifications and application programming interfaces are implemented as well as the version each implements. This information is presented in a neat table that helps you compare each specification and API version to earlier editions of the WebSphere Application Server product (that is, 5.1, 6.0 and 6.1).

Using the WebSphere architecture view

The main benefit of analyzing your WebSphere environment using this view is that it will provide you with the vocabulary to better understand the needs of application developers and architects and, equally important, to communicate back to them the special features the WebSphere environment may offer them as well as any possible restrictions imposed by security or other infrastructure characteristics.

An additional benefit provided by this view is that it offers alternatives to troubleshooting application related issues, as you will become more familiar with which JVM components are being used as the runtime environment for a given enterprise application.

WebSphere technology stack view

Finally, the third view covered in this chapter is that of the WebSphere environment technology stack. In other words, this view presents which technologies from the operating system to the WebSphere Application product are involved, highlighting the aspects related to security. This view is broken down into three categories, which are described in the following paragraphs. The stack and its categories are depicted in the diagram shown in the next sub-section.

OS platform security

At the bottom of the stack there are the primitive technologies. The term primitive in this context does not carry the meaning of backward, but rather that of foundation technologies. In the following diagram, the rectangular (bright green) area located at the bottom of the stack represents the OS platform layer.

In this layer, the presence of the underlying operating system can be observed. In the end, it is the responsibility of the OS to provide the low-level resources needed by the WebSphere environment. Furthermore, it is also its responsibility to enforce any security policies required on such resources. Two of the more prominent OS components as they relate to a WebSphere environment are the file system and the networking infrastructure. Both the file systems and the networking infrastructure are handlers of special resources.

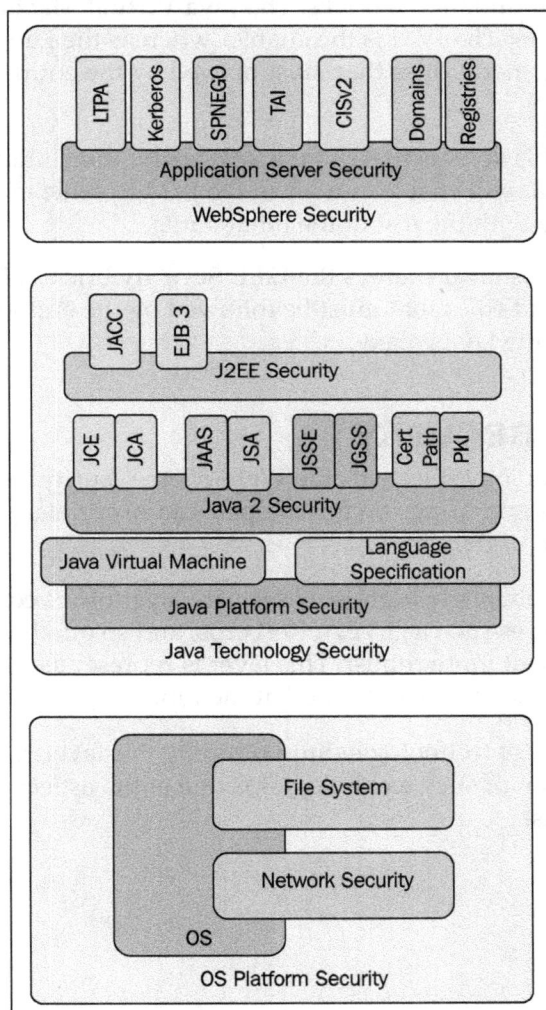

Java technology security

The next layer in this architecture is that of the Java technology. This layer comprehends the core Java technologies and APIs used within the WebSphere environment. In the previous diagram, the layer is represented by the rectangle (teal) in the middle of the stack.

The layer is further broken down into three distinct groups among the Java stack. At the bottom sit the foundational bricks. The **Java Virtual Machine** and the **Java Language Specification**. The JVM is the enabler whereas the Language Specification lays down basic and general rules that must obeyed by the entities that will populate the JVM.

The middle brick of this layer is that of **Java 2 Security**. It includes more sophisticated rules that will enable entities in the JVM to achieve more complex behaviors in harmony with the rest of the inhabitants.

Finally, at the top of this layer there is the **J2EE Security** brick. It brings additional enablers to the JVM and rules that must be followed by the entities that populate these remote areas of the Java galaxy.

WebSphere security

At the top of the technology stack, sits the WebSphere security layer. It builds up on the previous layers and brings on board open and proprietary security bricks to supplement the Java foundation.

In other words, the WebSphere high-level security layer offers conduits using a number of technologies such as LTPA, Kerberos, and so on, that make the WebSphere environment more robust. This layer is represented in the previous diagram by the rectangle (maroon) located at the top.

In general, the number of technologies supported by this layer as well as the implementation version of such technologies is one of the aspects that make up each new WebSphere release.

Using the technology stack view

One of the main benefits of the technology stack view is that it helps WebSphere practitioners involved in various roles to map the various technologies included in this stack to the functional blocks that make up the other two views. Some practitioners will benefit by selecting the most appropriate subset among the classes offered by the WebSphere environment to implement a required functionality. Other practitioners will benefit by integrating into the WebSphere environment the best infrastructure component that will help to enable a piece of functionality required by a hosted application.

Summary

This chapter presents an introduction to WebSphere security by taking the reader to a tour that helps him observe the environment from three different angles. Each of the views presented in a way supplements the other two. Aspects related to security are at the center of each of the views described. In this chapter and in the remaining part of the book experienced users will get acquainted with new security aspects offered by the IBM WebSphere Application Server Network Deployment version 7.0. In addition, and perhaps more importantly, the material covered in this chapter and the rest of the book is presented so no prior knowledge of WebSphere security (as in earlier versions of WebSphere) is required. This fact makes it easier for new WebSphere administrators to learn the security aspects of WebSphere version 7.0. Throughout the rest of the book, the terms WebSphere Application Server Network Deployment version 7 and WAS ND7 will be used interchangeably. Let's get started!

2
Securing the Administrative Interface

Did your parents, or other adults, ever tell you when you were a child, "make sure you lock the door when you leave the house"? Why was that? Normally, you have a lock on the front door so only those persons who have the correct key can get in the house. I say *normally*, because there may be people out there like my late grandfather in-law, who used to live in a small town in Tennessee. He would keep his house locked while he was at home and would keep it unlocked when nobody was home in case a relative or friend would need to go inside his home. The same applies to your WebSphere Application Server (WAS ND7) infrastructure. Not having a secured administrative interface (that is, having global security disabled) is equivalent to your house having a front door without a lock.

Out of the box, there is no security enabled. Why? IBM gives the freedom to use whatever user registry infrastructure is already used by your company. Such registry will contain a list of users and groups they belong to. Access to WebSphere resources will be granted by user ID and user groups defined in the registry.

This chapter describes the following topics:

- Concepts surrounding the WebSphere web-based administrative interface
- How security affects the overall WebSphere infrastructure
- Presents the pieces of information that required to secure the administrative interface
- A procedure to follow in order to secure the WebSphere global administrative infrastructure.

Information needed: Planning for security

Continuing our analogy, if you want to secure your front door, you need to know what tools and parts you will need to install a lock. Similarly, in order to implement global security for your WebSphere environment, we need to figure out what is needed to enable it and what procedure to follow to accomplish this task. Therefore the purpose of this major section is to identify possible values and sources for the parameters that are required throughout the *Enabling security* section. Consequently, there may be a need in the rest of this chapter to reference the table in the following subsection "The LDAP and security table", that summarizes this chapter's required parameters and values. So, it may be a good idea to place a bookmark on the page where the table starts for easy reference.

> In order to simplify references from the rest of the chapter to the table presented at the end of this section, it will be denoted as the **LDAP and security table**.

The type of information required to enable the administrative security varies. It will depend on the type of user registry. Most medium to large corporations would use a type of user registry based on LDAP as the underlying technology. Therefore, in this book, we will be using LDAP as our underlying user registry technology. **LDAP** stands for **Lightweight Directory Access Protocol**. Describing the LDAP technology itself is out of the scope of this book, as it would take a whole other book to describe it. However, in the next few paragraphs it will be highlighted along with the elements of LDAP-based registries that are needed in our task of enabling the administrative security, focusing on the values that can be used with each parameter. If you are interested in further exploring the concepts behind the LDAP technology, you can start with the book "Understanding LDAP", by IBM, available online at: http://www.redbooks.ibm.com/redbooks/SG244986/wwhelp/wwhimpl/js/html/wwhelp.htm. In addition, a description for each of the parameters is readily available from the LDAP configuration page, available by following the breadcrumb **Security | Global security | Standalone LDAP registry**.

> For all practical purposes, enabling the administrative security of WebSphere is equivalent to enabling WebSphere global security. Those terms will be used interchangeably in this book.

Best practice: Gather required information beforehand
Use the table provided next as an information template of data that needs to be collected before starting the process of enabling security. For instance, for each of your cells, create a spreadsheet which summarizes the required data.

The LDAP and security table

For LDAP-based global security configuration, you will need to gather the following parameters:

SSO domain name:

This refers to the LDAP realm. It is the common DNS domain shared across multiple applications. SSO stands for single sign-on. An example of SSO domain name would be the top portion of your domain name: **yourcompany.com**, which is the value to be used for this parameter.

Server user identity and password:

This will be the primary administrative ID for intercommunication within the WebSphere cell. Infrastructure WebSphere components, such as the deployment manager and node agents, will present these credentials to communicate with each other. We will use the ID **wasadm** also. Since this parameter is only available when the **Server identity that is stored in the repository** option is selected, just like the other IDs, the ID used for server user identity must already exist in the LDAP repository.

Server user ID

This ID must exist in the OS. It is the ID that will own the deployment manager process. We will use the value **wasid**.

WebSphere administrative identity and password:

This is an ID that already exists in the LDAP registry and which will be used to log in to the WebSphere Console (or more precisely, the Integrated Solutions Console) once global security is enabled. For our examples throughout this chapter, we will use the ID **wasadm**.

Bind distinguished name and password:

This ID must exist in the LDAP registry. It is the ID that WebSphere uses to connect to and authenticate with the LDAP registry. The major requirement for this ID is that it must have read privileges to users and groups under the LDAP domain. Specifically, it should be able to read starting at the LDAP base distinguished name. (See below for additional information.) This ID must be entered in an LDAP distinguished name format. We will use: **uid=wasbind,ou=service,o=yourcompany.com**.

LDAP server Host name:

The fully qualified domain host name of the LDAP server. We will use the value **jsdsdev01.yourcompany.com**.

LDAP server TCP port:

It is the TCP port to which the LDAP server is listening. (Verify with your LDAP team whether WebSphere should use plain or SSL protocol.) We will use the standard LDAP un-encrypted port, **389**.

LDAP base distinguished name:

Obtain this information from your LDAP administration team. We will use the value: **o=yourcompany.com**. Unless your environment uses multiple DNS domain names, yours may be similar to the one we are using. When selecting this value, extreme care must be taken to insure that the value selected, which is the root of all WebSphere LDAP queries, does not include branches that won't return any results. In other words, select this value to avoid global searches and only focus on the branches with the subset of users and groups that will be accessing the applications hosted in the WebSphere environment.

URL to the Integrated Solutions Console:

URL you normally use to access your deployment manager console.

Best practice: Personal WebSphere Administration IDs

When more than one person will be sharing the responsibilities of administrating a WebSphere environment, it is customary to define each user with the role of Administrator. In this way, a single ID could be used for the WebSphere administrative ID and server ID, reducing the overhead of having multiple IDs. In essence, you are reserving the administrative ID for operational use only.

Your LDAP administrator should be able to provide you with the appropriate distinguished name for your bind ID. As a prerequisite to enabling security, it is likely that you will need to request the LDAP team to create this ID.

Enabling security

After coming back from the hardware store with the parts (locks, keys, and so on) and tools (drill, screwdriver, and so on) and perhaps some advice from the hardware store assistant, you can confidently start the task of installing that lock system you just bought for your front door. In a similar way, now you can begin to configure your WebSphere global security.

As in many IT tasks, there may be more than one way to accomplish such a task. This section will guide you thru enabling global security using the **Integrated Solutions Console**. Throughout this chapter, we will also refer to the Integrated Solutions Console by the names of the **WebSphere Console** and the **Deployment Manager Console**.

> If your organization has a large base of WebSphere Application Server domains and you are considering enabling global security on multiple consoles, it may be a good idea to automate this task using the WebSphere administrative scripting interface, wsadmin.

The procedure we are going to follow in this section is carried out in three phases or stages as indicated below.

1. Set the domain name.
2. Configure the user registry.
3. Enable the administrative security.

As already mentioned in the planning section at the beginning of this chapter, the procedure described in this section will be using an LDAP-based registry. This type of registry will be applicable to most organizations. However, you are encouraged to experiment with another type of registry. In a laboratory setting, for instance, you could use the local OS authentication mechanism. Working with a different type of registry will help you better understand global security.

Setting the domain name

Our first task then, is to set the SSO domain name for the global security task. The sections that follow will walk you through the process.

Starting at the console

Log in to the WebSphere Console. Before global security is enabled, the Console will only have one field in which to enter an ID. This ID can actually be anything since we have not linked our WebSphere environment to any user registry. (The use of the term **User ID** may be misleading. At this stage, WebSphere uses that field as a temporary tag to label an area in which to save any changes that may be made during the session until they are either committed or discarded.) Access the Deployment Manager Console using a browser, enter a value for **User ID** and click the **Log in** button. Prior to enabling global security, part of the Console log in page will look similar to the portion shown in the following screenshot.

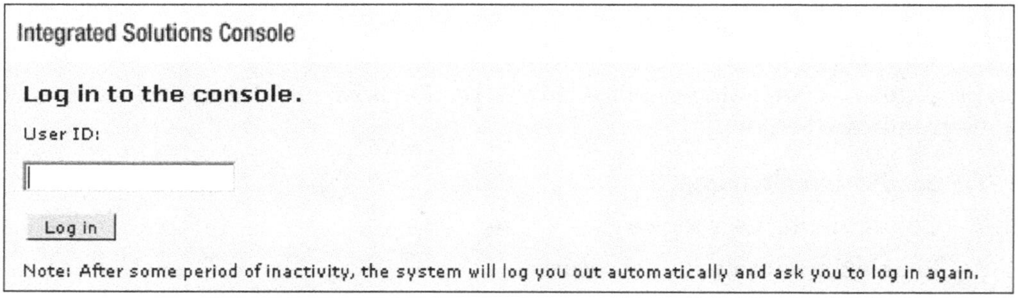

Integrated Solutions Console

Log in to the console.

User ID:

[   ]

[Log in]

Note: After some period of inactivity, the system will log you out automatically and ask you to log in again.

Continuing with the global security page

We first need to open the **Global security** page. After logging in, expand the **Security** leaf on the left pane of the console, and then click on the **Global security** link as shown in the following figure. The global security page will be displayed on the right hand pane.

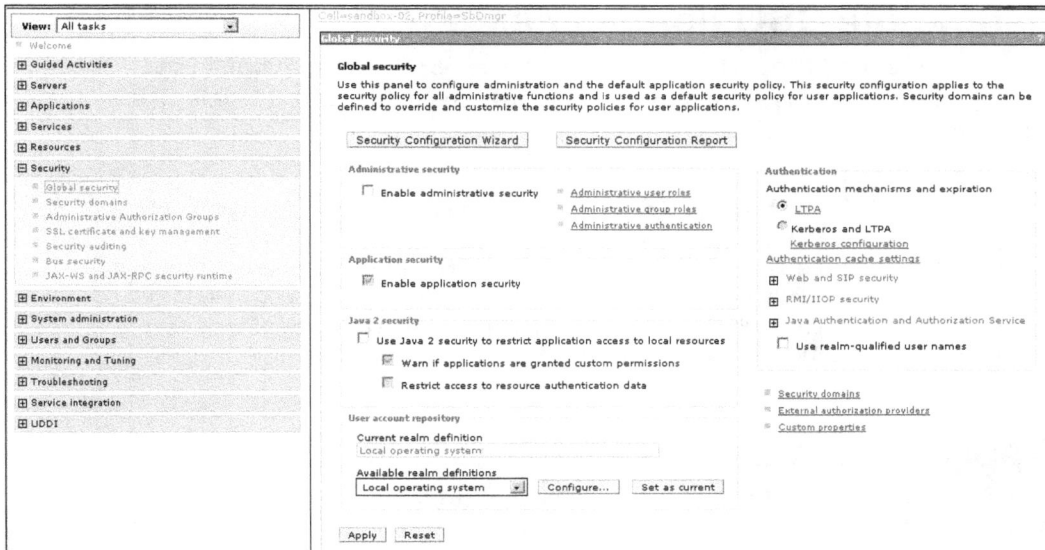

Onto the SSO page

Next, let's open the SSO page. Expand the **Web and SIP security** leaf under the **Authentication** section on the right section of the **Global security** page (figure shown previously). Click on the **Single sign-on (SSO)** link. A portion of the **SSO page** is shown in the next screenshot.

Setting the SSO domain name

Under the **General Properties** section, enter the **SSO domain name** in the corresponding field, as shown in the previous screenshot. Use the default selections for the rest of the parameters.

> If you check the **Require SSL** parameter, single sign-on will only be in effect for SSL communications. If your HTTP server resides in the same server as your WebSphere Application Server, you will normally not want to use SSL for communications between the WebSphere Plug-in running inside the HTTP server process, and the WebSphere Application Server hosting an application.

Applying and saving your changes

Keeping as a reference the previous screenshot under the section *Onto the SSO page*, saving the changes is in order. Click the **OK** button. You will be sent back to the **Global security** page. A **Messages** box is displayed at the top of the page giving you the opportunity to save your changes. The message is shown in the following screenshot:

```
□  Messages
     ⚠ Changes have been made to your local configuration. You can:
     ● Save directly to the master configuration.
     ● Review changes before saving or discarding.

     An option to synchronize the configuration across multiple nodes can be disabled in Preferences.
     ⚠ The server may need to be restarted for these changes to take effect.
```

Save your work as you normally would have for any other configuration modifications of your environment in the past, ensuring that the changes are propagated to all your existing nodes in this cell.

> **Learning WebSphere configuration internals**
>
> If you wish to learn which internal WebSphere parameters are modified, created or deleted as you apply various configuration tasks you may want to do the following. For this particular task, before you commit the changes, make a copy of the file: `<Dmgr_Profile_ Path>/config/cells/<cell_name>/security.xml`. As you save your work, you can compare the difference between the original copy and the active version of the file to observe what has changed.

It is important to ensure that any of the changes made while enabling global security are synchronized with all of the nodes in the cell as they are saved by the deployment manager. Failing to do this may prevent the nodes from getting the new configuration and they may be unable to communicate with the deployment manager.

Configuring the user registry

Once the SSO domain name has been set, we are now ready for the second phase in the securing of the WebSphere Console, and we can proceed to select the user registry. During this stage of the global security configuration, we are going to tell WebSphere which type of registry to use, what server and port to connect to and which user IDs and passwords to use. Once global security is enabled, WebSphere uses the information from this repository to grant or deny access to resources as they are requested (in accordance with settings in the enterprise applications and in their installed configuration.

Locating the user registry configuration area

Open the WebSphere Console Global security page. If you have closed your browser, you need to open the Deployment Manager Console and log in as you did in the first stage. (If needed, refer to the section "Starting at the Console"). Next, expand the **Security** leaf and click on the **Global security** link, as you did in the second step of the first phase. During this stage, we will pay attention to the User account repository section (shown in the following figure).

Registry type selection

We continue by selecting the user registry type. The first thing we need to tell WebSphere is the type of user registry to which we wish WebSphere to connect. The default type is the local OS authentication mechanism. The supported registry types are shown in the following screenshot:

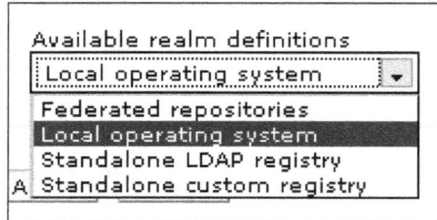

```
Available realm definitions
┌──────────────────────────────┬───┐
│ Local operating system       │ ▼ │
├──────────────────────────────┴───┤
│ Federated repositories            │
│ Local operating system            │
│ Standalone LDAP registry          │
│A Standalone custom registry       │
└───────────────────────────────────┘
```

In the next sections, we look very briefly at each of the options supported by WAS ND7.

Federated repository

The type **Federated repository** enables us to use a common interface to a collection of heterogeneous repositories. In addition, it establishes a common realm that WebSphere uses to query the user registry when needed. In other words, a federated repository provides a logical realm and a mapping between the logical entity types and the underlying repository entity types. There are four types of data stores that can be used in a federated repository: file-based, LDAP, database, and custom registry. In WebSphere, a federated repository is implemented using the **Virtual Member Manager**. Moreover, there is a restriction to whether or not two data stores can be logically combined, that each data store contains unique distinguished names from the others.

Local operating system

Next is the type **Local operating system**. As the name implies, it uses the host OS user and group schema as the repository for users. There are several limitations to using this type of repository. On the one hand, for distributed systems such as Unix, Linux and Windows OS, the authentication mechanism *must* use a domain controller when the cell expands to more than one host. On the other hand, the built-in authentication mechanism of the OS can be used as registry only if all of the cell components are hosted in the same OS server. Furthermore, if the process owner for the WebSphere environment is a non-root ID, the local OS cannot be used if the cell components are spread over multiple OS hosts.

LDAP

We continue with the type **Standalone LDAP registry**. The formal definition for
Lightweight Directory Access Protocol is: "provides access to distributed directory
services that act in accordance with X.500 data and service models" [RCF 4511:
Lightweight Directory Access Protocol (LDAP): The Protocol].

Standalone custom registry

Finally, the last type of supported registry is the **Standalone custom registry**. As
the name implies, this type of registry provides a custom access interface (or more
officially, custom adaptors) to a custom store. An example of a custom adaptor
(although written for WebSphere v6) can be found at: `http://www.ibm.com/
developerworks/websphere/library/samples/vmmsampleadapter.html`.

LDAP—the preferred choice

In most scenarios, it is likely that you will be using a type of standalone LDAP
server. Select the **Standalone LDAP registry** option from the **Available realm
definitions** pull-down menu. Once the standalone LDAP registry type is selected,
click the **Set as current** button. The value of the **Current realm definition** field
updates to the selected value as shown in the following screenshot:

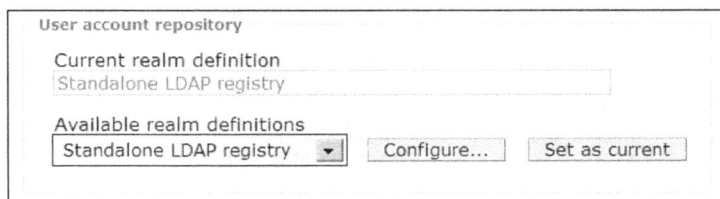

Reviewing the resulting standalone LDAP registry page

Simultaneously, as a result of the previous action, a warning message is displayed
at the top of the **Standalone LDAP registry** page, as shown in the next screenshot.
The deployment manager is just reminding us that the configuration we are about to
make will not become active until we turn on global security.

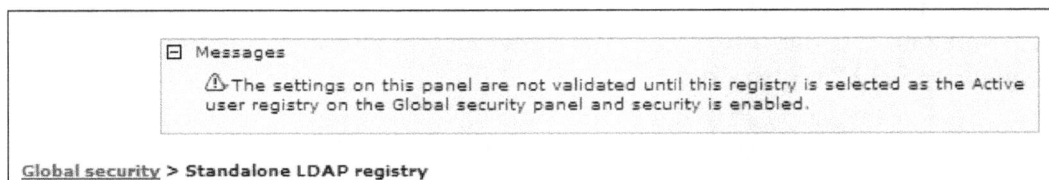

Defining the WebSphere administrative ID

Under the **General Properties** section, enter the value for the WebSphere administrative ID in the **Primary administrative user name** field. For the purposes of this chapter, we are using the fictitious value **wasadm**, as shown in the following screenshot. For additional information on this value refer to the *LDAP and security table* section.

General Properties

* Primary administrative user name

    wasadm

    Server user identity

    ⦿ Automatically generated server identity

    ○ Server identity that is stored in the repository

Setting the type of LDAP server

Next, we need to select the type of LDAP server. The default type is the **IBM Tivoli Directory Server**. The supported LDAP server types are shown in the next screenshot. Obviously, your choice will depend on the type of LDAP server used by your company.

Type of LDAP server

    IBM Tivoli Directory Server ▾

    IBM Tivoli Directory Server
    IBM SecureWay Directory Server
    Sun Java System Directory Server
    IBM Lotus Domino
    Microsoft Active Directory
    Novell eDirectory
    Custom

Entering the LDAP server parameters

Using the values you gathered in the first section of this chapter, *Information needed: planning for security*, enter the **LDAP server host name** value in the **Host** field. The fictitious value **jsdsdev01.yourcompany.com** is being used in our example. Next, enter the **LDAP server TCP port** value in the **Port** field. We are using the standard **TCP port 389**. The following screenshot shows how these values are displayed in the **Standalone LDAP registry** page.

```
Type of LDAP server
Sun Java System Directory Server  ▼

✳ Host
jsdsdev01.yourcompany.com

Port
389
```

Providing the LDAP bind identity parameters

Once the primary parameters that identify the LDAP server have been specified, we need to designate the parameters to be used by WebSphere to connect to the LDAP registry. In the field designated as **Base distinguished name (DN)**, enter the value for **LDAP Base Distinguished Name** identified in the *Information needed: planning for security* section. We will be using the value **o=yourcompany.com**. Next, enter the **Bind Identity** value in the **Bind distinguished name (DN)** field. The full value shown in the following screenshot is **uid=wasbind,ou=service,o=yourcom pany.com**. Finally, enter the corresponding password for the bind ID in the field that is designated as **Bind password**. These values are shown as displayed in the **Standalone LDAP registry** page in the following screenshot:

```
Base distinguished name (DN)
o=yourcompany.com

Bind distinguished name (DN)
uid=wasbind,ou=service,o=you

Bind password
••••••••
```

Confirming other miscellaneous LDAP server parameters

In general, the default value of the remaining parameters for the LDAP server works just fine in most situations. Normally, there will be no need to modify the default values shown in the following screenshot. However, if for instance, the LDAP server to be used with this particular WebSphere environment only accepts SSL connections, that fact would have to be reflected by checking the **SSL enabled** check box under the **SSL settings** section of the **Standalone LDAP registry** page. In a similar way, if your particular LDAP server has other requirements that are not covered by the default selections shown in the following figure, adjust the corresponding parameter accordingly.

Applying and saving the standalone LDAP configuration

At this point, all that is left to complete the configuration of the standalone LDAP registry is to commit the new configuration values just entered. Click the **Apply** button, located at the bottom of the page. In the resulting page, a **Messages** section appears at the top of the page. Use the appropriate link to save your work, always insuring that the changes are synchronized with any existing node agent.

Confirming the configuration

Before concluding this portion of the configuration, it is best practice to confirm that the deployment manager can connect and log in the LDAP server. Identify and click on the **Test connection** button located near the top of the page, just above the **General Properties** section. If your configuration is correct, a **Messages** section is displayed at the top of the page, similar to the one shown in the next screenshot. If an error occurred, a corresponding message will be displayed. Correct the error and test the connection again.

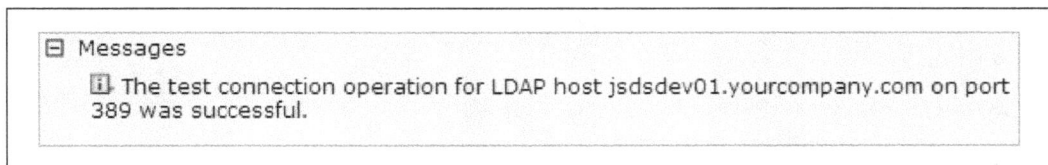

> ⊟ Messages
> ⓘ The test connection operation for LDAP host jsdsdev01.yourcompany.com on port 389 was successful.

> Common errors that may take place while testing the LDAP connection include mistyped hostnames, IDs and passwords. Another type of error, a little more difficult to detect, could be that WebSphere cannot connect to the LDAP server. This could be due to a possible firewall issue (by either a real firewall appliance or a firewall application running on the LDAP server host OS), or a temporary network slowdown.

Enabling the administrative security

Once the two first stages have been completed, we are now ready to start the last phase in the securing of the WebSphere Console and can proceed to turn on the administrative security.

> **Best practice: node activation**
> Ensure that all of the node agents in your cell are operational. If they are not, the node agents will not be able to receive the changes to the global security and additional steps will be required to allow them to connect to the deployment manager.

By enabling administrative security, we are effectively turning on global security. In order to enable the administrative security perform the following steps.

Locating the administrative security section

Open the WebSphere Console **Global security** page. If you have closed your browser, you need to open the Deployment Manager Console and log in as you did in the previous two stages. (If needed, refer to the first step of the first stage.) Next, expand the **Security** leaf and click on the **Global security** link, as you did in the second step of the first stage. This time we are going to focus on the **Administrative security** section, as shown in the following screenshot:

Global security

Use this panel to configure administration and the default application security policy. This security configuration applies to the security policy for all administrative functions and is used as a default security policy for user applications. Security domains can be defined to override and customize the security policies for user applications.

   [Security Configuration Wizard]   [Security Configuration Report]

Administrative security

   ☐ Enable administrative security   Administrative user roles
                                 Administrative group roles
                                 Administrative authentication

Application security

   ☐ Enable application security

Java 2 security

   ☐ Use Java 2 security to restrict application access to local resources

      ☐ Warn if applications are granted custom permissions

      ☐ Restrict access to resource authentication data

User account repository

Current realm definition
Federated repositories

Available realm definitions
[Federated repositories ▼] [Configure...] [Set as current]

Authentication

Authentication mechanisms and expiration
   ◉ LTPA
   ○ Kerberos and LTPA
      (This function is currently disabled. See the IBM Support site for possible future updates.)
      Kerberos configuration
Authentication cache settings

  ⊞ Web and SIP security

  ⊞ RMI/IIOP security

  ⊞ Java Authentication and Authorization Service

    ☐ Use realm-qualified user names

  Security domains
  External authorization providers
  Custom properties

[Apply] [Reset]

Performing the administrative security configuration steps

Under the **Administrative security** section, check the **Enable administrative security** box. You will notice that the box labeled **Use Java 2 security to restrict application access to local resources** is checked automatically. Normally, you do not want this box to be checked, so remove the check from Java 2 security. The main reason for choice is that it is not uncommon for enterprise applications to require Java 2 security access that surpasses the default security policies. When this fact is present, enterprise applications are likely to either fail or function differently as designed. Therefore, modifications to the application's app.policy or was.policy, as appropriate, would be required. Additional information about these files can be found at http://publib.boulder.ibm.com/infocenter/wasinfo/v7r0/topic/com.ibm.websphere.nd.doc/info/ae/ae/rsec_rpolicydir.html. An alternative to employing Java 2 security is to use an external access control policy manager, for example, IBM Tivoli Access Manager or the popular CA SiteMinder Policy Server. Moreover, Chapter 3 describes alternative locations in the administrative console where the Java 2 security can be enabled for a limited number of applications that require it.

Your selections should be as those shown in the following screenshot:

Applying and saving your changes

On the same **Global security** page, scroll down. Click the **Apply** button, located at the bottom. It is likely that WebSphere may display a long **Messages** section as the one shown in the next screenshot:

⊟ Messages

⚠ The security configuration is enabled or modified in a Network Deployment environment. The following steps need to be followed so that all the processes in this environment have the same security run-time settings: 1) Verify that all nodes are synchronized with these security configuration changes before stopping these processes. 2) If any node agents are currently stopped, issue a manual **syncNode** command before starting that node agent. 3) Stop all of the processes in the entire cell, including the deployment manager, node agents, and Application Servers. 4) Restart all of the processes in the cell; restart the deployment manager and node agents first, then Application Servers.

⚠ If the Restrict access to local resources option is not enabled, the Java virtual machine (JVM) system resources are not protected. For example, applications can read and write to files on file systems, listen to sockets, exit the Application Server process, and so on. However, by enabling the Restrict access to local resources option, applications might fail to run if the required permissions are not granted to the applications.

ℹ If any of the fields are changed, save the configuration and then stop and restart the server.

⚠ Changes have been made to your local configuration. You can:

● Save directly to the master configuration.

● Review changes before saving or discarding.

An option to synchronize the configuration across multiple nodes after saving can be enabled in Preferences.

⚠ The server may need to be restarted for these changes to take effect.

Summarizing these warning messages, they tell us what to do if one or more node agents belonging to this cell are not active in order to propagate our configuration changes to each node agent configuration repository.

Propagating new configuration

After reading the warning messages, click on the **Save** link to commit your changes to the WebSphere configuration repository. However, if you have not enabled automatic synchronization with the nodes after each save, then click on the **Review** link instead so you have the chance to indicate that you wish these changes to be propagated to the nodes in the cell.

Logging off from the console

Once you have saved your changes, you need to allow WebSphere to make those changes active. This is accomplished by restarting the deployment manager. Although not necessary, it is always good practice to log off the console. If there were pending tasks to be saved, the deployment manager would display a message to either save or discard any pending changes before allowing you to log off.

Changes in the deployment manager console URL

Pay close attention to the URL used to access the WebSphere Console until this point. The protocol used is HTTP. Make note of the port being used. This port matches your WC_adminhost TCP transport. After you activate the global security, this URL will change. First, the protocol changes to HTTPS. Secondly, the port also changes. This time your browser will be redirected to the WC_adminhost_secure TCP transport. You can still use the old URL; the deployment manager console will redirect your browser to the secure port.

When describing procedures that need to take place at the OS level, in this book it will be assumed that we are working on a Unix or Unix-like environment. If you are working on a different type of OS, it is likely that you are already familiar with the various commands used and can perform the equivalent operations in your particular OS.

Restarting the deployment manager

Log in to the command line interface of your OS on the server where the deployment manager process is executing. Switch to the user ID used to stop and start the deployment manager process as you normally do. Use the following command:

`<Dmgr_Profile_Path>/bin/stopManager.sh`

(Use stopManager.bat in Windows; or the Windows service for WAS). Now you can start the deployment manager. Use the following command:

`<Dmgr_Profile_Path>/bin/startManager.sh`

(In Windows, use startManager.bat or the Windows services interface). Ensure that the output does not display any errors.

Keep in mind that global security will take place only after the deployment manager and all of the nodes in its cell are restarted.

Logging in to the deployment manager console

Using your browser, connect to the WebSphere Console using the same URL you have used before. WebSphere will attempt to redirect you to its secure administrative port. However, your browser will show you a warning message stating the SSL certificate presented by the site is invalid. The deployment manager is presenting its self-signed certificate and the warning message means that your browser does not have a root CA certificate to validate it. This is fine, since it was the configuration we just did that created the SSL certificate. Click on the **OK** button. Depending on the browser being used you will be presented with the option to cancel or continue. Firefox presents an **Or you can add an exception** link. IE presents a **Continue to this website (not recommended)** link. Accept the SSL certificate.

The **Integrated Solutions Console** opens. One can tell that global security is on by observing that the log in page now has two fields. One field is for the **User ID** and the other is for the **Password**. Enter the appropriate credentials (WebSphere administrative ID and password) and click on the **Log in** button.

Congratulations! You have successfully enabled global security.

> When global security is enabled you will be asked to provide a user ID and its corresponding password in order to issue commands that are required to communicate with the WebSphere administrative infrastructure (for example, node agents.) The parameters to supply to most command line scripts are **-username** and **-password**. For instance, to see the status of the deployment manager process, you would enter: `<Dmgr_Profile_Path>/bin/serverStatus.sh -username wasadm -password <mysecretpwd>`

Administrative roles

Let's assume for a moment that the type of lock system you installed in your house is a very sophisticated one. With that lock system, you have the capability to issue different kinds of keys. The master key, which very likely you will take charge of, would be enabled to open all of the locks installed throughout your house. There would be other keys that may not have the same capability. All of the keys will open the front door. In addition, some may open the kitchen pantry and the door to the garage; other keys may open the office but not the locks in the kitchen to the pantry or the garage. OK, I admit: this is stretching the front door analogy a little bit too far. Nevertheless, I hope the point is made.

WebSphere provides several user roles; the most common ones will be briefly described next.

- **Monitor**: Capable of viewing the current WebSphere configuration and the state of the application servers (JVM's).

- **Configurator**: In addition to being able to do what the Monitor does, the configurator is capable of performing activities related to configuration of the application servers and the deployment of applications (for example, creating resources like virtual hosts, mapping application servers, and so on.)

- **Operator**: Entitled to the same privileges of a Monitor, an Operator has the ability to change the runtime status of the application servers.

- **Deployer**: In addition to be able to perform the tasks of a Monitor, a Deployer has the capability to perform configuration and change run status of applications.

- **Administrator**: Capable of performing any of the tasks of the previous roles plus can assign **add user** to any of the roles, affect the configuration and runtime status of the WebSphere infrastructure (for example, deployment manager and node agents).

> Additional information about roles can be found in the IBM WebSphere V7 Information Center: http://publib.boulder.ibm. com/infocenter/wasinfo/v7r0/index.jsp?topic=/com. ibm.websphere.nd.doc/info/ae/ae/rsec_adminroles.html.

For most organizations, using Monitor and Administrator will suffice. If there is an Operations group in your company, you probably have written (or will write) simple scripts to stop and start enterprise applications, thus there is no need for Operations folks to need access to the WebSphere Console.

Disabling security

Like many analogies, there is always a place where they don't completely hold. Our front door lock scenario is no different and it falls short when it comes to disabling security, unless removing the front door lock would make any sense and it could be considered as a possibility.

There are going to be situations in which you will need to temporarily disable global security. For instance, during the installation of WebSphere Portal, which installs on top of a WebSphere Application Server layer, you are asked to disable global security to perform some of the configuration tasks.

In this chapter so far, we have been using the WebSphere Console. You will see in the next few paragraphs how easily global security can be disabled. The word 'easily' in the last sentence implies simplicity, not that it is unsecure. For this task, you will need the following additional information:

- **Connection type**: Protocol to be used between the wsadmin.sh JVM and the deployment manager. We will use SOAP.

- **Port**: The SOAP TCP transport to which the deployment manager is listening.

> The TCP ports used by the deployment manager are stored in the properties file **portdef.props** which is located under the properties directory of the deployment manager profile, that is, <Profile_Root_Directory>/properties/portdef.props

In addition, it is recommended to always create a backup of the XML configuration file for global security, security.xml located in <Profile_Root_Directory/ config/cells/<Cell_Name>/security.xml. This file can be restored if there are difficulties with security configuration modifications.

1. Log in to the command line interface.

   Using either SSH or telnet, log in to the host where the deployment manager is running.

> Actually, you could log in to any host where a WebSphere 7 profile is installed and using the administrative script interface, log in to the deployment manager.

2. Switch to the user who owns the deployment manager process.

   Using sudo or another similar mechanism, switch to the OS user ID used to start and stop the WebSphere administrative components such as the deployment manager. In our case, it will be the wasid.

3. Change your working directory to the profile's bin directory.

   Change your working directory to the deployment manager's bin directory, that is, <Dmgr_Profile_Path>/bin. This is not necessary but it will ensure that you are invoking the correct script (in case you have multiple profiles on a host.)

4. Start the WebSphere administrative command line interface (`wsadmin`).

   Since you have global security turned on, in order to connect to any of the administrative components using various scripts, including `wsadmin.sh`, in addition to any script's required parameters, you will need to supply the administrative ID and password. To start the administrative command line interface, issue the command:

   ```
   <Dmgr_Profile_Path>/bin/wsadmin.sh -conntype SOAP -host mydmgr
   -port 10005 -user wasadm -password <mysecretpwd> -lang jython
   ```

   > If this is the first time you use Jython as scripting language, the command will issue a long list of libraries being loaded.

At the end of the output you should see similar lines to the ones shown next.

WASX7209I: Connected to process "dmgr" on node sb02Dmgr using SOAP connector; The type of process is: DeploymentManager

WASX7031I: For help, enter: "print Help. help()"

wsadmin>

1. `wsadmin.sh` commands to execute to disable GS.

   In order to verify that global security is enabled, type the command:
   `AdminTask.isGlobalSecurityEnabled()`

   Which should return **true**. To disable global security, type the command:
   `AdminTask.setGlobalSecurity ('[-enabled false]')`

   If the command is successful, it should return the value **true**. Now to confirm the current status of global security, repeat the first command of this series. It should return **false** this time. In order to commit this change you need to save it to the WebSphere repository. Issue the command:
   `AdminConfig.save()`

   This should return an empty string (''). You can now exit the **wsadmin** interface.

   > Food for thought: What would happen if you restart the `dmgr` process and then attempt to re-enable global security in this wsadmin session? Why is this?

2. Synchronize the changes with the other nodes in the cell.

Use your favorite method to synchronize all of the nodes in this cell.

3. Restart the deployment manager.

    In order to make the change active you need to restart your administrative environment, that is, the deployment manager and all of the node agents.

4. Log in to the WebSphere Console.

    When you log in to the Administrative Console, you will notice that the Log in page will look like the beginning with only a field for User ID.

5. Revert the change and re-enable global security.

    Log off the WebSphere Console. Start the `wsadmin` interface. You can use the command used before but you do not need to include the user and password parameters. When you get the `wsadmin>` prompt, issue the following command:

    ```
    AdminTask.setGlobalSecurity ('[-enabled true]')
    ```

    The output of this command should be **true**, if there were no issues. Confirm that global security is enabled using the command `AdminTask.isGlobalSecurityEnabled()` as you did before. Save your results. Synchronize the changes with the nodes. Restart the administrative components.

    Your environment has global security turned on again.

Summary

In this chapter, you have learned about locks. Well, not really what you have learned is that there are different types of user registry, LDAP being the most common. You also learned the type of information you will need to be able to configure global security. In addition, you learned that setting the SSO domain name and selecting and configuring the user registry are prerequisites to enabling the administrative security. Furthermore, you gained experience setting up global security using the WebSphere Console. You now know some of the most common security roles that could be used in your organization. Finally, you learned how to disable global security using the administrative command line interface and how to re-enable it using the same interface. This is quite an accomplishment. Congratulations. Time for a coffee break, you've earned it!

3
Configuring User Authentication and Access

Not too long before this chapter was written there was an interesting turn of events that could help us visualize our topic. In November of 2009, the President of the United States of America hosted a State Dinner honoring the Prime Minister of India. In this type of formal and ceremonious event, there are well-defined groups of participants. For instance, you may have the hosts, the guests of honor and other important guests, security personnel, military members, service people, media, and on occasions, crashers. The underlying principles that surround a State Dinner may help us to better understand the concepts of security domains, user registries, authentication, and authorization of users as they pertain to a WebSphere application server environment.

This chapter deals with users, how they can be organized and managed to grant access to the information and resources they are entitled to. In the next sections:

- You will be exposed to the concepts of security domains and user registries.
- The chapter provides a hands-on approach to creating security domains using scripting.
- A mini project at the end will help you understand the various concepts presented by protecting an application server. In this project, the chapter describes the use of federated repositories by creating and managing users and groups. It then uses that structure to deploy and protect an application.

Security domains

In terms of our State Dinner proceedings, we would observe that there may be several organizations working in harmony with the sole purpose of making sure the occasion is a successful one, and perhaps even memorable for all participants involved. At first glance, we would observe two distinct groups: participants and service. These two generic groups could be divided further down, at least a level. On the one hand, take the participants, for instance. This group would be made of hosts, guests of honor, important guests from the hosting government, and perhaps important guests from the honored country. On the other hand, we have the service group which would be made of the security organization, the press and the service provider group. Each of these groups helps the event coordinator to delegate responsibilities, so managing the occasion is feasible. In version seven, WebSphere has introduced the use of multiple security domains.

Just as in the State Dinner analogy, where groups are assembled to manage a group to accomplish a task, in WebSphere there is now the concept of multiple security domains. With this new feature introduced in Version 7, it is now possible to use multiple security settings at different levels or scopes in the WebSphere infrastructure. In other words, a scope in the context of security defines where the settings are applicable. Therefore, if there are differences in terms of the security requirements among two or more enterprise applications, Version 7 makes it easier to configure many of the security parameters customized to the need of each of those enterprise applications.

> **Best practice: use multiple security domains**
>
> Take advantage of this new feature to increase the security of your WebSphere infrastructure. Make a habit to *define at least two security domains*. In other words, the global security domain should be reserved for the administrative component of the WebSphere infrastructure.

WebSphere Version 7 supports the following scopes, which can include their own custom security domain:

- Global security
- Cells
- Clusters
- Servers
- Service Integration Buses

Keep in mind that in order to be able to configure a security
domain for cells, clusters, servers, or service integrations
buses, global security must be enabled and configured.

What is a security domain

A WebSphere security domain is a well-defined collection of security-related
parameters and settings that guide how resources are to be protected in a given
scope, as well as what type of services may be provided to entities requesting them.

There are a large number of settings that make up a security domain. A group
of those settings can only be defined at the global security level. The rest of the
security settings can be customized at lower security domains. Among the security
settings that can be superseded by non-global security domains, we can find the
following categories:

- Enablement of application security
- Java 2 security
- User realm (registry)
- Trust Association Interceptor (TAI)
- SPNEGO Web authentication
- RMI/IIOP Security (CSIv2 protocol)
- JAAS
- Authentication mechanism attributes
- Authorization provider
- Custom properties

On the other hand, the categories of security settings that can only be defined at the
global security domain are as follows:

- Web attributes (single sign-on)
- Secure communications attributes (SSL)
- Security auditing
- LTPA authentication mechanism
- Kerberos authentication mechanism

Scope of security domains

In light of this new feature, an obvious question arises: given an enterprise application, which security configuration would apply? The issue of which security element can be applied to an enterprise application hosted in a WAS ND7 environment is determined by the following:

- When an enterprise application is executing on an application server or a cluster and there is a security domain defined at either of those levels, security parameters defined at the security domain level will be applied to the enterprise application. Any security parameter that is not defined at the security domain level will be obtained from the global security configuration. This is applicable even if a security domain at the cell level is defined.

- When an enterprise application is running on an application server or cluster that does not have an associated security domain, but there is a security domain at the cell level, security values defined at the cell security domain will be applied to the enterprise application. Any other security value not defined in the cell security domain will be gathered from the global security configuration.

When the previous two scenarios do not apply, security parameters will be obtained from the global security configuration.

Therefore, in order to help us answer this question, let's refer to the next diagram. In this diagram, global security has been defined, which is a prerequisite to define additional security domains (as was stated earlier in this chapter). This fact is illustrated by the long rectangle at the top of the diagram. In addition to the global security, a security domain has been defined and assigned to the cell scope. In our diagram, this security domain is represented by the rectangle underneath the global security domain. In this diagram, we have two application servers. They could very well be servers of other types or clusters or service integration buses. In this diagram, both application servers are protected, using security settings (that is, security is enabled).

In any event, the application server represented by the green rectangle and denoted by the letter 'A' on the left of the diagram does not have a security domain defined. Finally, the application server represented by the blue rectangle and denoted by the letter 'B' is configured with its own security domain. Let's focus now on the enterprise applications shown at the bottom of the diagram in order to see which security domain governs them.

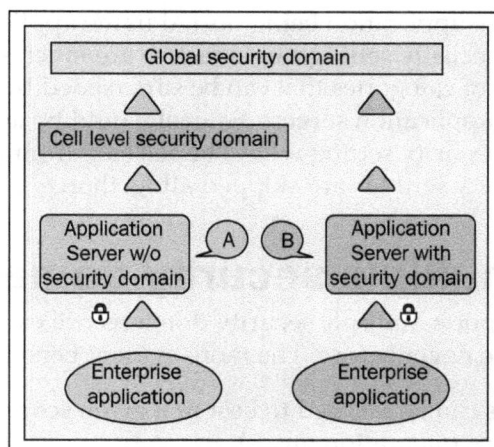

```
┌─────────────────────────────────────────────┐
│  ┌───────────────────────────────────────┐  │
│  │        Global security domain         │  │
│  └───────────────────────────────────────┘  │
│         △                    △               │
│  ┌─────────────────────┐                     │
│  │ Cell level security domain │              │
│  └─────────────────────┘                     │
│         △                    △               │
│  ┌───────────┐  ⟨A⟩ ⟨B⟩  ┌───────────┐      │
│  │Application│           │Application│      │
│  │Server w/o │           │Server with│      │
│  │security domain│       │security domain│  │
│  └───────────┘           └───────────┘      │
│     🔒 △                    △🔒              │
│  ⟨ Enterprise ⟩         ⟨ Enterprise ⟩       │
│  ⟨ application ⟩         ⟨ application ⟩      │
└─────────────────────────────────────────────┘
```

Scenario 'A' background: Global security is enabled. Cell scope security domain is defined and enabled. Application server security is enabled, but it is not mapped to a specific security domain.

The enterprise application represented by the oval is running on the application server 'A'. Since this server has security enabled but is not mapped to a custom security domain, any security settings from the group of categories that can be superseded by non-global security domains and would be defined at the cell scope (for example, the enablement and configuration of trust association) would be applied to this application. This fact is represented in the diagram by the middle small triangle, located between the cell and the application server. Furthermore, any security setting from the group of categories that can be superseded by non-global security domain and would not be defined at the cell scope (for example, authorization provider), would be applied from the global security domain. This situation is represented in the diagram by the top small green triangle, located between the global security domain and the cell level security domain.

Scenario 'B' background: Global security is enabled. Cell scope security domain is defined and enabled. Application server scope security domain is defined and enabled.

Finally, for the enterprise application being hosted in the application server 'B', the rules to identify which security settings are effective are much simpler. Any security settings from the group of categories that can be superseded by non-global security domains defined at the application servers 'B' level would be used for the enterprise application. Any other security setting would be selected from the global security domain. Cell level security settings are skipped altogether.

Benefits of multiple security domains

Since WebSphere 7 supports multiple security domains, we can see an added amount of flexibility like never before. The more evident benefits are as follows:

- Security settings can be tailored to best fit a given scope (cells, clusters, servers, or service integration buses).
- Since certain security configuration will take precedence at a given scope over the global security configuration, a security domain can focus solely on the aspects that need to be customized, and continue to use suitable parameters from the global security.
- It is now possible to segregate administrative security configuration from application configuration.

Limitations of security domains

There are some points that we need to keep in mind since they are not supported. However, if we look closely at such restrictions, it may be to our benefit not to have those settings at all levels.

Among the limitations, it can be mentioned that the categories of security settings available for configuration are at the global security level and cannot be overridden.

Additionally, another limitation is the fact that there is only one federated repository, and this can only be defined at the global security level.

Administrative security domain

For the State Dinner analogy, it would be assumed that the local government has the final word in terms of the implementation of the security for the event. One official, or one department or group within a department, would be made responsible for managing the event security. Let's denote this entity as the **State Dinner Security Management Team (SDSMT)**. It is likely that there would be other groups, possibly not affiliated with the SDSMT, which would be delegated the overseeing of security management for a specific aspect of the proceedings. For instance, one of the responsibilities of the contracting agency would be to receive bids for the food services. The contracting agency would have received, as part of its delegation of authority, the guidelines for a food services provider. It would be the duty of the contracting agency to ensure such guidelines are met by the selected food services contractor. If there was a group providing certain types of services for which the SDSMT would have not made the corresponding delegation of authority, the SDSMT would have to directly oversee that particular group. Therefore, the party ultimately responsible for any security related affair would be the SDSMT.

In WebSphere version 7 it is now possible, as mentioned earlier, to have multiple security domains. When global security is enabled, an administrative security domain should be defined. The security parameters defined at the global level will be applied down to the application server or service integration bus levels. You have already had some hands-on experience setting up the administrative security domain in the *Setting the domain name* on *Chapter 2*, *Securing the Administrative Interface*. For this chapter's project, an alternative procedure will be described.

> **Best practice: using the global security domain as the administrative domain**
>
> Since WebSphere version 7 now supports multiple domains, it is highly recommended to *set aside the global security domain uniquely for administrative purposes*. Therefore, you also must create at least one other security domain. If you are planning to use only one additional security domain, define it at the cell level.

Configuring security domains based on global security

When global security is configured and enabled, it becomes by default the global security domain. After you enable global security as described in *Chapter 2, Securing the Administrative Interface* if you were to open the **Security** domains page (that is, expand the **Security** leaf and click the **Security** domains link) you will see that it is empty. Assuming that you wish to use multiple security domains, you may wish to clone the global security domain and use it as it is, or with some customization at the cell level. For instance, you may wish to use the federated repository realm for global security and a standalone LDAP registry for the cell security domain.

In this section, we will learn to manipulate security domains by doing the following:

- Creating a global security clone and assigning it to the cell level using the administrative console.
- Creating security domains from scratch using the wsadmin scripting tool.

In this section, the wsadmin tool will be used to create the administrative security domain. The procedure that will be used is broken down in two stages. In the first one, the security domain is created. In the second stage, the security domain is mapped to a scope.

Creating a global security domain clone

This task will be demonstrated using the Deployment Manager Console. Log in to the console, then expand the **Security** leaf and open the **Security domains** page. In order to clone the global security domain, click the **Copy Global Security** button. In the page that is displayed, type in a name for the domain and a description. For simplicity, we will call it cell.yourcompany.com. Click the **Apply** button in order to remain on the same page. When the page re-displays, several more sections are added. Under the section **Assigned Scopes**, check the cell box as it is shown in the following screenshot:

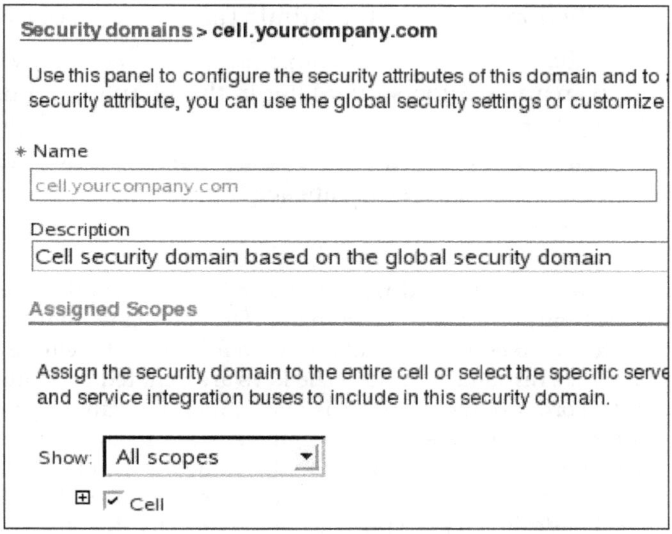

Security domains > **cell.yourcompany.com**

Use this panel to configure the security attributes of this domain and to
security attribute, you can use the global security settings or customize

✳ Name

cell.yourcompany.com

Description

Cell security domain based on the global security domain

Assigned Scopes

Assign the security domain to the entire cell or select the specific serve
and service integration buses to include in this security domain.

Show: All scopes   ▼

⊞ ☑ Cell

Finally, scroll down and click the **OK** button to make the changes on the configuration. Save and synchronize the changes.

Creating a security domain using scripting

The security domain secappsrv01.yourcompany.com will be created, and the "**Security domain for SecureAppServer01**" will be set as its description. In order to create this security domain using the wsadmin scripting tool, follow the procedure shown next:

1. Log in to the Deployment Manager command line.
2. Change working directory to the bin directory.
3. Start the wsadmin command.
4. Issue the following command:

   ```
   ./wsadmin.sh -user wasadm -password <yourpwd> -lang jython
   ```

> **Best practice: use Jython as your scripting language**
> IBM encourages using Jython as your primary, if not the only, scripting language to administrate your WebSphere application server environment.

5. Create a security domain using the AdminTask wsadmin object.

We will create the asecappsvr01.yourcompany.com security domain. It will be assigned to an application server later in this chapter and used in the mini project at the end of it. At the wsadmin> prompt, enter the following code:

```
AdminTask.createSecurityDomain('-securityDomainName secappsvr01.
yourcompany.com -securityDomainDescription "Security domain for
SecureAppServer01" ')
```

In the code above, the **AdminTask** wsadmin object offers the createSecurityDomain command. The command, in its string syntax form, takes a string that follows a format that includes two keys and their corresponding value. The keys are denoted by a preceding dash. The order of the elements is key, value, key, value (without the commas.) The value for the parameter securityDomainName is the name desired for the domain; the value for the key securityDomainDescription is a string surrounded by double quotes that designates the purpose of the security domain.

6. Save the configuration.

Use the wsadmin object AdminConfig and its command **Save** to make your configuration changes permanent.

You can log in to the Deployment Manager console and go to the **Security domains** page following the crumb trail **Security | Security domains**. The page should include the security domain just created, as shown in the following screenshot:

Select	Name ◇	Description ◇
⊞ Preferences		
New	Delete	Copy Selected Domain...	Copy Global Security...		
Select	Name ◇	Description ◇
You can administer the following resources:		
☐	cell.yourcompany.com	Cell security domain based on the global security domain
☐	secappsvr01.yourcompany.com	Security domain for SecureAppServer01
Total 2		

User registry concepts

It is likely that at the State Dinner there would be several lists that would help manage all of the people expected to be on site at the event. There would be lists of organizations that have personnel at the event site. It would be also probable that each individual organization involved in the proceedings by offering services would make available a roster of employees assigned to work at the event. Similarly, there would be lists of guests. These lists would probably come from different organizations as well, such as the local government and the embassy of the foreign guest of honor.

In WebSphere, are the equivalents to the lists used at the State Dinner. They are the user registries, also denoted as user repositories. These registries will contain lists of groups, individuals, and perhaps other entities relevant to the operation of an organization.

What is a user registry

As briefly mentioned in *Chapter 2, Securing the Administrative Interface* there are various types of user registries. In essence, a user registry is a collection of records that contains information about users. The fields, which represent the type of information kept about users, who make up a record, will vary immensely. Each field will be associated with relevant information about the users in the repository. However, it is likely that at least some records will contain a field that stores the user identification (user ID), and a field for storing an authentication token of some sort, such as an encrypted password. In addition, the registry may include a hierarchy of groups that best fit the needs of an organization. It is customary that each user in the registry will be assigned to at least one of the groups.

Applications and a variety of IT systems will take advantage of this organization of groups and users to provide different types of services according to an established design. Let's see how the WebSphere application server uses these stores.

WebSphere use of user repositories

User repositories are used by WebSphere mainly for two purposes. Firstly, the information available through a user repository may be used to certify that a user is who the user says he is. This is known as **authentication**. Secondly, once a user is authenticated, the information stored in the registry indicates the resources a user is entitled to access. This is known as **authorization**. Let's look at each of these uses.

Authentication

In our State Dinner analogy, a roster of authorized employees would be provided by a food services company to the security agency handling the event. An entrance at the location holding the State Dinner would be designated as the point of entry for personnel working in matters relating to the banquet. In the diagram shown next, a worker of the company offering food services is denoted as "Bill". His job is to help fix a portion of the meal to be served to the guests. When Bill is ready to report to work, he would be directed to the entrance assigned for the food services personnel. His initial goal is to go to the kitchen or cooking area to be used for this event. His purpose is represented in the diagram by the yellow rectangle labeled "Going to the kitchen". A security guard, identified in our diagram as "Kim", would stand at the entrance, ensuring that anyone wanting to enter presents the proper credentials, for example, a photo ID provided by their employer. The security guard would then insure that the name bored in the credential matches the name in the roster list the guard received. The list is illustrated in the diagram by the oval labeled **Food Services Roster**. Additionally, the guard would ensure that the person presenting the ID is a match with the picture in the ID. We will assume that Bill has been asked to work at the event and his name is on the roster. Kim will then give the OK and provide an event badge that Bill must wear while working at the event.

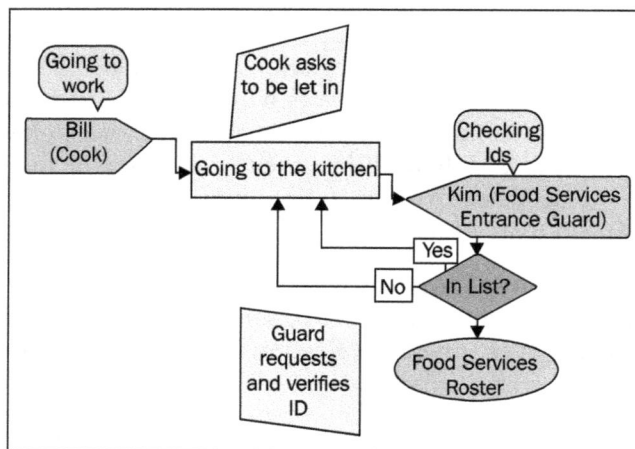

In WebSphere, at an abstract level, the mechanism used to verify the identity of a user is very similar to our State Dinner analogy. Consider the following diagram:

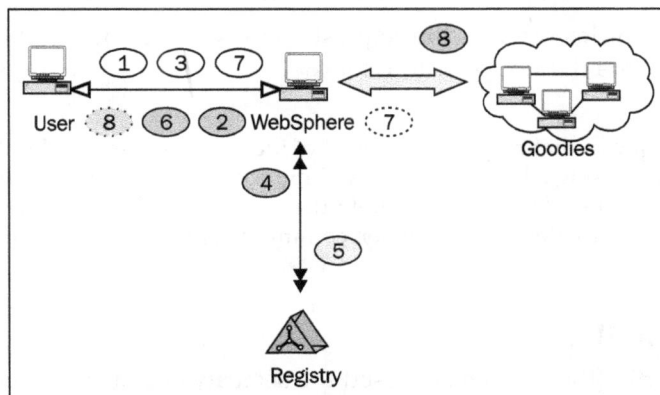

In this simple diagram, **User** wants to get some **Goodies**. Let's find out what interactions take place between the different components of the system. Interactions are presented as a sequence of communications numbered from 1 through 8 and depicted in small ovals. Ovals **1**, **3** and **7** represent communications or messages sent by User; Ovals **2**, **4** and **6**, in turn, represent messages originated from WebSphere; **5** is a message sent by Registry; and finally, **8** indicates communications sent by Goodies. The sequence in the diagram is as follows:

1. **User** sends an identifier, such as a URL, of a resource or service requested.

2. **WebSphere** replies by asking for credentials (for example, a user ID and password combination) in order to with grant the request. Let's assume that User is entitled to access to the resource or service in question.

3. User provides an identification (for example, a login ID) and a password.

4. **WebSphere** asks Registry to validate if the ID and password match its records.

5. Since we are assuming that User is entitled to the resource or service requested, Registry responds to WebSphere in the affirmative. At this point, many other subprocesses may take place, but for our purposes, we assume that this is all that is required.

6. WebSphere answers User in the affirmative and, along with the answer, it sends a token that User can include in subsequent requests. Again, other subprocesses may take place at this point, which will be ignored until later.

7. User makes the same request, but includes the token provided earlier by WebSphere; WebSphere finds the token in the request and forwards it to Goodies. (This is represented by the dotted line oval number 7.)

8. Finally, **Goodies** receives the request and responds back to WebSphere, who then forwards the response to User.

> Requests that may require proof of identification are not limited to users using a browser. More and more applications interact with each other. Therefore, it is not uncommon to find an application A, having to identify itself when communicating with application B.

Authorization

When our friend Bill (the cook) has passed the security entrance, he would be led to the area where he is expected to perform his job. In our State Dinner analogy, badges that personnel wear represents their credentials, whereas the specific location each of the workers attempts to go to represent the sought resource. In other words, when Bill enters the premises, his blue badge would give him access to the kitchen. If Bill wants to take a peek at the guests and attempts to go to the ballroom or the lawn, when he tries to enter another area by presenting his badge, the security person at that checkpoint would deny him access based on the color of his badge. The security guard at the checkpoint would have received a list that summarizes what color badges can enter that specific location. Such a list represents our registry concept. There would be other people working at the State Dinner that would have access to more than one working area. An example of this type of case would probably be the security personnel at the event. Let's remember Kim, who checked out Bill's credentials at the food services entrance. She probably would have been granted access to all exterior areas. This would include all of the points of entry to the building, the various gardens and the lawn where the banquet is to take place. With that type of access, Kim can perform different duties. Each duty will place her at a specific location of her assigned access areas. However, she cannot go into the kitchen or the ballroom since they, being interior locations, fall outside of her assigned areas of access. Essentially, the type of badge an employee is carrying will indicate which areas this employee is authorized to go to based on custom lists used at each checkpoint.

In WebSphere, these principles apply as well. Let's make our User-WebSphere-Registry-Goodies a little more complex. Refer to the diagram shown next. In it, the **Goodies** component has been blown up. In this improved version, Goodies contains three different areas, which could be mapped to applications with a unique context root. One of the applications, Public, only requires that the user be registered (for example, authenticated). There is no change in behavior between accessing Public in this second revision and accessing Goodies in the first revision. Another Goodies application, HR, in addition to be authenticated requires that the user belongs to Registry group **Human Resources**. By design, any member of Human Resources would also belong to the Registry group **Employee**. The final application, **Employees**, in order to be accessed requires that the user be authenticated and that also belongs to Registry group **Employee**.

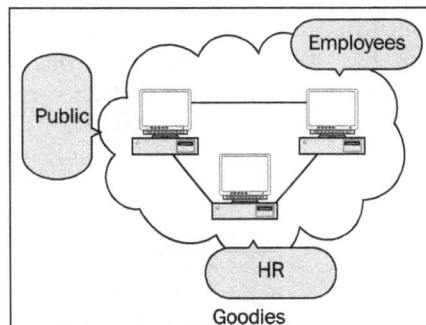

Supported user registry types

User registries may vary from one another along many dimensions. WebSphere version 7 supports four types of user registry:

- Local operating system
- Stand alone LDAP
- Stand alone custom registry
- Federated repositories

With the possibility of using multiple security domains, it is also possible to use several user registries within a cell. A specific type of registry would have to be mapped to a given security domain. It is therefore possible to have shared user registries between two or more security domains.

> **Best practice: use stand-alone LDAP**
>
> Most organizations use LDAP as the user registry. This is because many IT components outside of a WebSphere environment that require user authentication already make use of LDAP-based user directory services as a central corporate user repository. LDAP-based repositories can be used to grant access to employee's workstations, Notes e-mail, Blackberry enterprise applications, and so on. It is natural then to map WebSphere with an LDAP-based user repository.

Local operating system

Under this user registry type, WebSphere would use the users and groups defined at the OS level where the **Deployment Manager** is executing. This principle is depicted in the next diagram. In it, the deployment manager and other WebSphere components (for example, node agents and application servers) are executing under the same host, identified by the creative label **'Local OS'**. Any security-related operation within the WebSphere environment will draw its information from the OS users and groups defined.

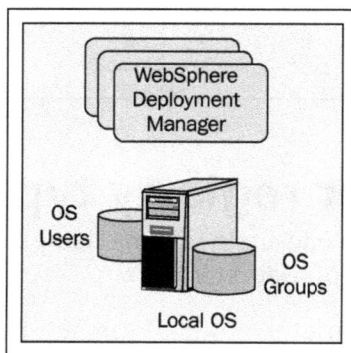

> It is not recommended to use this type of repository if the following two circumstances are met different WebSphere components execute on different hosts hosts do not have a synchronized authentication mechanism. In other words, each host has its own user repository.

In our State Dinner analogy, an equivalent approach to the local OS registry is highly unlikely. Let's see what would be the implications. From our past discussions, there are multiple groups that are responsible for selected personnel. This is equivalent to using multiple servers. Each group handles its own roster, so it would not be possible to use a particular group's roster approach simply because it would contain only that group's employees and no other personnel. For the local OS type of registry to be feasible, it would require that each participating service group (for example, Secret Service) would have to include all persons expected to be at the dinner in its own roster. So, it is practically not possible.

Standalone LDAP

For the State Dinner occasion, let's recall that there will have been created individual event (that is, official) badges that indicate the bearer is who the badge says the person. In addition, the color of the badge will provide access to one or more areas on site. Bill would present his official badge, after getting it from Kim, to any security personnel who would ask for it on his way to the kitchen. All event badges were ordered by only one group (after getting the rosters from all organizations involved). So a single organization (most likely the security group) would handle the distribution of the badges.

In the IT world, and in particular in WebSphere environments, an LDAP-based server handles groups, users, and any specific objects that suit the needs of a corporation. In the following diagram, WebSphere is running in a cluster model. For any authentication or authorization needs, it will draw the required information from the LDAP server and pass it on to the enterprise application, which will act accordingly.

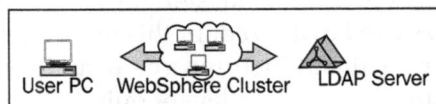

Standalone custom registry

WebSphere gives a lot of flexibility. Among the low-level behavior that can be altered is how authentication and authorization is carried out. This is not a new feature in WebSphere Version 7. Essentially, in order to use a custom registry, the WebSphere Java interface `com.ibm.websphere.security.UserRegistry` must be implemented. Since the implementation requires not only a good understanding of what an application needs, but programming to create a Java class that implements the `UserRegistry` interface, it is outside of the scope of this book.

> For those readers who would like to learn more about this interface, you can go online to the WebSphere Version 7 information center at: http://publib.boulder.ibm.com/infocenter/wasinfo/ v7r0/index.jsp?topic=/com.ibm.websphere.nd.doc/ info/ae/ae/xsec_customuser.html

Federated repositories

In our State Dinner scenario, we saw earlier that having a single master roster as a source is impractical. The security group could be assigned the task of creating a master roster from multiple sources. Let's designate the sub-group within the security group as the **Master Roster Management** group (**MRM**). MRM would probably split the task into major efforts: collecting a list of all guests from different sources; and gathering employee/contractor rosters from all of the non-guests which would probably include the press plus the various service contracting agencies. MRM would turn this master roster to whatever group is in charge of defining categories of participants and what type of person would be assigned to each category. Once the master roster and the master participant categories have been combined, the event badges can be ordered. In this way, all non-guests involved in the event have been identified and their records would contain the same type of information. This information would be relevant only to the occasion.

The purpose of a federated repository is very similar to the State Dinner scenario. There will be times in which information needed to provide users of a WebSphere application authentication and access may be stored on more than one repository, even perhaps using different storing techniques. Federated repositories make transparent to WebSphere the actual source of the information. The types of user registry supported in a federated repository are:

- File-based
- Database
- LDAP

- Custom

- Local OS (see note below)

> Initially in version WebSphere 7.0, only the first four registry types were supported. Since fix pack 5, local OS is also supported as a potential member of a federated repository.

In the following diagram, our former scenario seems a bit more complex. From the WebSphere applications, perspective, nothing has changed. The fact that there may be more components as back-end repositories is transparent to the enterprise applications and other WebSphere components requiring this type of security information. One of the additions to the diagram as compared with the *LDAP-based registry* diagram is the presence of the VMM component. **VMM** stands for **Virtual Member Management**. VMM is a component of the WebSphere ND v7 architecture. It is used to create an interface with the federated repository. In the diagram, four types of back-end registry make up the federated repository. Therefore, for any authentication and authorization needs, WebSphere will obtain the required information through its VMM infrastructure.

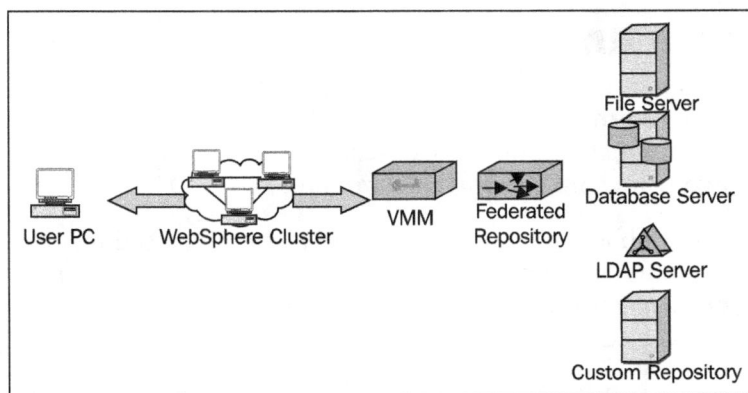

However, there are certain restrictions in using a federated repository. The chief restriction among them is that there can only be one federated repository per cell, and it can only be used at the global security level. Another limitation is that a user must be unique among all of the federated back-end repositories. If there is a query a user to the federated repository, an exhaustive search is performed on all of the federated repositories. If the result of the search returns more than one result, an exception will be returned.

Protecting application servers

In this section, a simple process to enable security on an application server will be shown in the form of a mini-project. At the end, you are expected to have a secured application server that will challenge users with authentication credentials.

There are some prerequisites that need to be completed. Most of them, if not all, are probably already familiar to you. The very next section states what elements are expected to be available and ready to be used. You should not be required to perform any task.

WebSphere environment assumptions

This mini-project assumes that the following architecture is available: one WebSphere cell environment with at least one node federated to the cell. All of the WebSphere environment components can reside on a single OS host. As before, the procedures shown below are being carried out on a Linux OS.

The second assumption is that the original WebSphere file-based federated repository is available. The name of the file is `fileRegistry.xml`. It is deployed when a deployer manager is created in the directory: `<Profile_Root_Directory>/config/cells/<Cell_Name>`.

The third and final assumption is that the IBM-provided enterprise application `DefaultApplication.ear` is available for deployment. If not already deployed on the application server server1, you should find it under the directory `<WASND_Install_Directory>/installableApplications`.

> If `DefaultApplication.ear` was not deployed on your installation, run the WebSphere installer (`install.sh`) on your media distribution, and select to add the Sample Applications feature to your existing installation.

Prerequisites

As stated earlier, the tasks included in this section should be familiar to you. Therefore, only a brief description of what is needed will be provided. You may want to use the deployment manager console or the wsadmin scripting interface to carry out the tasks. Let's have fun.

Creating an application server

For this project, you need to add a new application server. In our example it is called SecureAppServer01. You can give a name that best suits your organization standards. The name is not relevant. The default parameters, when creating an application server, can be used, as there are no special requirements other than that the server must be the application server type.

Creating a virtual host

Create the `employees_vh` virtual host. Add the Web Container default and administrative ports to it, making sure to remove any other ports added by default.

Creating application JDBC Provider and DataSource

Both a JDBC Provider and a DataSource at the application server SecureAppServer01 level are required. On the one hand, the requirements for the JDBC Provider are shown in the next screenshot:

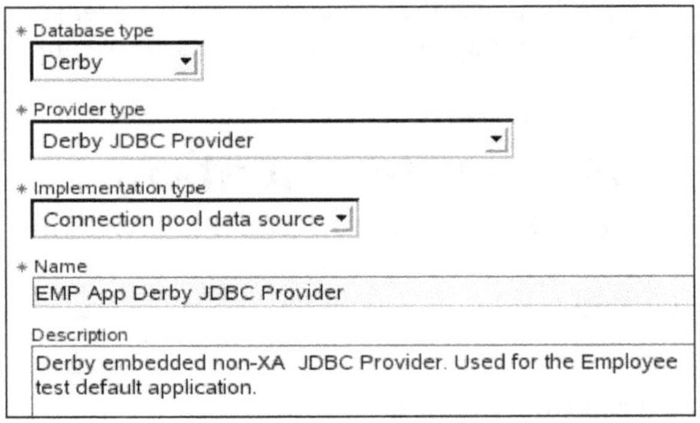

On the other hand, the requirements for the DataSource are as follows:

Use the JDBC Provider just created. Name: **Employee Data Source**. JNDI name: **EMPDataSource**. Database name: **${APP_INSTALL_ROOT}/${CELL}/EmpDefaultApplication.ear/DeafaultDB**.

Configuring the global security to use the federated user registry

You probably already have a WebSphere environment with the global security enabled. If that is not the case, you can refer to the previous chapter (*Securing the Administrative Interface*). Insure to select **Federated repositories**, under the **Available realm definitions** pop-up menu. Click the **Set as current** button to make federated repositories the new realm definition.

> If you had to make this change, do not forget to restart the environment (deployment manager and node agent or agents) so the switch of repository becomes effective as you continue your work.

Creating a security domain for the application server

This is probably a recent skill that you have acquired. If you are using the same environment as when you created your first security domain in the administrative security domain section, you can use the cell security domain as the basis for the new one. Name the domain secappsvr01.yourcompany.com. Keep in mind that the name of the security domain does not need to follow the format of a FQDN name, so you could omit the yourcompany.com portion.

> If you are creating the security domain from scratch, you could go to the **Security domains** page as you have done before and click on the **Copy Global Security...** button to ensure that this new domain uses the federated registry as its realm.

Configuring user authentication

In order to make the sets of actions clearer, let's continue working with our **User-WebSphere-Registry-Goodies (UWRG)** scenario. In this section, we will be creating a couple of users and groups and will add them to our federated repository.

> **Federated repository feature**
>
> Currently, in WebSphere Version 7, only the federated repository is supported for reading and writing to the back-end registry. The other supported repository types are supported for reading only.

Creating groups

Our goal in this section is to create two groups from the UWRG scenario. Drawing our requirement from the diagram in the *Authorization* section, one group will be **Employee** and the other, **Human Resources**. In order to create groups in the federated repository follow the steps described next:

1. Log in to the **Deployment Manager** console.

2. Open the **Manage Users** page.

   Expand the **Users and Groups** leaf on the left, click on the **Manage Groups** link. The **Manage Groups** page is displayed as shown in the following screenshot. Initially it is blank, as we have not defined any groups.

3. Add the groups to the federated repository.

   Click the **Create...** button. The **Create Group** page opens, as shown in the following screenshot. Enter **Employee** in the **Group name** field. Optionally, type **All Employees** in the **Description** box. Once the fields are completed, click the **Create** button. You should get a notification stating that **The group was created successfully**. Click the **Close** button. You are sent back to the **Manage Groups** page, this time listing your newly created group.

   Create a Group

   * Group name

   Employee

   Description

   All employees

   [Create]   [Cancel]

   Repeat the steps to create the **Human Resources** group. Optionally, create the group **Authenticated**.

4. Display existing groups.

   On the **Manage Groups** page, click the **Search** button. The groups just created should be displayed in the results area; your screen should look similar to the following screenshot. (The description fields may not match those in the screenshot, but that does not have any relevance.)

   Search for Groups

   Search by   * Search for   * Maximum results
   Group name ▼ *   100

   [Search]
   3 groups matched the search criteria.

   [Create...] [Delete] Select an action ▼

Select	Group name	Description	Unique Name
☐	Authenticated	Registered User at YourCompany INC Website	cn=Authenticated,o=defaultWIMFileBasedRealm
☐	Employee	Regular employees of YouCompany INC	cn=Employee,o=defaultWIMFileBasedRealm
☐	Human Resources	HR Dept of YouCompany INC	cn=Human Resources,o=defaultWIMFileBasedRealm
Page 1 of 1			Total: 3

Creating users

The approach followed to create users follows similar mechanics as creating groups. There are a few extra steps, however, in order to assign users to groups. Our goal is to create at least two users. One, Ravi Employee, will be assigned to the Employee group. The second is Lola HR, who is part of the Human Resources group.

1. Open the **Manage Users** page.

    Expand the **Users and Groups** leaf on the left, click on the **Manage Users** link. The **Manage Users** page is displayed as shown in the following screenshot. Initially it is blank, as we have not defined any users.

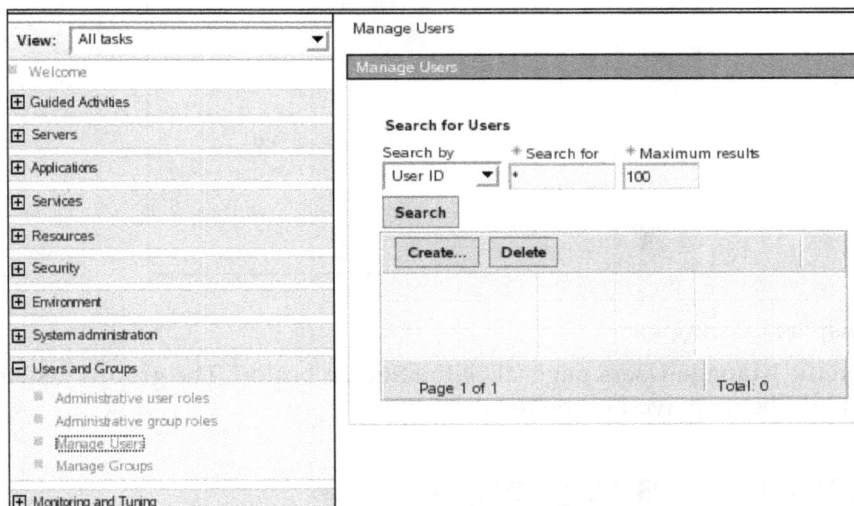

2. Add the users to the federated repository.

    The information needed for each user to be entered is: User ID, Name and **Last name**, and **password**.

ID	Name	Last name
ravi	Ravi	Employee
lola	Lola	HR

Click the **Create...** button. The **Create User** page opens, as shown in the next screenshot. Fill the fields with the information provided. (Passwords are at your discretion.) Then click **create**. A notification indicating the user creation was successful is displayed. Repeat for the other user.

```
Create a User

* User ID
[ravi]                              [ Group Membership ]

* First name                        * Last name
[Ravi]                              [Employee]

E-mail
[                    ]

* Password                          * Confirm password
[****]                              [****]

[ Create ]  [ Cancel ]
```

3. Display existing users.

   On the **Manage Users** page, click the **Search** button. The groups just created should be displayed in the results area.

Assigning users to groups

The final sub-task of this section is to assign users to groups. It is rather simple, as you may imagine. Open the **Manage Groups** page. After doing so, click the **Employee** group link. The **Group properties** section is then displayed. Click the **Members** tab. In the section that is displayed next, click the **Add Users...** button. In the new section that appears, click the **Search** button. Select the users **ravi** and **lola** from the list, as shown in the next screenshot. Click the **Add** button. A confirmation screen is shown stating that the addition was successful.

Add Users to a Group

Group name

Employee

Search for users that will be members of this group.

Search by	* Search for	* Maximum results
User ID ▼	*	100

Search

5 users matched the search criteria

lois
travi
sam_visitor
samples
wasadm

** Add**   **Close**

> As a simple exercise, go to the **Employee** group page and confirm that the users are now members of the group.

Configuring access to resources

For the State Dinner scenario, people working at the event would need access to the kitchen, hallways around the official gathering and residence surroundings and the dining area. These areas are equivalent to resources in the WebSphere scenario. Each area would be designated with a color-code that would match the color of the official badges. Workers belong to a particular company or sub-contractor. Companies and sub-contracting agencies are equivalent to the groups in our federated user registry.

Thankfully, it is very likely that you will not be in the business of managing users and groups as most corporations use an LDAP type of registry. However, it is always good to get a feel for what is under the hood, so to speak, when you have to troubleshoot applications in the future.

What is left for this task is extremely easy to carry out since most of the work has already been completed. Let's use a procedure so you can repeat this task easily in the future.

1. Go to the required security domain page.

   Open the `secappsvr01.yourcompany.com` security domain page. (Expand **Security**, click the **Security domains** link, click the `secappsvr01` link.)

2. Assign the security domain to the application server.

   In the section, **Assigned Scopes**, expand the cell tree all the way to the **SecureAppServ01** application server. Check the corresponding box.

3. Enable security at the application server level.

   In a similar way, expand the **Application Security** tree. Click **Customize** for this domain, and check the **Enable application** security box.

4. Save the changes.

Simple, wasn't it? What is left is also simple, but may take a while longer.

Testing the secured application server environment

In order to test that we have enabled security for the application server, we will deploy, as stated at the beginning of the *Protecting application servers* section, the enterprise application DefaultApplication.ear.

Deploying and securing an enterprise application

Deploy the application using the Deployment Manager Console, as you normally do with other enterprise applications. The following screenshot shows the start of installing an enterprise application. To get to this page follow the breadcrumb **Applications | New Applications | New Enterprise Application** (not shown). The arrow indicates where to start.

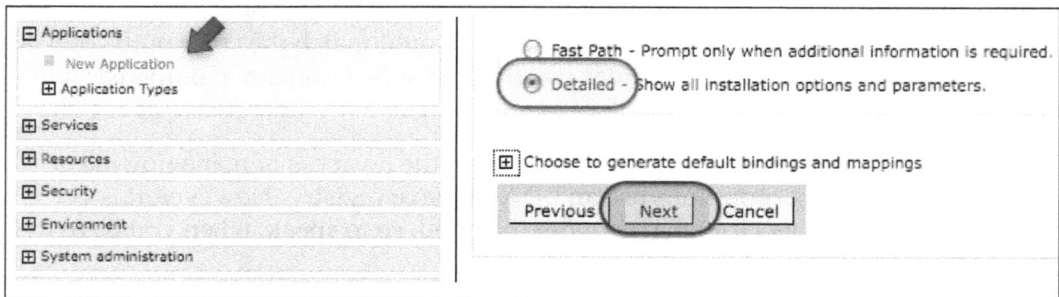

Perform the EAR installation with the following specifics:

- Use **Detailed** installation (as opposed to **Fast Path** shown in the screenshot above, and focus on the brown oval).

- Use the default values, with the following exceptions:
    - ○ In Step 1, change the **Application name** to `EmpDefaultApplication`: (this name must match the DataSource database name).

☑	Distribute application
☐	Use Binary Configuration
☐	Deploy enterprise beans

Application name

`EmpDefaultApplication`

☑	Create MBeans for resources

    - ○ In Step 2, map the modules to SecureAppServer01.

Module	URI	Server
Increment EJB module	Increment.jar,META-INF/ejb-jar.xml	WebSphere:cell=wasmasterCell01,node=wasmasterNode01,server=SecureAppServer01
Default Web Application	DefaultWebApplication.war,WEB-INF/web.xml	WebSphere:cell=wasmasterCell01,node=wasmasterNode01,server=SecureAppServer01

    - ○ In Step 9, map the EJB module to the DataSource you created.

Select	EJB module	URI	Target Resource JNDI Name	Resource authorization
☐	Increment EJB module	Increment.jar,META-INF/ejb-jar.xml	EMPDatasource Browse...	Resource authorization: Per application

    - ○ In Step 10, do the same as Step 9.
    - ○ In Step 11, map to the `employees_vh` virtual host.
    - ○ In Step 12, set the context root to `/emp/`.

- Step 13 is the big one. Note that initially there are no users or groups mapped to the application defined **All Role** role. Perform the following:

  1. Map the **Employee** group to the **All Role** role.

     Select the **All Role**. Click the **Map Groups** button. Click the **Search** button. Add the **Employee** group to the **Selected** column. Click the **OK** button.

  2. Confirm that the group appears on the step summary.

     Observe that under the column **Mapped Groups**, **Employee** is listed as the only group.

     For the rest of the steps, click the **Next** button and the **Finish** button on Step 15.

Save and synchronize with the nodes. Then start the new application server.

Accessing the secured enterprise application

The last step is to access the application. Using your browser, open the application server URL: `http://<your-hostname>:<virtual-host-port>/emp/snoop`. If everything worked as expected, you should see a pop-up window asking for your credentials as shown in the following screenshot:

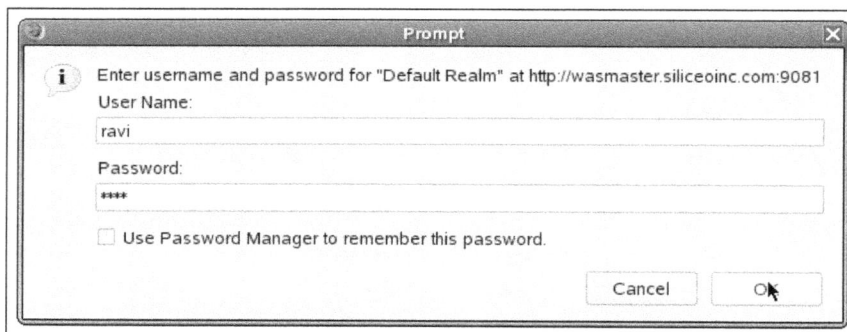

If your credentials are correct, your browser will display the familiar snoop servlet.

Congratulations!

Summary

In this chapter, you have learned about a new feature in WebSphere Version 7—that of using multiple security domains. You also learned about user registries to be used in the security domains as their realm. In addition, you gained hands-on experience creating security domains and assigning them to a scope. You can do several of the tasks using the administrative console and the wsadmin scripting tool. You went through all of the steps to secure an application server using a custom security domain, created groups and users and deployed an application that was protected by that security domain. Way to go! Time for another break. How 'bout tea this time?

4
Front-End Communication Security

Let's think for a few minutes about corporate (snail) mail. Our scenario would be a large company with multiple locations, say in the same city. An external party to this company would be trying to communicate with an employee of the purchasing department using post office mail. It would be likely that the address on the envelope would have a general street address for the company plus a mail stop of the purchasing department or another group within the company. The external party would not know by the address, the actual location of the employee. However, that information is irrelevant. The combination of company street address, mail stop, and employee name would be enough for the intra-corporate mail to deliver the envelope. This company mail scenario is similar in a way, to how WebSphere front-end communication architecture security works. Now, don't be skeptical.

You have already learned what's been described in the first three chapters. Let's see how everything is fitting together. Consider the diagram shown next. The outer-most rectangle (teal), labeled **Global Security**, represents the key concepts learned in Chapter 2, *Securing the Administrative Interface*. Among such concepts, we have the following:

- **Global Security**: This notion is extremely important. Without it there cannot be security at the application level. Therefore, in our diagram, global security encompasses all of the other security topics described so far.

- **Administrative Security**: In that same chapter, administrative security was explained, as well as how to configure it. The concept is represented in the diagram by the long rectangle (golden), labeled **Administrative Security**, at the bottom.

- **User registry**: In that same chapter, an introduction to user registries was provided as it pertains to the selection of a repository to be used with the global security. Since a more in-depth description of the topic was offered in Chapter 3, the rectangle (blue), labeled **User Registry**, on the left overlaps portions of Chapter 2 (the rectangle labeled **Global Security**) and Chapter 3.

The rectangle (maroon) labeled **Authentication and Authorization** illustrates the key concepts reviewed in Chapter 3, *Configuring User Authentication and Access*. They are listed as follows:

- **Security domains**: Just like global security was the most important concept in Chapter 2, the notion of the security domain is the chief idea in Chapter 3. This is expressed in what was already mentioned in Chapter 3, when there is only one security domain, it is equivalent to global security as everything (that is, all scopes) in such cells will be dependent on the global security configuration.

- **User registries**: Another very important principle described in Chapter 3 is that of user registries. Such registries help to secure resources based on the presence of a user in the registry (authentication), and the memberships such user holds that grant the user access to the services of an application (authorization).

- **Protecting Application Servers**: As a practical application of the concepts covered in Chapter 3, a project to protect a J2EE Application Server was detailed, presenting the necessary steps to secure the JVM hosting an application.

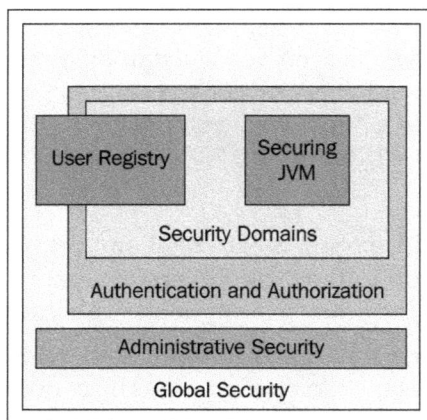

By the end of this chapter, we will be adding to this diagram the concepts described in the next sections. A WebSphere enterprise application may be accessed either by users via browsers or by client applications. This chapter describes the most common communication channels used on the front-end of the enterprise architecture.

At the end of the chapter you will learn about:

- Common front-end infrastructure architectures
- Best-practice architecture
- Secure Socket Layer protocol
- Certificate Authorities
- Public and private encryption keys
- Key databases or store keys

You will conclude this chapter by applying all of these concepts in securing through encrypted communications the environment created in the last chapter.

Front-end enterprise application infrastructure architectures

Let's recall the enterprise application server architecture view from Chapter 1. During this chapter, we will concentrate on the front-end portion of the architecture. The following figure shows the front-end of a classic WebSphere clustered environment topology:

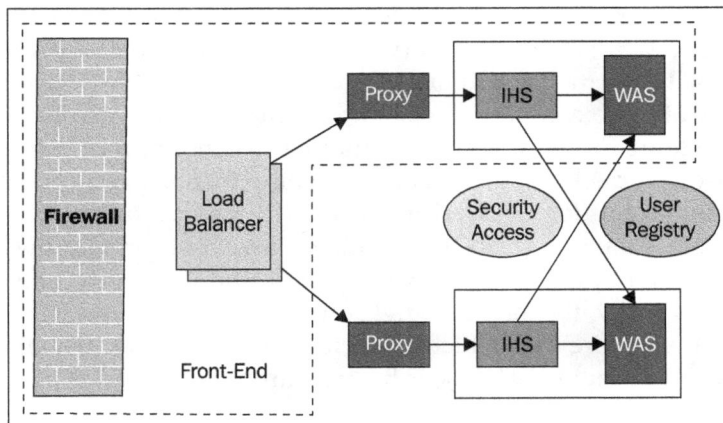

[✎ The main purpose of the architectures presented in this section is to limit in-bound network traffic from the Internet into your organization service networks.]

WebSphere horizontal cluster classic architecture

The diagram shown in the previous figure is a simplification of the classic WebSphere horizontal cluster architecture. In such topology, each of the rectangles (green) labeled **WAS** represents a WebSphere node, which may include a node agent (the WebSphere notation for the name of the process is nodeagent) and one or more Java application servers. This node is hosted on its own [OS] server. Therefore, in the diagram, we have two servers hosting a WebSphere node each. It is in this layer, Java Application Server, where the enterprise application executes.

[✎ Keep in mind that the Java Application Server, often referred to simply as Application Server, executes in IBM's **Java Virtual Machine (JVM)**.]

In addition, going back to the previous diagram and taking a step closer to the Internet (that is, moving towards the left), the rectangles (light blue) labeled **IHS** represent the IBM HTTP Server version of the open source Apache HTTP server. Since in this topology we are using proxy servers, it is common to place the IHS server on the same OS host as the one used for the WebSphere node infrastructure. As it is expected, the IHS component provides the HTTP/S layer to the environment. Furthermore, taking another step towards the Internet, the rectangles (dark blue) labeled **Proxy** represent HTTP proxy servers. They provide both performance and security functionality to the architecture. Depending on the technical requirements, the functionality of a proxy server can be implemented with WebSphere Edge Components' Caching Proxy or even with another instance of IHS, just to name a few options based on the WebSphere family of components. In any event, the proxy servers are hosted in a different physical server. Moreover, moving one step closer to the Internet, the rectangles (teal) labeled **Load Balancer** represent the function of the load balancer. Normally, only one will be active and the second one is used for high-availability. Finally, the long rectangle (orange) labeled **Firewall** at the left-most position represents the firewall, which is our first line of security. The firewall is the only internet-facing component of the infrastructure.

The flow of a request made by a browser or an application client would be as follows. The inbound network transactions from Internet entities would go through the Internet firewall and be passed to the load balancer, which transparently would forward the request to the corresponding proxy server. The proxy server will terminate the traffic flow and create a new request that would be sent to the IHS/WebSphere hosted application for processing. The result of such transaction will be picked up by the proxy server and create a response to the Internet entity that made the request in the first place.

The advantages, from the viewpoint of security, of this type of architecture are as follows:

- Infrastructure is protected from Internet traffic via a firewall, which must be configured to only allow traffic to specific service ports (for example, HTTP, HTTPS, DNS).
- Proxy servers break the communication link between the browser (or entity making the HTTP/S request) and the WebSphere host.

WebSphere horizontal cluster using dual-zone architecture

A variant of the horizontal cluster classic architecture is one in which several of the components are placed across two security zones. The horizontal cluster using dual security zones architecture is shown in the following diagram. In this type of architecture, an additional firewall (labeled DMZ firewall) has been placed to create security network zones. For simplicity, the components used for authentication have been omitted from the previous diagram.

It is a common practice to house the WAS/IHS servers in the corporate network zone, in many cases referred as the **intranet** zone. The intranet zone has as its front-end boundary the DMZ firewall. In addition, the outer most components of the architecture are proxy servers and load balancer. This outer zone is normally referred as the Demilitarized Zone (**DMZ**). As shown in the diagram, its front-end boundary is made up by the Internet firewall and its back-end boundary is marked by the DMZ firewall. The functionality of each of the components shown is the same as in the previous case. The main difference of this architecture is the presence of a second inner firewall. Its function is to provide further protection to the WAS infrastructure in case a proxy server is compromised.

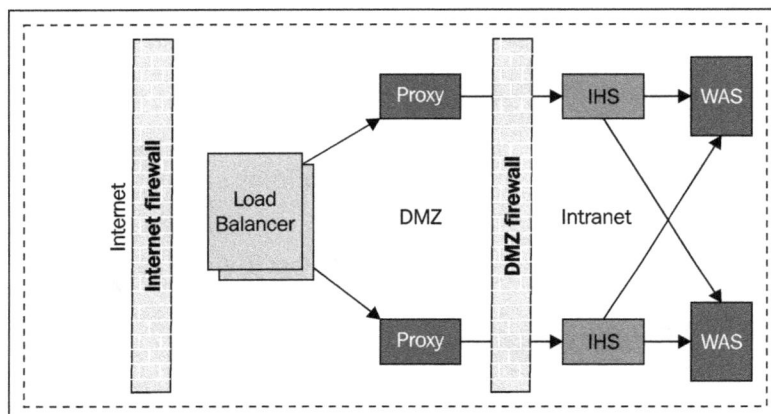

The way in which network traffic flows is as follows. Request traffic will originate from browsers and possibly application clients located in the Internet. The traffic flow would go through the Internet firewall and would pass to a load balancer, which transparently would forward the traffic to the corresponding proxy server. The proxy server would terminate the inbound network traffic and create a new request to the IHS/WebSphere hosted application.

In addition to the benefits from the classic architecture, the dual-zone architecture provides the following features:

- All in-bound network traffic is terminated in the DMZ zone.
- As an obvious offspring of the previous benefit, no inbound network traffic into the intranet is originated in the Internet.

- Application Server hosts and authentication infrastructure are further protected by a second firewall in case a proxy server is compromised by potential intruders.

- Flexibility of locating IHS and WAS servers on the same or different OS hosts.

WebSphere horizontal cluster using multi-zone architecture

Many corporations are under the belief that the dual-zone architecture is very secure against potential intruders. The fact of the matter is that such architecture, although popular, misses protecting against internal threats. Therefore, we show next the horizontal cluster with multi-security zones architecture. This architecture is based on the dual-zone topology, with the addition of a third firewall (Production firewall) placed between the service networks (DMZ and production) and the corporate intranet as shown in the following diagram.

In this type of layout, inbound traffic into the DMZ zone may come from either the Internet or the corporate intranet. The rest of the network traffic flow is the same as in a dual-zone architecture environment. In addition, the diagram shows an additional player, the WebSphere administrative user. Strictly speaking, this element is not part of the front-end topology, however, it is included in the diagram to show another use of the production firewall.

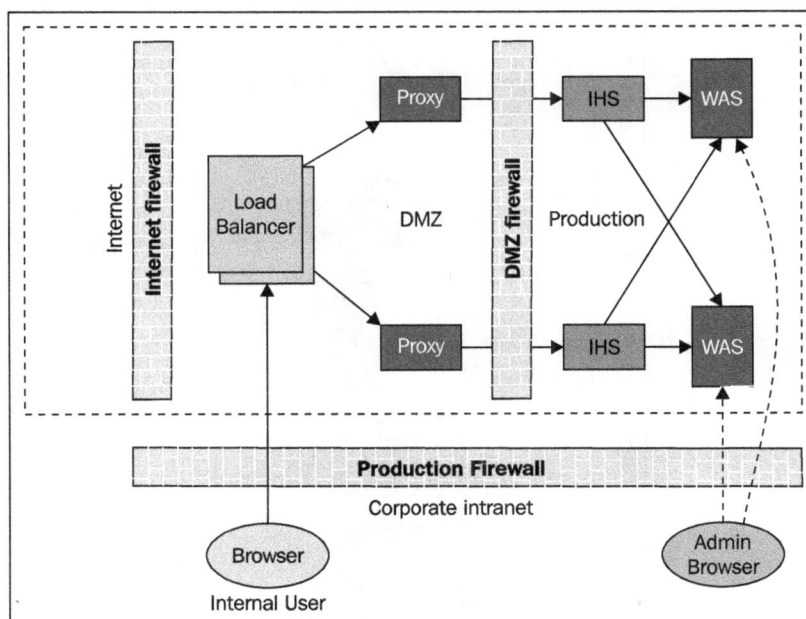

The added advantages of this architecture have been implicitly mentioned in the previous paragraphs. In addition to the benefits provided by the classic and dual-zone architectures, the multi-zone architecture provides the following advantages:

- Protection against potential internal threats by the use of a third firewall
- Added protection to accessing the administrative components of the infrastructure

Best practice: Use a multi-zone architecture

In industries where the flow of network traffic contains highly confidential and sensitive data such as the banking and healthcare industries, using the horizontal cluster with multi-security zones is the recommended architecture.

SSL configuration and management

The architectures discussed in the previous section provide the next step in securing a java enterprise application server infrastructure, specifically at the front-end of the architecture. In order to visualize this fact, we are in a position to add to the diagram introduced at the beginning of this chapter. The updated diagram, which includes architecture concepts, is shown as follows. The two dotted rectangles represent the concepts to be reviewed in this and the next sections.

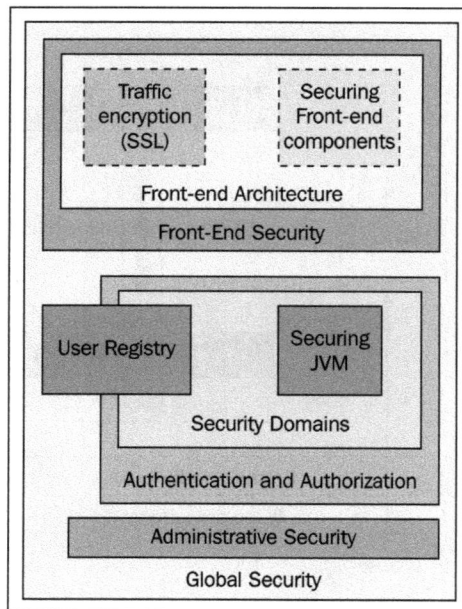

What is SSL

SSL stands for Secure Socket Layer. It is a protocol that offers security at the transport layer. In addition, security is increased by using encryption of data at that layer. What does all that mean? According to the Internet Protocol Suite documentation (cf. RFC-1122 *"Requirement for Internet Hosts – Communication Layers"* `http://tools.ietf.org/html/rfc1122`) there are four major Internet protocol layers, as shown in the following diagram. The most used protocol used on the web is HTTP, which would reside on the top-most layer, the **Application Layer**. In contrast, SSL is a foundational protocol as with others on the **Transport Layer**. Application Layer protocols rely on the Transport Layer protocols to operate. In other words, HTTP uses TCP as its transport layer, whereas HTTPS uses SSL as its transport layer.

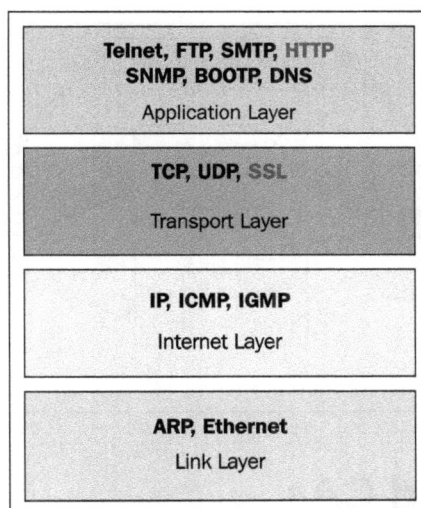

How SSL works

It's been my experience that in order to understand a concept better, having an example that employs such a concept makes things much clearer. With that in mind, let's refer to the following diagram to see SSL in action. The objective in the diagram is for the client to establish a series of secure transactions with the server. This communication will take place using the HTTPS protocol. Using a simplified version of the protocol, let's see the communications that take place. In the diagram, the client (most likely, a browser) will send an HTTPS request, initially as an anonymous user, to the server. Being this, the very first communication of the server with this client, (a.k.a. session) the server will send its public SSL key 'inside' a signed SSL certificate. This is denoted in the diagram by the label **S-Public-Key** inside the rectangle (maroon) labeled **Server Certificate**.

Normally, the signer of a server certificate is a well-known Certificate Authority. (Cf. next section for further details about CA's). In such case, the client will trust the certificate sent by the server and retrieve the server's public key. From this point on, the client will use the server public key to encrypt the data to be sent to the server. The next step then to close the initial handshake is for the client to use the S-Public-Key to encrypt its own **C-public-key** and send it to the server. The server would use its S-Private-Key to decode the message sent by the client and would use the client C-public-key to encrypt its communications to the client. The SSL topic is very extensive and, therefore, it's out of the scope of this book to provide a more detailed review of the technology. If you are interested in learning more about SSL please refer to the Internet Draft document: The SSL Protocol Version 3.0 (available online at `http://tools.ietf.org/html/draft-ietf-tls-ssl-version3-00`).

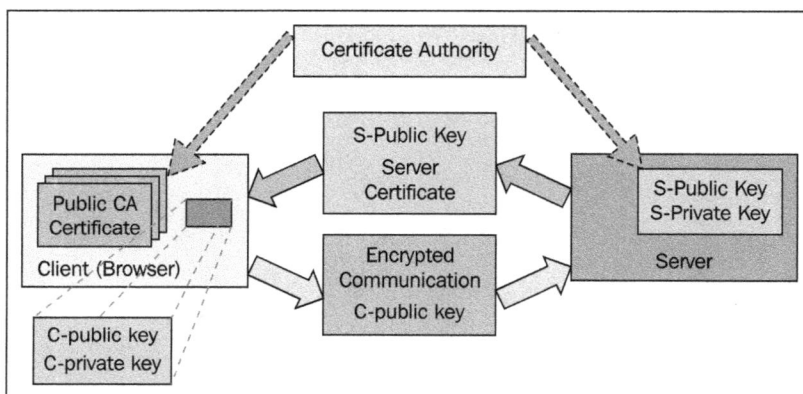

Certificates and CAs

In the previous section, **Certificate Authorities** (**CA**) were briefly mentioned. They are the Internet official organizations that guarantee that an SSL certificate is genuine and it comes from the server that sends it. **CA root certificates** refer to certificates created by these organizations and such certificates would be normally included by software vendors in browsers and client applications. This fact is very important, as for a browser to trust a server certificate, the signer (CA) must already exist in the client (browser) certificate vault, or keystore. The following diagram is an extension of the previous diagram. In it, a server (or another entity within the server's organization) generates a pair of asymmetric SSL keys to be used for encryption (private key) and for decryption (public key).

During this process, a Certificate request is created that includes the server's public key. This request is then sent to one of the CA vendors, which after some identity verification and exchange of currency, will return a signed certificate that includes the server public key. Once the signed certificate is received, it will be installed, along with the corresponding private key, in the server's keystore. This process is shown by the process flow in our diagram:

- Generate certificate/keys
- Certificate Request
- Receive Certificate Request
- Sign Certificate
- Signed Certificate

Once the signed certificate is installed, the client-server communication process is as described in the previous section.

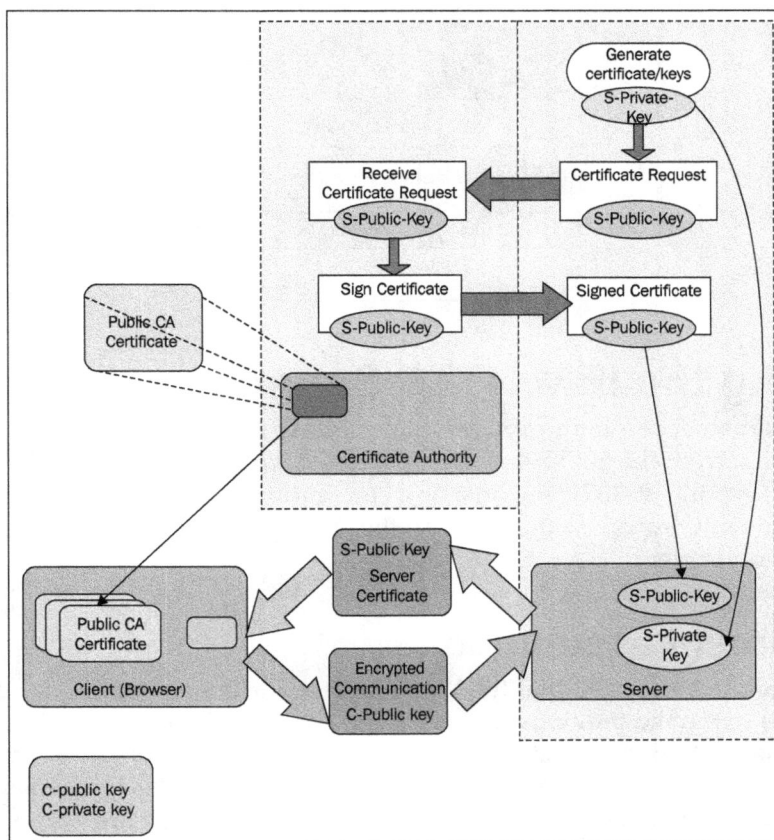

Securing front-end components communication

The concepts related to SSL, CAs, and so on, covered in the previous section help us to add a new block to our road map. This new block is labeled **Traffic encryption (SSL)**. In this section, we will be able to finalize the diagram started at the beginning of the chapter; filling in the details for the dotted rectangle in the diagram.

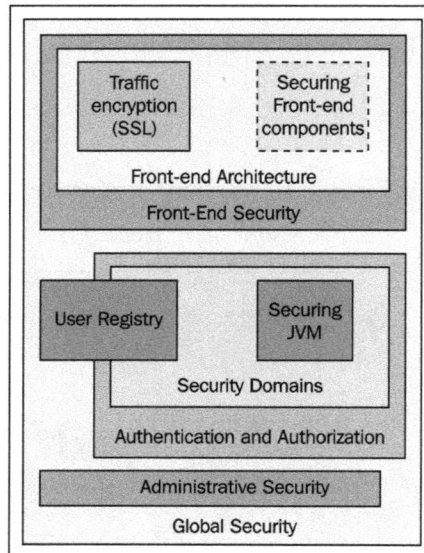

Securing the IBM HTTP Server

In this final subsection, a mini-project will be used to secure the front-end communication from the HTTP server down to the Application Server. A the end, you should have an IHS listening on a non-conventional port using HTTPS to communicate with browsers; and through the WebSphere Plug-in, use SSL to talk to the Application Server.

Environment assumptions

For the project, it is expected that the WebSphere environment would be very close to how it was left in the previous chapter; that is, there would be a secure application server hosting the Snoop servlet. It is also expected that an installation of the IBM HTTP Server at least the same version level than that of the WebSphere version. This IHS installation must include the security components that are part of the IHS distribution software.

> In order to verify that the security components are included in your installation, insure that the ikeyman utility is installed in the IHS bin directory.

In addition, for the project to be successful, the environment must have already IHS integrated with WebSphere, that is, the Application Server virtual host must be configured to listen to the port IHS listens to and IHS must have the WebSphere Plug-in configured and loaded. Finally, the certificate to be used at the IHS level will be self-signed. In a production environment, you would need to use SSL certificates signed by a Root CA.

SSL configuration prerequisites

As in the previous chapter, the tasks mentioned in this section should be already familiar as they are activities performed by WebSphere administrators on routine basis.

Add SSL ports to WebSphere employees_vh virtual server

There will be two ports needed (listening ports, that is) in this setting. The first one will be assigned to the HTTP server and it will be used as its HTTPS port. The second port is already in use by the Application Server web container. It is the port designated as **WC_defaulthost_secure** in the server's end points.

Select a port for the HTTPS communication that is not utilized (in this project, the port will be 8444). Add this port to the WebSphere virtual host employees_vh, created in the last chapter.

> **Best practice: Avoid using the wildcard * (star or asterisk) as the host name.**
>
> Limit the range to the actual server (or servers) involved. Using wildcards may leave your application vulnerable for an address spoofing attack. For the host alias being added, replace the wildcard and use the server host name value.

In order to enable the second port, **WC_defaulthost_secure**, its value must be added to the **employees_vh** virtual host, making sure to replace the wildcard with a hostname value.

Creating the SSL system components

Out of the box, the IHS installation does not include the basic elements needed to enable SSL. The reason for this is that many companies choose to break the SSL link at the load balancer or reverse proxy levels. However, if the data is sensitive, it is highly recommended to continue the SSL link down to the IHS.

In this section, the following components or items will be created:

- A directory to store the various files related to the keystore
- A keystore in the format supported by IHS (CMS)
- A self-signed certificate with its public and private keys

Create the IHS SSL keystore

The first order of business is to create a place to save the IHS certificate that will be created shortly. The item needed is a key database or keystore. There are multiple ways to create one. However, keep in mind the following.

> The type of keystore needed is a CMS keystore. (CMS refers to the algorithm used, Cryptographic Message Syntax, to store the data.) There are other types, but IHS v7 only supports this type.

One of the methods to create this type of keystore is to use the IHS command **gsk7capicmd**, located in the bin directory.

> **Best practice: create a dedicated directory in which to keep the files related to the certificates used.**
>
> In this project the directory **certs** will be created immediately underneath the IHS root directory.

Execute the commands:

```
cd <IHS_Root>/certs

../bin/gsk7capicmd -keydb -create -db ws1key.kdb -pw <password> -stash
```

> If desired, use the command **gsk7capicmd -help** to review the various objects and actions available.

The command **gsk7capicmd** takes as a first argument an object. In the command above, it is **-keydb**, the object representing the keystore. The second parameter is an action to perform on the object. In the command above, it is to create a keystore. The rest of the commands are options to the first pair. The name of the database, which is a file, is given by preceding the file name with the keyword **-db**. Next, is the password to be assigned to the keystore (argument to the -pw keyword). The final keyword indicates to the command to create a file where the password will be stashed. In future interactions with the keystore, when a password is provided, the system will first check if a stash file exists and use that value to authenticate the action. If the file does not exist, the system will decrypt the password form within the actual keystore.

In order to verify the success of the command, perform a directory listing. You should see a list of files similar to the one shown next:

```
ls
    total 129
    drwxr-x---   2 root root     176 May 23 18:04 .
    drwxr-xr-x  25 root root     664 May 23 17:59 ..
    -rw-------   1 root root      80 May 23 18:04 ws1key.crl
    -rw-------   1 root root  115080 May 23 18:04 ws1key.kdb
    -rw-------   1 root root      80 May 23 18:04 ws1key.rdb
    -rw-------   1 root root     129 May 23 18:04 ws1key.sth
```

List built-in CA certificates included in keystore

This next step is not required; however it shows interesting information included in the keystore created in the previous step. It is the built-in list of Root CAs. Any certificate that is signed by one of the CA's certificates in this keystore will be trusted by the server.

```
../bin/gsk7capicmd -cert -list all -db ws1key.kdb -pw <password>
```

The following is the list of CA certificates included:

```
Certificates found:
* default, - has private key, ! trusted
!   Thawte Personal Premium CA
!   Thawte Personal Freemail CA
!   Thawte Personal Basic CA
!   Thawte Premium Server CA
!   Thawte Server CA
!   VeriSign Class 3 Secure Server CA
!   VeriSign International Server CA - Class 3
!   VeriSign Class 4 Public Primary Certification Authority - G3
```

```
!   VeriSign Class 3 Public Primary Certification Authority - G3
!   VeriSign Class 2 Public Primary Certification Authority - G3
!   VeriSign Class 1 Public Primary Certification Authority - G3
!   VeriSign Class 4 Public Primary Certification Authority - G2
!   VeriSign Class 3 Public Primary Certification Authority - G2
!   VeriSign Class 2 Public Primary Certification Authority - G2
!   VeriSign Class 1 Public Primary Certification Authority - G2
!   VeriSign Class 3 Public Primary Certification Authority
!   VeriSign Class 2 Public Primary Certification Authority
!   VeriSign Class 1 Public Primary Certification Authority
!   Entrust.net Global Secure Server Certification Authority
!   Entrust.net Global Client Certification Authority
!   Entrust.net Client Certification Authority
!   Entrust.net Certification Authority (2048)
!   Entrust.net Secure Server Certification Authority
```

Create self-signed certificate

It is now time to create the self-signed certificate that this IHS server will use in its secure communications. The command takes as an object a certificate object, denoted by the keyword **-cert**. The action to perform on the object is **-create**. The syntax for the keystore and password is the same as before. The **-label** keyword takes as an argument a string that will be used by the humans to identify the certificate. (This label will be used later on, when configuring httpd.conf). The next keyword, **-dn**, represents the distinct name. Its format is similar to the structure used for LDAP. The available fields are:

- CN=common name
- O=organization
- OU=organization unit
- L=location
- ST=state, province
- C=country
- DC=domain component
- EMAIL=e-mail address

Only CN is required. The only thing to be aware of is that for the field CN, no spaces are allowed. If using additional fields, surround the distinct name with double quotes. The rest of the keywords used below are optional. The keyword **-size**, indicates the size of the public and private keys to be generated. Valid values are from 512 to 4096. The default value is 1024. To designate the certificate as the default certificate of the keystore, use the keyword **-default_cert**, and provide the value 'yes'. Finally, the length of validity of the certificate, in days, is provided using the keyword **-expire**. Valid values are from 1 to 7300, which is equivalent to 20 years. The default value is 365. Use the following command:

```
../bin/gsk7capicmd -cert -create -db ws1key.kdb -label ihs1.wasmaster -pw
<password> -dn "CN=wasmaster.yourcompany.com" -size 1024 -default_cert
yes -expire 365
```

> The default values for the parameter's size and expire were used in the command above so it is easy to remember.

Confirm the creation of self-signed certificate

In order to confirm the creation of the certificate, list all certificates.

```
../bin/gsk7capicmd -cert -list all -db ws1key.kdb -pw <password>
```

The start of the output generated by the command is shown below. Notice that our certificate, ihs1.wasmaster is listed and designated as: 1) default (*); 2) with private key (-); and is trusted (!).

```
Certificates found:
* default, - has private key, ! trusted
*-!     ihs1.wasmaster
!       Thawte Personal Premium CA
```

Finally, list content of self-signed certificate. The action keyword used is **-details**. In order to identify which certificate to list, the keyword **-label**, must be used. Use the following command.

```
../bin/gsk7capicmd -cert -details -label ihs1.wasmaster -db ws1key.kdb
-pw ws1key
```

```
Label         : ihs1.wasmaster
Key Size      : 1024
Version       : X509 V3
Serial Number : 70647a8370bde1fe
Issuer        : cn=wasmaster.yourcompany.com
Subject       : cn=wasmaster.yourcompany.com
Valid From    : Saturday, 22 May 2010 21:54:21 PM
```

```
To            : Monday, 23 May 2011 21:54:21 PM
Finger Print : 0x0a0740e0b2b69e1960640dfb2eb00220000ae381
Extensions    : NULL
Signature Algorithm: 1.2.840.113549.1.1.5
Trusted       : enabled
```

Configuring IHS for SSL

After having created the SSL components we will proceed to configure the IHS server to use these components. This configuration is made of the following stages:

- Modifications to the httpd.conf file
- Extraction of the WebSphere CA certificate
- Adding the certificate to the Plugin
- Validation of the SSL configuration

Modifications to httpd.conf

Enabling SSL in the httpd.conf file will be done using a virtual host to define the HTTPS server. The lines below can be added at the end of the configuration file, replacing the label **Server_IP** in bracket with the IP address of your server:

```
LoadModule ibm_ssl_module modules/mod_ibm_ssl.so
Listen [Server_IP]:8444
<VirtualHost [Server_IP]:8444>
SSLEnable
SSLServerCert ihs1.wasmaster
SSLProtocolDisable SSLv2
</VirtualHost>
KeyFile /opt/IBM/HTTPServer/ihsserverkey.kdb
SSLDisable
```

The first line in our code indicates IHS to load the module that implements the SSL protocol and enables HTTPS. The next two lines are standard IHS directives used for virtual hosts. Next, the first line inside the virtual host indicates to enable SSL form that point down until either we tell it to disable it or the end of the file, whichever occurs first. The next line, which contains the directive **SSLServerCert**, is to configure the label associated with our self-signed certificate, as it was indicated in the previous section (under *Create self-signed certificate*). The last line inside the virtual host indicates that we do not speak ancient languages, well not really. It just means that we won't support the old version 2.

> **Best practice: Do not use SSL protocol version 2 (SSLv2)**
> SSLv2 has several serious issues as stated in http://www.
> kb.cert.org/vuls/id/386964, which makes it unsuitable for
> secure communications.

The first line after the virtual host definition block indicates the file that contains the keystore. The last line in our code indicates that SSL is disabled for the main HTTP server.

> **Best practice: Isolate SSL configuration**
> Implementing an SSL-enabled IHS server is best done using virtual
> hosts. It is easier to administer and troubleshoot.

Extract the WebSphere CA certificate

In order to enable the SSL communication between the Plug-in loaded in the IHS and the application server (**SecureAppServer01**) hosting the application in question (**DefaultApplicationSecure**) perform the procedure described that follows.

1. Open the **NodeDefaultTrustStore** page of the node where **SecureAppServer01** executes.

   Traverse the following breadcrumb trail: **Security | SSL certificate and key management | Key stores and certificates | NodeDefaultTrustStore** (scope: (cell)wasmasterCell01:(node)wasmasterNode01 –in my particular case; your cell and node names will vary).

2. Verify the filename of the trust store.

   On that page, identify the location of the trust store for the node. Under the **General Properties** section, find the value for the **Path** field. Its value will be similar to:

   ${CONFIG_ROOT}/cells/wasmasterCell01/nodes/wasmasterNode01/trust. p12

   Insure that the filename is **trust.p12**.

3. Open the signer certificates.

   Then, under the **Additional Properties** section, to the right of the page, click the **Signer Certificates** link.

4. Identify the node's CA certificate.

   From the list of certificates, find the one whose alias is **root**. Select it by clicking the check box to its left.

5. Extract the CA certificate.

   Click the **Extract** button. The **Extract signer certificate** page is displayed. The goal now is to save the file that contains the WebSphere node signer certificate in the same directory as the IHS key store files, that is, **<IHS_Root_Dir>/certs**. In the field **file name**, enter a value for the CA file, for instance: **<IHS_Root_Dir>/certs/wasrootcert.arm**. (The extension 'arm' is customary for certificate files.)

Add WAS self-signed certificate to the plug-in

The two components between the HTTP server and the application server that will engage in the SSL transactions are the Plug-in, loaded in IHS, and **SecureAppServer01**. Therefore, the final configuration step is to add the certificate extracted in the last section to the plug-in key store.

1. Find the location of the plug-in configuration file.

   Do a search for the term **WebSpherePluginConfig** in the **httpd.conf** file. The value of that directive is the location of the plug-in configuration file. Its value may be similar to: **<IHS_Root_Dir>/Plugins/config/<Server_ID>/plugin-cfg.xml**.

2. Find the location of the plug-in key store.

   Open the file found in the previous step. Perform a search for the term **keyring**. Insure that the definition is within the block that corresponds to the **SecureAppServer01** server. The value may be similar to: **<IHS_Root_Dir>/Plugins/etc/plugin-key.kdb**.

3. Add the **SecureAppServer01** root certificate.

   Change your working directory to the directory where the plug-in key store is. For the next commands, you will need the password for the key store. Unless you have changed it, the default password should be WebAS. Execute the following command in order to display the current list of certificates found in the key store

   ```
   <IHS_Root_Dir>/bin/gsk7capicmd -cert -list all -db plugin-key.kdb
   -pw WebAS
   ```

Next, use the following command to add the certificate to the key store:

```
<IHS_Root_Dir>/bin/gsk7capicmd -cert -add -db plugin-key.kdb -pw
WebAS -label SecureAppServer01RootCert -file /opt/IBM/HTTPServer/
certs/wasrootcert.arm
```

In this command, the object is **-cert** and the action is **-add**. The other required options provide information about the key store, **-db**; its password, **-pw**; the tag to be used to identify this certificate in the key store, **-label**; and the location of the file that holds the certificate, **-file**. Repeat the listing of certificates command to insure that the label **SecureAppServer01Root** appears in the list.

Validation of the SSL configuration

Now, the moment that we have been waiting for — to see how all this ties together. Restart the **SecureAppServer01** application server. Restart the HTTP server. Open a brand new browser. Enter the IHS SSL address, similar to `https://<yourserver>.yourcompany.com: :8444/emp/snoop?Hello`

Your browser will alert you that the SSL certificate is not signed by a CA. The Firefox browser warning looks similar to the following screenshot:

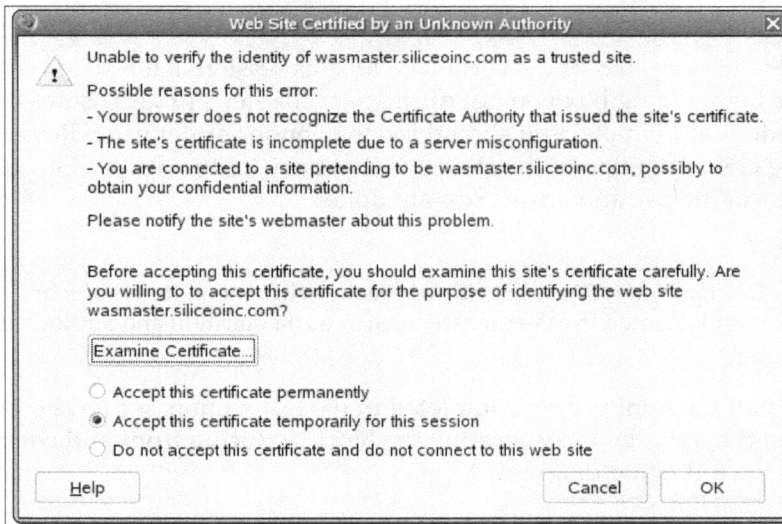

Click the **Examine Certificate** button. Verify that the DN you entered in the creation of the certificate appears in the details window. For the Firefox browser running under Linux, the screenshot is shown next.:

Certificate Viewer:"wasmaster.siliceoinc.com"	✕

General | Details

Could not verify this certificate for unknown reasons.

Issued To
Common Name (CN)	wasmaster.siliceoinc.com
Organization (O)	<Not Part Of Certificate>
Organizational Unit (OU)	<Not Part Of Certificate>
Serial Number	B1:DB:23:FC:41:FD:A0:7C

Issued By
Common Name (CN)	wasmaster.siliceoinc.com
Organization (O)	<Not Part Of Certificate>
Organizational Unit (OU)	<Not Part Of Certificate>

Validity
Issued On	06/11/2010
Expires On	06/12/2011

Fingerprints
SHA1 Fingerprint	A3:FB:07:90:EA:1B:DF:9E:CA:2E:CC:27:15:55:01:78:77:D5:86:86
MD5 Fingerprint	C3:08:FF:B6:33:FF:35:1F:CE:C2:4E:4F:5A:49:88:31

Click the close button. Accept the certificate for this session. After this, you should see the same login dialog box you got during last chapter's project. Enter the required credentials. Finally, you should see the Snoop servlet page. Review the page, paying close attention to the elements that have to do with an SSL connection, such as protocol (https), and so on. You are done!

[SSL by itself will not provide a secure environment. It needs to be supplemented by other means such as authentication and authorization.]

With the help of the mini project completed in the last section, we have completed the road map diagram, by incorporating the block 'Securing front-end components', as shown in the following diagram:

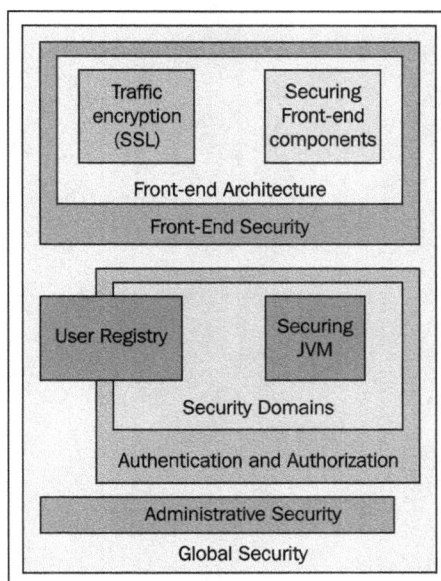

Summary

In this chapter you have learned the principles that will help you secure the front-end of your J2EE Application Server architecture infrastructure, such as the following:

- Front-end architectures
- SSL encryption, including CAs, private and public keys and key stores

We finished by putting all this new material into a mini project where you can do the following:

- Created a key store
- Created a self-signed certificate
- Added the certificate to the key store
- Created a virtual host in IHS that uses the HTTPS protocol
- Configured the WebSphere Plug-in to communicate via SSL with the back end application server

Well done! It's time for another well-deserved break. I do not know about you, but I am going to check if there are any FIFA World Cup matches. I heard that Germany was giving a spanking to somebody; I'm going to find out to whom.

Securing Web Applications

5

Securing web applications can be viewed differently, depending on the role of the person. This chapter helps the administrator to gain an understanding of the security components in which a team of developers may be most interested. It then describes the aspects of securing web applications that will have an effect on or that will be influenced by external components in the enterprise infrastructure. The chapter describes the following:

- How to secure a WebSphere web application
- The function of groups in securing an application
- The function of roles in securing an application
- The use of deployment descriptors in securing applications
- Identify the type of information provided by deployment descriptors at the time of application deployment that plays a role in security
- A procedure to build, package, and deploy a secure application made of multiple modules

Securing web applications concepts

J2EE Applications can be made up of dynamic/Java web applications and EJB applications. Dynamic web applications may consist of a combination of components such as dynamic Java components (Servlets, JSP's, and so on) as well as static components (for example, HTML, CSS, images--JPEG). Therefore, WebSphere offers the capability to customize access to both types of applications: dynamic/ Java web applications and EJB applications. This chapter explores securing Java web applications whereas the following chapter covers the securing of EJB applications. In the next couple of sub-sections you will learn of two different views of web application security.

Developer view of web application security

In most cases, developer teams having a J2EE background outside of a WebSphere environment tend to see security of their applications from a purely programmatic point of view. Skilled developers use methods provided by the J2EE security API.

Through such a API, an application can gather information about the user making the request. For instance, the API provides methods to obtain information such as the request for user ID or to query the request object to find out if the user is enabled with a particular role, to mention a couple of methods. Knowing the role of a user will be useful to make decisions such as displaying or hiding objects on a resulting web page.

This book will not cover the API, as it is a topic that falls within the development realm. For our purposes, we will just mention one of the methods of the **javax. servlet.http.HttpServletRequest** object: **getRemoteUser()**, which returns the user ID value as a **String** object. This method will be used in this chapter's min-project later in the chapter.

Administrator view of web application security

The other view of web application security is based in making declarations about J2EE components and the attributes that define how and by whom a particular component may be made available. The places where these declarations are made are called deployment descriptors. For instance, as we saw in Chapter 3, WebSphere, through a user registry, is able to offer user information about the group or groups a user belongs to. In addition, applications will include declarations about types or classes that can have access (rights) to the application. These types or classes are denoted as roles. Therefore, creating relationships from groups to roles, an application can be made available only to the users that have, certain role. The group-role mapping creates a relationship between users and roles, and therefore, which users can access a given application.

Securing a web application

In this section, a mini-project will be used to enhance the understanding of the concepts described earlier in the chapter in a pragmatic way. The methodology to be followed is the declarative security approach. Get a cup of coffee and let's get to work.

Project objectives

The purpose of this mini-project is to deploy and secure a Java web application made up of three modules. Each module will be configured so that it will only be available to a segment of the users. In order to accomplish this, the project will rely on some of the concepts and assets from previous chapters.

The modules that make up this enterprise application are:

- **allemp.war**: A module available to all employees of yourcompany.com
- **hronly.war:** A module available only to the Human Resources department of yourcompany.com
- **open.war**: A module available to anyone that authenticates to the server yourcompany.com
- **CommonAssets.war**: An optional module which contains a component that could be use by any of the remaining modules in yourcompany.com

Assumptions

As in the previous chapter, the first assumption is that the current environment is very close as to how it resulted at the end of last chapter. In essence:

- In the WebSphere environment, the global security domain is mapped to the default federated user repository.
- There is an application server (**SecureAppServer01**), which has been protected and is mapped to its own security domain. (**secappsvr01. yourcompany.com**)
- There is a WebSphere virtual host (**employees_vh**) configured to the correct TCP ports.
- There are at least three users defined in the user repository.
- There are at least three user groups defined in the user registry.
- There is an IHS installation with a defined server (webmaster). Moreover, the **webmaster** server is integrated with WebSphere through its Plug-in module.
- You have experience deploying enterprise applications onto a WAS ND v7 environment.

Prerequisites

For this project, you are going to need some additional tools and J2EE knowledge not related to security. In order to create and package an enterprise application you will need:

- A J2EE IDE. In this project, the screenshots and directions will be drawn from the IBM product WebSphere Application Tool (AST). This application is part of the WebSphere Application Server ND distribution.

[
The IBM product file that contains the AST as available through their Passport Advantage program is C80UMML.tar.
]

- An alternative to AST is IBM Rational Application Developer. Furthermore, you could also use the Eclipse platform (version 3.5.2 was the one tested) which is available from: http://www.eclipse.org/downloads/.

- In addition, the project requires that the administrator have knowledge of fundamental J2EE concepts such as EAR, WAR, deployment descriptor, JSP, Servlet, and so on.

Enterprise application architecture

As mentioned briefly in the *Project objectives* section, above, the project uses four web modules and a number of users classified into groups.

Application groups

The application has been designed to work with three different groups that contain users and, in some circumstances, other groups. The required groups are shown in the screenshot below. As mentioned earlier, these groups are assumed to already exist. (Cf. Chapter 3 for details).

Select	Group name	Description	Unique Name
	Authenticated	Registered User at YourCompany INC Website	cn=Authenticated,o=defaultWIMFileBasedRealm
	Employee	Regular employees of YouCompany INC	cn=Employee,o=defaultWIMFileBasedRealm
	Human Resources	HR Deptartment of YouCompany INC	cn=Human Resources,o=defaultWIMFileBasedRealm

Page 1 of 1   Total: 3

Application users

In addition, each group hosts at least one user and perhaps a group. The required users are shown in the following screenshot. These users were created in Chapter 3. Refer to that chapter if necessary.

Select	User ID	First name	Last name	E-mail	Unique Name
☐	lola	Lola	HR	lola@yourcompany.com	uid=lola,o=defaultWIMFileBasedRealm
☐	ravi	Ravi	Employee	ravi@yourcompany.com	uid=ravi,o=defaultWIMFileBasedRealm
☐	sam_visitor	Sam	Visitor	sam@visitor.com	uid=sam_visitor,o=defaultWIMFileBasedRealm

Page 1 of 1   Total: 3

Application memberships

Each of the required groups must have members as indicated next. Since it is desired that anybody who authenticates to the application is able to access the open.war application we must perform some configuration to define this behavior.

There are two choices to assign access to resources. One choice is to form an ACL by manipulating the structure of the user registry groups. On the other hand, an ACL can be created by mapping, in a different way than before, user registry groups to application roles.

ACLs based on user registry groups

In the first approach, user registry groups are configured so it is possible to configure a group, using registry tools, to contain the necessary users. After doing so, the group can then be mapped to the application role on a one-to-one relationship. For instance, for the open.war web application should be accessed by anybody that authenticates to the application. Basically, it is desired to add to the registry group **Authenticated** any external user that has an ID on the website, for example they have registered with the site. On top of the external users, the group **Authenticated** must also contain all of the employees of the fictitious *YourCompany INC*. Before we address this fact let's analyze the registry group **Employee**. Once that's done, we will return to how best to add the employees to the **Authenticated** registry group.

The registry group **Employee** includes, or should include, all of the employees of YourCompany INC. There are many ways in which this could be achieved. For this project, which does not focus on designing user registry architectures, all regular '*individual*' employees will be added directly to this group, plus the group **Human Resources**. (In the above expression, interpret the term 'individual' as the person's ID). The group **Human Resources** will contain only the members of the HR department. So in this particular design, when a person working in HR is registered to the system, they will be assigned to the Human Resources group and through that group the new HR person will *inherit* the group **Employees**. The following screenshot depicts what was just discussed:

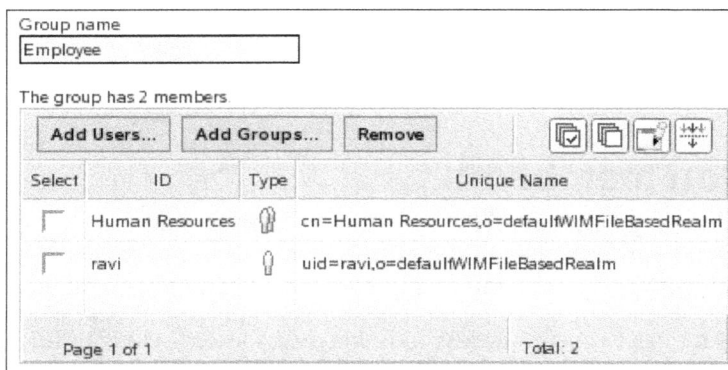

Therefore, returning to the membership of the **Authenticated** group; based on the definition of the Employee group, we can now add the **Employee** group to the **Authenticated** group; solving our dilemma of how to include all of the employees of this organization. The group membership is illustrated next:

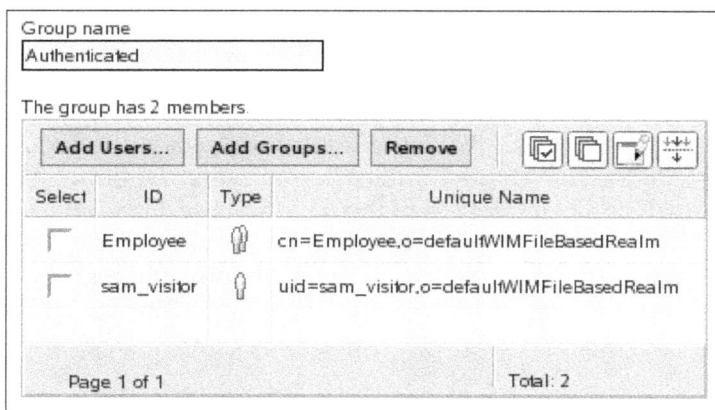

Finally, membership of the user registry group **Human Resources** is very simple, compared to the other two. This group contains employees assigned to the HR department. The group membership is shown in the screenshot that follows:

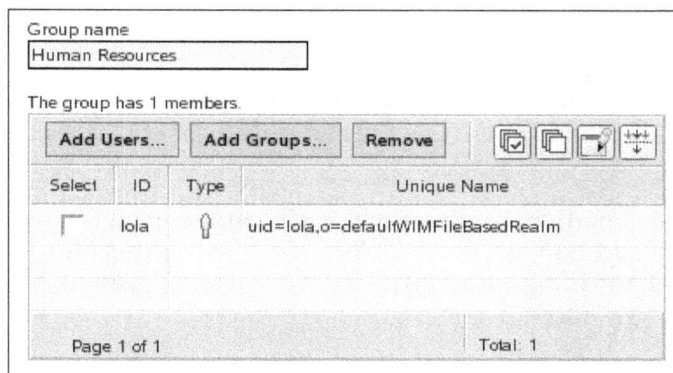

ACLs based on application roles

In the second methodology, user registry groups would contain mainly individuals. In this case, during the packaging of the web application, a many-to-one relationship would be created between groups and application roles. For the same example as above, open.war, the groups **Employee** (which would not contain the Human Resources group) and **Human Resources** would be mapped to the **Employee Role**; the group **Human Resources** would be mapped to the **HR Role**; and the groups Authenticated, Employee and Human Resources would be mapped to the Authenticated Role.

> **Best practice: use group-based ACLs**
>
> Group-based ACLs are more flexible than application-role-based ACLs. If changes are needed in terms of an ACL, they can take place at the user registry level, whereas role-based ACL may require modifying the application deployment descriptor in order to modify the groups to role mappings. Furthermore, from the security standpoint, a security team could be charged with administering groups-to-role administration.

As a result of this comparison in approaches, this project will use the group-based ACL methodology.

Dynamic web modules

The enterprise application is made up of three modules. One of the modules, `allemp.war`, uses an additional module that contains a servlet. There is nothing to the complexity of the modules. The application has been broken down in this way to point out how the ACLs are being enforced.

In any event, the three modules are almost identical. Each contains a welcome file (either an HTML document or a JSP—which is only an HTML document to which a servlet redirects).

The project uses the modules to define which URI pattern and HTTP methods are to be protected. In addition, the module declares to which role (or roles) is mapped. On the other hand, the project uses its deployment descriptor to define the roles and how user registry groups map to them.

Securing a J2EE web application

It is now time to put everything learned in this chapter into practice. This section describes the procedure followed to create, pack, and deploy the **YourCompanySite** enterprise application.

> As stated earlier, this project uses AST to package the enterprise application archive. As this book deals with security, those aspects of packaging an EAR that deal with security will be highlighted. Other aspects of the packaging process will be only briefly mentioned, as the full process of packaging EAR files is outside of the scope of this book. For those of you who would like to know about the packaging and deployment of EAR files in more detail, refer to the following on-line publication: *WebSphere Application Server V7: Packaging Applications for Deployment* (Red Paper 4582 http://www.redbooks.ibm.com/redpapers/pdfs/redp4582.pdf)

Creating the enterprise application project

Most J2EE IDE's require the creation of projects. We will be creating several during this mini-project. In order to create our enterprise application project follow the given steps:

1. Launch your IDE (AST in our case).
2. Select a convenient location for your workspace.
3. Close the **Welcome** page.

4. From the **Window** menu, scroll down to **Open Perspective** and from that menu select **Other…**. A new window, **Select Perspective**, opens.

5. From that new window, highlight and select the **J2EE** option. Click the **OK** button.

Once in the J2EE perspective, carry out the next steps:

1. Select the **Enterprise Applications** branch. Right-click your mouse.

2. Select **New** from the pop-up menu.

3. Select the **Project…** option from the menu that follows. A wizard window opens.

4. Expand J2EE and select Enterprise Application Project.

The next steps will guide you in naming the project:

1. Click the **Next** button.

2. Enter **YourCompanySite** in the **Name** field.

    This is depicted in the next screenshot:

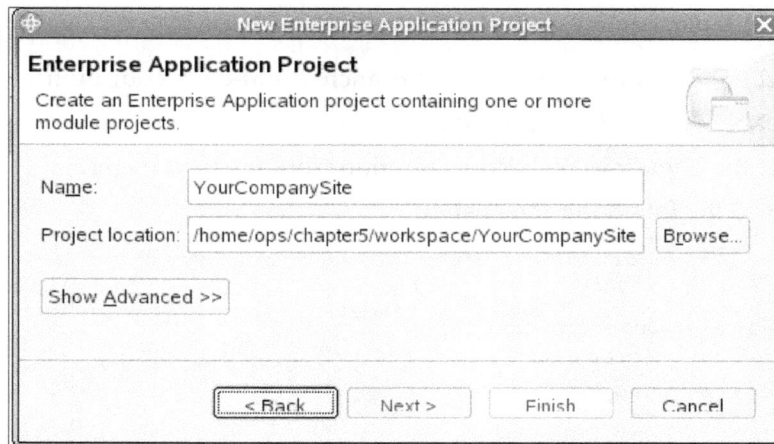

3. Click the **Finish** button.

The new project appears under the **Enterprise Applications** branch. There may be a 'problem' listed under the Problems section towards the bottom of the AST window. This can be safely ignored. It means that the project contains no modules. For the enterprise application, the file that would be of most interest is named `application.xml`, which contains the deployment descriptor of the application. It can be accessed in different ways. One is by traversing the project tree as indicated by the breadcrumb, as will be shown next.

Enterprise Applications | YourCompanySite | META-INF | application.xml

Double click `application.xml` to open the deployment descriptor editor. Review the various sections. When you are done, close any open editor.

> **Additional learning: Deployment descriptor**
>
> If you wish to get more familiar with the deployment descriptor, click **Source** at the bottom of the editor. This file contains the XML code that describes the descriptor. It is a very simple file when an EAR is just created. Come back to this file as more items are added to the project so you see how it is populated.

Creating the dynamic web application projects

The process for creating a dynamic web application project follows a similar pattern to the procedure used to create the YourCompanySite project.

There is one assumption at this point, and it is that AST is still open. If that is not the case, refer to the previous section in order to open the same workspace.

Once in the J2EE perspective, complete the following steps:

1. Select the **Dynamic Web Projects** branch. Right-click your mouse.
2. Select **New** from the pop-up menu.
3. Select the **Dynamic Web Project** option from the next menu.

   Refer to the following screenshot:

   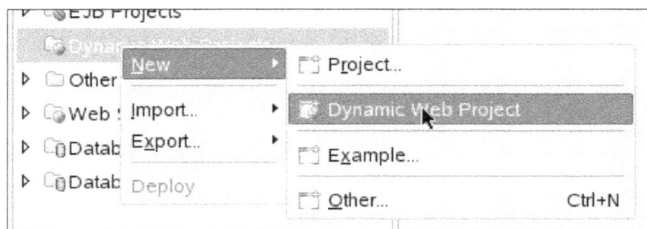

   A wizard window opens.

4. Enter name (**allemp**) and click the **Show Advanced** button.
5. Click the **EAR project** pop-up menu.
6. Select the **YourCompanySite** option.
7. Modify, if necessary, the context root field to `/allemp/`.

8. Leave the other options with their default values.
9. Click the **Finish** button.

The new dynamic web application, **allemp**, is listed now under the Dynamic Web Applications. In addition, note that the problems listed when **YourCompanySite** has been removed. If desired, go back to **YourCompanySite** and open the `application. xml` file. Observe the additional XML declarations; a definition for our module has been added.

Repeat this procedure for the modules **hronly** and **open**. Using the values shown in the screenshot, create the **hronly** project:

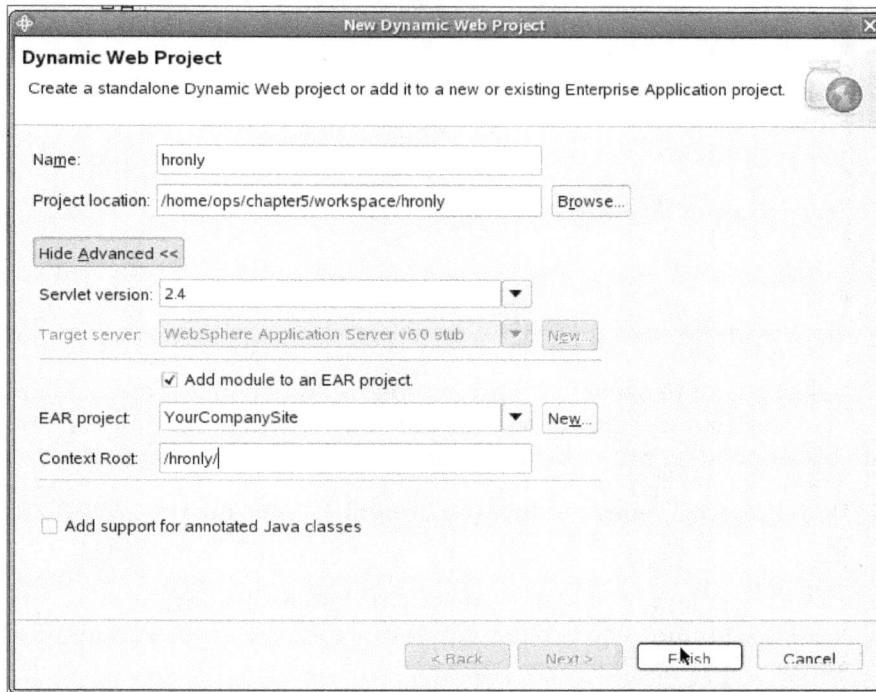

Likewise, using the values shown in the next screenshot, create a dynamic web project for the **open** module:

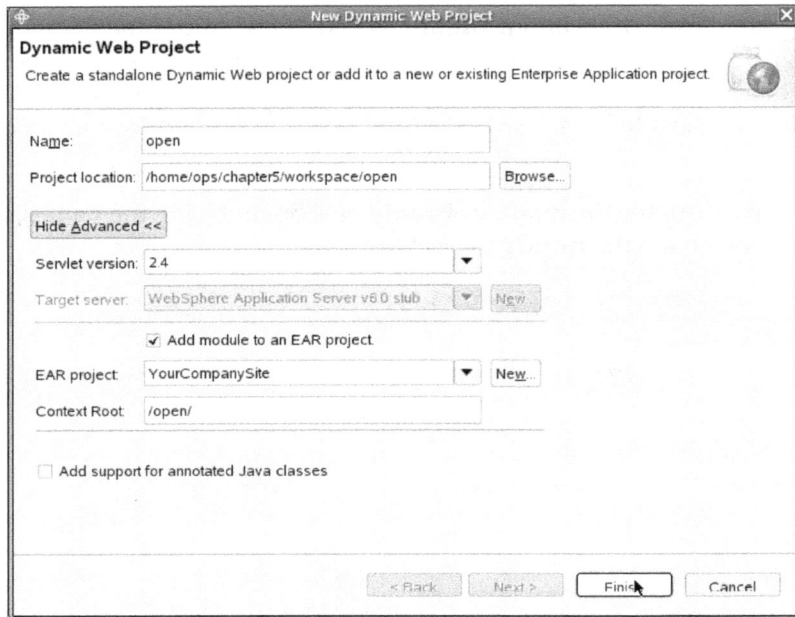

If desired, select any of the web application projects and open its deployment descriptor. For a dynamic web application, the deployment descriptor is named web. xml. It can be accessed by following the breadcrumb:

Dynamic Web Projects | your module (e.g., open) | WebContent | WEB-INF | web.xml

Double-click web.xml and review its content. Notice that it is very simple at this stage. Close all the editors once you are done with your review of web application projects content.

Configuring dynamic web applications

We now turn to customizing each of the modules with the values that will enable the enterprise application serve their content to the appropriate audience.

Defining welcome files

By default, a long list of files (six) is included in the file web.xml. For our project, only one will suffice.

For the **open** module, carry out the following steps:

1. Open the deployment descriptor editor (double-click the **Deployment Descriptor: open** branch).
2. Click the **Pages** tab at the bottom of the editor.
3. In the editor, expand **Welcome File List** located under the **Welcome Pages** section.
4. Select all but **index.html**. Refer to the following screenshot:

5. Click the **Remove** button.
6. Save your changes.

If desired, open the file source (web.xml) by clicking the editor **Source** tab. Notice that the list has reduced to one entry.

For the module **hronly**, execute the same steps as for the module open with the exception of keeping the file named index.jsp. The resulting **Welcome Pages** list should similar to the following screenshot:

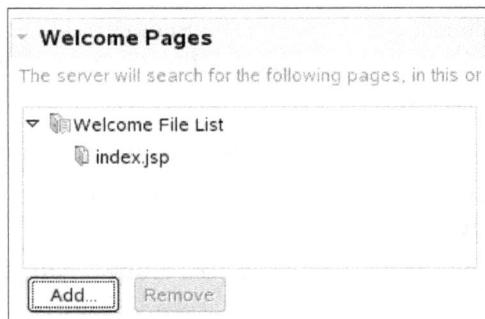

In a similar fashion, for the module `allemp`, reduce the Welcome Pages list to `default.jsp`.

Adding log in information

For all of the three modules (dynamic web applications) created, we now are going to turn to define the type of authentication requested. Perform the following directions for all of the web applications:

1. Open the deployment editor.
2. Select the **Pages** tab.
3. Scroll down to the **Login** section.
4. Set the value of **Authentication method** to **BASIC**.
5. Set the value of **Realm name** to **YourCompanyINC**.

Use as a reference the screenshot shown next:

Defining protected URI patterns and methods

At this moment, we need to define which URI patterns must be protected for each of the dynamic web applications along with the HTTP methods that are allowed. The series of steps to accomplish this is described below. Use the same steps for all modules, except as noted.

1. Open the deployment editor. Select the **Security** tab. Scroll down to the **Security Constraints** section. Click the button **Add**. A wizard opens.
2. Enter the following values:
    *   For the `allemp` module: **Constraint name<-Employee constraint**
    *   For the `hronly` module: **Constraint name<-Human Resources constraint**
    *   For the `open` module: **Constraint name<-Authenticated constraint**

3. Click the **Next** button.

4. On the next window enter the following values:

   For the `allemp` module enter:
   - ° **Resource name<-Employee**
   - ° **Description<-Employee area**
   - ° **HTTP methods<-GET, POST**
   - ° **Pattern<-/***

   For the `hronly` module enter:
   - ° **Resource name<-Human Resources**
   - ° **Description<-Human Resources area**
   - ° **HTTP methods<-GET, POST**
   - ° **Pattern<-/***

   For the `open` module enter:
   - ° **Resource name<-Authenticated**
   - ° **Description<-Authenticated area**
   - ° **HTTP methods<-GET, POST**
   - ° **Pattern<-/***

5. Click the **Finish** button.

6. Save the configuration.

Creating application roles

Once the URI's patterns and methods have been created, it follows to create the application roles. Later on, in the next section, these roles will be propagated to the enterprise application level.

For each of the dynamic web application projects execute the series of steps that follow:

1. Open the deployment editor for the module (`web.xml`). Select the **Security** tab. Scroll up or down to the **Security Roles** section. Click the button **Add**. A wizard opens.

2. Enter the following values.

For the `allemp` module:

- **Name<-Employee Role**
- **Description<-All regular employees role**
- For the `hronly` module:
- **Name<-HR Role**
- **Description<-HR department members exclusive role**

For the `open` module:

- **Name<-Authenticated Role**
- **Description<-All authenticated users role**

3. Click the **Finish** button.
4. Save the changes.

Assigning the application role

Next, it is required to assign the roles that will have access to the application. Use the following methodology to make the assignments for each of the web modules.

1. Open the web module deployment editor. Select the **Security** tab. Scroll down to the **Security Constraints** section. Select the corresponding constraint.

   - For the `allemp` module: **Employee constraint**
   - For the `hronly` module: **Human Resources constraint**
   - For the `open` module: **Authenticated constraint**

2. Scroll down to the **Authorized Roles** section.
3. Click the **Add** button. A **Define Authorization Constraint** dialog box opens.
4. For each module perform the following.

   For the `allemp` module:

   i. Set **Description<-YourCompany.com employee area**.
   ii. Check the **Employee Role** box.
   iii. For the `hronly` module:
   iv. Set **Description<-HR restricted area**.
   v. Check the **HR Role** box.

For the open module:

    i.   Set **Description<-YourCompany.com OPEN area to authenticated users**.

   ii.   Check the **Authenticated Role** box.

An example of the **Define Authorization Constraint** box is shown for the al-lemp module in the following screenshot:

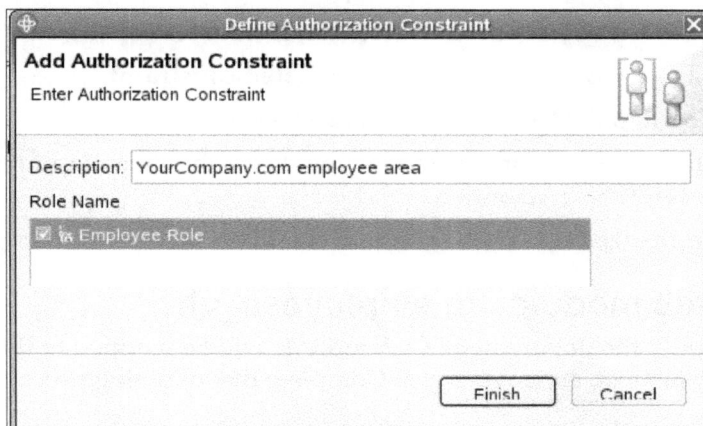

5.   Click the **Finish** button.

6.   Save the changes.

The summary of this definition (in the Security tab of the deployment descriptor editor) is shown in the next screenshot:

Defining client-server transport type

In the next task for the web modules it is necessary to define the type of client-server transport to be used to access the module. Perform the following procedure.

1. Open the web module deployment editor. Select the **Security** tab. Scroll down to the **Security Constraints** section. Select the corresponding constraint.
   - For the `allemp` module: **Employee constraint**
   - For the `hronly` module: **Human Resources constraint**
   - For the `open` module: **Authenticated constraint**
2. Scroll down to the **User Data Constraint** section.
3. For each module perform the following: From the Type pop-up menu select the **CONFIDENTIAL** option.
4. Save the changes.

Mapping web modules to employees_vh

In order to simplify the deployment, each module will be mapped to the designated WebSphere virtual host, `employees_vh`. Complete the following procedure for each web module:

1. Open the deployment editor for the module (`web.xml`).
2. Select the **Overview** tab.
3. Scroll up or down to the **WebSphere Bindings** section.
4. Replace the default value, `default_host`, with the value `employees_vh`.
5. Save the changes.

Configuring enterprise applications

There are different configuration objects that will be needed by the enterprise application modules. This section states what needs to be defined and the procedure to do it.

Defining roles

The roles that had been defined at the web module level are:

- Authenticated role
- Employee role
- HR role

Carry out the following steps in order to define the roles in `application.xml`:

1. Open the *enterprise application* deployment editor.
2. Select the **Security** tab.
3. In the **Security** section, click the button **Gather**.
4. Immediately, the three roles appear under the Security section.

   The following screenshot shows the state of the editor:

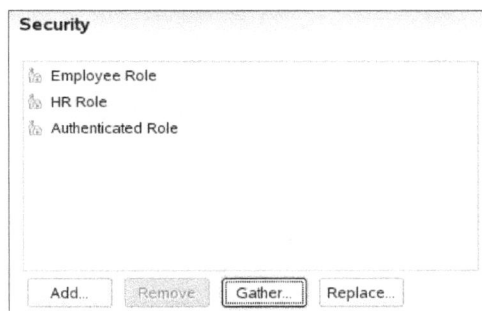

5. Save the changes.

Mapping groups to roles

Next after defining the roles it is necessary to indicate to what user registry groups they must be mapped. The groups that will be mapped, which come from the user registry are:

- Authenticated
- Employee
- Human Resources

Starting from the **Security** page in the application deployment descriptor, complete the following steps:

1. Identify the **WebSphere Bindings** section on the **Security** page.
2. Click on the first role under the **Security** section, **Authenticated Role**.
3. Check the **Users/Groups** box.
4. Scroll down to the **Groups** section.
5. Click the **Add** button. A wizard opens.
6. Enter the value **Authenticated** in the **Group name** field.

7. Repeat steps 2-3 for the second role, **Employee Role**, using the value **Employee** in the **Group name** field.

8. Repeat steps 2-6 for the last role, **HR Role**, using the value **Human Resources** in the **Group name** field.

9. Save the changes.

A screenshot of the editor highlighting how the mapping between roles and groups is displayed is shown next:

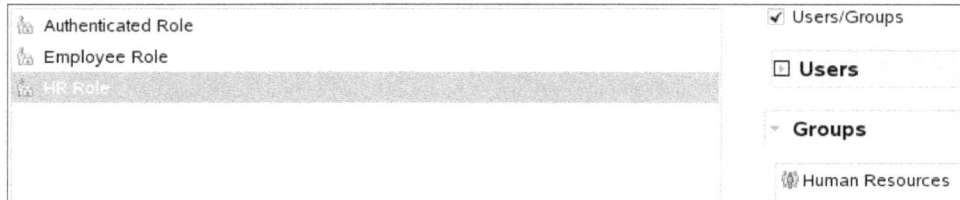

If so desired, click the **Source** tab to review the additions made to the `application.xml` file.

Adding content to dynamic web applications

Up to this point we have focused on the configuration portion of the project. Thankfully, we are not very ambitious and we will create just extremely simple HTML.

Adding web files

This project will use three types of files: HTML, a JSP and a servlet. The general methodology to add files is as follows. Start with all of the branches collapsed under the Project Explorer.

1. Open the **Dynamic Web Projects**.

2. Right-click the desired *web module*.

3. Follow the breadcrumb

   Dynamic Web Projects | `<WebModule>` | **New** | **Other...**

4. Click the **Other...** menu item. The Select wizard opens.

At this point, the process may vary slightly, depending on the type of file. For HTML and JSP files we can use this trick:

1. From the **Select wizard**, scroll down and expand the **Simple** folder.
2. Select the **File** option.
3. Click the **Next** button.
4. On the next screen, **New File**, expand the web module tree and highlight the Web Content folder.
5. Type the name of the HTML or JSP file in the File name field.
6. Enter the file name:
   - For the module `allemp`, use the name **empindex.jsp**.
   - For the module `hronly`, use the file name **index.jsp**.
   - And for the module `open`, use the file name **index.html**.
7. Click the **Finish** button. The file is added under the path `allemp/WebContent` and a generic editor opens with the blank file.

   The content of the `empindex.jsp` file, which is part of the `allemp` module, is shown in the screenshot that follows:

```
empindex.jsp

 1 <%@ page contentType="text/html"%>
 2 <%@ page info="Employee module home page"%>
 3 <!DOCTYPE html PUBLIC "-//W3C//DTD HTML 4.01 Transitional//EN"
 4     "http://www.w3.org/TR/html4/loose.dtd">
 5 <html>
 6 <head>
 7 <TITLE>YourCompany.com Employee Intranet</TITLE>
 8 </head>
 9 <body bgcolor="cornsilk">
10 <!-- <img src="banner.gif" alt="banner image"><p> -->
11 <H1>Welcome to YourCompany.com site</H1>
12 <pre>
13
14
15
16 </pre>
17 <% String id = request.getParameter("name");
18        if (id == null) id = "faithful Employee"; %>
19 <blockquote>Hello <%= id %>! This is your site</blockquote>
20 </body>
21 </html>
```

8. Enter the code as shown and save the file.

As stated before, we are not really concerned with the content of the application but that the content is protected in the correct way. The code for each of the file types includes only the barebones of the language or markup language as can be derived from the previous screenshot.

The analysis for empindex.jsp is as follows. **Lines 1-2** are basic JSP declarations regarding the document and some of its characteristics. **Lines 3-4** are the standard HTML document type declaration. **Lines 5 and 21** delimit the HTML portion of the document. **Lines 6-8** define the HEAD element of the document. **Lines 9-16 and 20** contain simple HTML directives. **Lines 17-18** include simple Java commands that attempt to gather the user name information from the HTTP request object in order to provide some personalization of the page. **Line 19** is a mix of HTML and JSP directive retrieving the value of the variable id, defined in the previous JSP block, line 17.

The file index.jsp, part of the module hronly, is defined as a member of the **Welcome File List**. The file content is shown in the next screenshot. In addition, index.jsp is equivalent to empindex.jsp from the functional standpoint. In terms of its content, it is just tailored to the hronly module.

```
index.jsp ✕
1 <%@ page contentType="text/html"%>
2 <%@ page info="HR module home page"%>
3 <!DOCTYPE html PUBLIC "-//W3C//DTD HTML 4.01 Transitional//EN"
4     "http://www.w3.org/TR/html4/loose.dtd">
5 <html>
6 <head>
7 <TITLE>YourCompany.com: Human Resources Intranet</TITLE>
8 </head>
9 <body bgcolor="cornsilk">
10 <!-- <img src="banner.gif" alt="banner image"><p> -->
11 <H1>Welcome to the Human Resources restricted site</H1>
12 <pre>
13
14
15
16 </pre>
17 <% String id = request.getParameter("name");
18     if (id == null) id = "talented HR team member"; %>
19 <blockquote>Hello <%= id %>! This is your site</blockquote>
20 </body>
21 </html>
```

The file index.html, shown in the following screenshot, is an equivalent although older version, from the presentation point of view, of the previous two files. It uses the same HTML directives. However, it lacks the personalization offered through the JSP directives.

```
 index.html ⊠
 1 <!DOCTYPE html PUBLIC "-//W3C//DTD HTML 4.01 Transitional//EN"
 2     "http://www.w3.org/TR/html4/loose.dtd">
 3 <html>
 4 <head>
 5 <TITLE>YourCompany.com OPEN site</TITLE>
 6 </head>
 7 <body bgcolor="cornsilk">
 8 <!-- <img src="banner.gif" alt="banner image"><p> -->
 9 <H1>Welcome to YourCompany.com OPEN site</H1>
10 <pre>
11
12
13
14 </pre>
15 <blockquote>Hello friend! Welcome to our OPEN site</blockquote>
16 </body>
17 </html>
```

Adding Java components

The final web module component is a servlet that will act as the home page for the
allemp module. This servlet, after 'performing' its function, will redirect the data
flow to the empindex.jsp component that will render the output returned as the
result of the request. Follow the course of action described next to add a servlet to
a web module. We assume we are starting the AST with all of the Project Explorer
branches collapsed.

1. Expand the Dynamic Web Projects branch according to the breadcrumb:
    Dynamic Web Projects | allemp | Java Resources | JavaSource .

2. Right-click the **JavaSource** folder. A menu pops up. From the menu, follow
    the breadcrumb: **JavaSource | New | Other...** .The **Select a wizard** window
    opens.

3. Scroll down the list of wizards to the **Web** collection/folder. Expand it. Select the **Servlet** wizard. This is shown in the following screenshot:

4. Click the **Next** button. Enter the value **HomePage** under the **Name** field. Note that by doing so, the URL mapping, **/HomePage**, is automatically added.

5. Under the **URL mappings** section, click the **Add** button. The **URL mappings** dialog opens. Enter the value **/index.html**.

6. Check the **Generate an annotated servlet class** box. Once that is completed, click the **OK** button to apply these values. Then, click the **Next** button to continue to the next screen.

7. In the screen that follows, **Servlet**, most of the fields are pre-populated. In the **Java package** field enter the value **yourcompany.common**. After you finish reviewing the screen, click the **Next** button. A new wizard screen opens.

8. Review values and selections of the modifiers, interfaces, and methods. Don't change the default values; such values will work for this simple project. When you finish reviewing the default values, click the **Finish** button.

9. Save the web.xml deployment descriptor. In the editor window, select the **Servlets** tab. Observe what has been added.

10. Under the **Servlets and JSPs** section, select the **HomePage** servlet. Observe that as you do it, the fields under the **Details** section become populated with the information gathered by the wizard.

11. If necessary, scroll down so you can review the content under the URL mappings section. Save the changes.

> If so desired, the Servlet could have been added to a fourth dynamic web project in a similar way. The new project then would be added to the enterprise application project. The content of this new web module would then be available to any of the other web modules. As an optional exercise, create a dynamic web project for it. You can name the DWP, navigator, if so desired.

Completing the Java code

Close any open deployment descriptor editors. If the Java editor is not open, drill down following the breadcrumb **Dynamic Web Projects | allemp | Java Resources | JavaSource | yourcompany.com | HomePage.java** and open the Java file. We will not analyze in detail the content of the file since development of Java assets is out of the scope of this book. We will, however, briefly describe the sections in the class file. Then, we will zoom in at the points where necessary additions and modifications are needed to accomplish our goal with this component, that is, to redirect the HTTP request to a JSP file.

Analysis of the initial servlet code

Lines 1-7 declare the package for the class being defined in the file and the external class dependencies needed. **Lines 8-21** contain servlet interface documentation in the form of comments. **Lines 22-25 and 43** include the class definition and the class annotation and reference in the form of comments. **Lines 26-28** define the class constructor. **Lines 29-42** consist of the **doGet** and **doPost** methods and their interface annotation. Refer to the screenshot below:

```
22  public class HomePage extends javax.servlet.http.HttpServlet implements javax.servlet.Servlet {
23      /* (non-Java-doc)
24       * @see javax.servlet.http.HttpServlet#HttpServlet()
25       */
26      public HomePage() {
27          super();
28      }
29
30      /* (non-Java-doc)
31       * @see javax.servlet.http.HttpServlet#doGet(HttpServletRequest arg0, HttpServletResponse arg1)
32       */
33      protected void doGet(HttpServletRequest arg0, HttpServletResponse arg1) throws ServletException, IOException {
34          // TODO Auto-generated method stub
35      }
36
37      /* (non-Java-doc)
38       * @see javax.servlet.http.HttpServlet#doPost(HttpServletRequest arg0, HttpServletResponse arg1)
39       */
40      protected void doPost(HttpServletRequest arg0, HttpServletResponse arg1) throws ServletException, IOException {
41          // TODO Auto-generated method stub
42      }
43  }
```

Completing the servlet code

What is needed to add to the code in order to enable the servlet to redirect the request to the renderer component, that is, JSP, is rather simple.

The following screenshot shows the two additional packages needed by the coded that will be added shortly:

```
7  import javax.servlet.http.*;
8  import javax.servlet.*;
```

The main *contribution* to the servlet is shown in the following code. A private **String** variable is defined in line **32**. Its role is to hold the value of the context root embedded in the HTTP request object. **Lines 34-40** show a private method (**doForwardRequest**) whose function is to perform the actual redirection by using a handful of methods from the **RequestDispatcher** object. Our method requires an **HttpServletRequest** object, an **HttpServletResponse** object, and a **String** object holding URL to which the request will be forwarded.

```
28      /**
29       * Context root
30       *
31       */
32      private String context;
33
34▽     private void doForwardRequest(final HttpServletRequest myReq,
35              final HttpServletResponse myResp, String myURL) throws IOException,
36              ServletException {
37          RequestDispatcher dispatcher = getServletContext()
38                  .getRequestDispatcher(myURL);
39          dispatcher.forward(myReq, myResp);
40      }
```

In the code shown below, the **HttpServletRequest** methods **doGet** and **doPost** have as their main responsibility to build the target URL to which the **request** and **response** objects will be forwarded. Both methods are identical. **Lines 55 and 68** retrieve from the request object the context root. With that information, in **lines 56 and 69**, the methods build the required URL and invoke the private method **doForwardRequest** that will do the actual forwarding.

```
52▽    protected void doGet(HttpServletRequest request,
53             HttpServletResponse response) throws ServletException, IOException {
54         //        Just redirect to JSP
55         context = request.getContextPath();
56         doForwardRequest(request, response, context + "empindex.jsp");
57     }
58
59▷    /*
65▽    protected void doPost(HttpServletRequest request,
66             HttpServletResponse response) throws ServletException, IOException {
67         // Just redirect to JSP
68         context = request.getContextPath();
69         doForwardRequest(request, response, context + "empindex.jsp");
70     }
```

A no-no.

Please note that including the value empindex.jps within the code is not encouraged. It was done in this way for the project in order to keep modules as simple as possible so they are not a distraction. In production systems, your development team probably can use properties files to declare such values. Properties can be customized every time the servlet class is deployed into a web application.

Our enterprise application project is ready for deployment.

Packaging an enterprise application

Our goal in this section is to export an EAR ready for deployment into our WebSphere v7 environment. The following steps will help us:

1. Follow the breadcrumb: **Enterprise Applications | YourCompanySite**.

2. Next, right click the **YourCompanySite** branch and follow the breadcrumb **YourCompanySite | Export | EAR file**. The **EAR export** wizard opens.

3. Enter a full path to where you wish to export your packaged project in the **Destination** field.

4. Check the **Include project build paths and meta-data files** check box.

5. Click the **Finish** button.

Open a terminal window and review the content of your EAR. Use the following command to list the content of the EAR file:

```
<WAS_Root>/java/jre/bin/jar -tvf <Absolute_Path>/YourCompanySite.ear
```

The output to the command should look similar to the listing shown in the next screenshot:

```
# /opt/IBM/WebSphere/AppServer/java/bin/jar -tvf YourCompany.ear
     25 Fri Jun 18 12:41:54 EDT 2010 META-INF/MANIFEST.MF
    580 Thu Jun 17 19:11:34 EDT 2010 .project
    812 Thu Jun 17 19:11:34 EDT 2010 META-INF/.modulemaps
   1171 Fri Jun 18 02:41:08 EDT 2010 META-INF/application.xml
    379 Thu Jun 17 23:53:08 EDT 2010 META-INF/ibm-application-bnd.xmi
    924 Thu Jun 17 23:53:10 EDT 2010 META-INF/ibmconfig/cells/defaultCell/applica
tions/defaultApp/deployments/defaultApp/deployment.xml
    235 Thu Jun 17 23:53:10 EDT 2010 META-INF/ibmconfig/cells/defaultCell/applica
tions/defaultApp/deployments/defaultApp/variables.xml
    226 Thu Jun 17 23:53:10 EDT 2010 META-INF/ibmconfig/cells/defaultCell/securit
y.xml
   3029 Fri Jun 18 12:41:54 EDT 2010 hronly.war
   2887 Fri Jun 18 12:41:54 EDT 2010 open.war
   4148 Fri Jun 18 12:41:54 EDT 2010 allemp.war
#
```

Deploying the enterprise application

As a final step to creating, configuring, and packaging an enterprise application process, we have arrived at deploying it to our environment.

1. Log on to the Deployment Manager console. Go to the page **New Application** and select **New Enterprise Application** for the type of application to be installed.

2. In the next screen, provide the location of the EAR file containing the application you just packaged in the previous section. Click the **Next** button to go to the following screen.

   The way in which the EAR was configured enables the administrator to perform a deployment using the **Fast path**. However, we will use the **Detailed** option so we can observe how the various configuration settings that were done during the creation of the enterprise application project fall neatly into place.

3. In the screen that gets displayed you can observe several configuration choices, many of which the install wizard has populated for you. Take a look around and when finished, click the **Next** button, as this page does not require any modifications.

4. The **Map modules to servers** page appears. Assign all three modules to the **SecureAppServer01** JVM. After doing so, click the **Next** button.

5. The **JSP reloading options for Web modules** page is shown next. Review the settings. There is no need to change anything. Click the **Next** button.

6. The **Map shared libraries** page is displayed. Similarly to the previous step, review the settings and click the **Next** button when ready.

7. The Map shared libraries relationships page follows. We can also skip this page. Click the **Next** button to advance to the following page.

8. The **Map virtual hosts for Web modules** page is shown. If you recall, while creating the EAR, we spent some time making this mapping. Since the value shown (employees_vh) is the one desired, we can skip this page as well. Click the **Next** button to continue.

9. The **Map context root for Web modules** is now displayed. Again, the values that appear are the values that are desired. We can continue without having to make any modifications. Click the **Next** button.

10. The **Map security roles to users or groups** page appears next. Notice also how this page has been populated with the groups. Click the **Next** button.

11. The Summary page appears. Review the current settings to insure that all the values are correct. When done, click the **Finish** button.

12. As the last series of steps: save the changes, re-generate the plugin-cfg.xml file. Restart all JVM's (dmgr, nodeagent and SecureAppServer01).

As stated earlier, the EAR file could have been deployed using the fast path method since all of the required settings were already part of the EAR.

Testing the enterprise application

In order to ensure that the application has been configured correctly, we need to test scenarios for all three types of users. The goal of the test is to have each of the users attempt to access all three modules. The results should match the following descriptions.

Module **open**, https://<yourserver>.yourcompany.com:8444/open/, should be available to anyone that can log in to the server. Module **allemp**, https://<yourserver>.yourcompany.com:8444/allemp/, should be open to YourCompanyINC regular employees as well as members from the HR department. Finally, module **hronly**, https://<yourserver>.yourcompany.com:8444/hronly/, should be available to members of the HR department.

In order to carry out the test, log in as one of the users defined by attempting to access the **open** application. Every time that a new user is logged in, the certificate warning will be displayed. Remember to only accept it only for that session. If the configuration is correct, after accepting the certificate a log in box will challenge you. Enter the user ID and password. You should see for any accepted ID the welcoming page (titled: YourCompany.com OPEN site). Start with the ID **sam_visitor**. Sam should only be able to access the **open** module. Using the same browser, have Sam access the allemp and hronly modules. For both attempts, you should get a 403 HTTP error: Authorization Failed.

Proceed the same way for the other two users, **ravi** and **lola**. Each time that you test for a different user, make sure to start a new browser. User **ravi** should be able to access open and allemp, whereas he should get a 403 error. Finally, user lola should be able to access all sites.

Summary

In this chapter you have learned the following:

- More about infrastructure front-end security
- The importance of group-role mapping in fine-tuning access to specific modules within a web enterprise application
- The locations inside an EAR that contain security data
- The security application attributes that need to be defined
- How to build, configure, and package securable EARs

6
Securing Enterprise Java Beans Applications

In the programming paradigm **Model-View-Controller (MVC)**, an application design/functionality is broken down into three main areas or layers: the model layer, which represents the logic of an application; the view layer, which deals with the presentation (sometimes referred as rendering) aspect of an application; and the controller layer, which is that portion of an application that directs the flow between the other two layers. Under the J2EE umbrella, EJBs often implement the model layer of an application, whereas Servlets implement the controller layer, which leaves the presentation layer to JSPs. In this chapter, you will:

- Learn the concepts surrounding security of EJB applications
- Design a simple EJB application in which the security concepts can be used and observe the application behavior
- Create an EJB project using a GUI programming tool (RAD and Eclipse)
- Write code for your EJB application and perform the configuration of your EAR package
- Deploy and test your EJB project

The approach followed in this chapter is very similar to the one used in the previous chapter. It starts with some *theory*, in this case, some EJB concepts required to help you understand the security configuration that surrounds this type of application. The chapter then goes into a description of a mini-project in which a very simple application that uses at its core an EJB will be developed, packaged, and deployed onto a WebSphere v7 environment. This mini-project will be leveraging on the previous two chapters' mini-projects. Portions of the full mini-project for this chapter will not be included here as they are, by now, familiar to you and they will be left as exercises to reaffirm the concepts reviewed in the previous chapters.

For instance, this chapter mini-project will not address the HTTP server component; it will be left as an exercise for you to complete its integration. You can use as a starting point what you learned in *Chapter 4, Front-End Communication Security* under the section *Securing front-end components communication*.

EJB application security concepts

As in other Java enterprise applications, there are two main aspects to the securing of an EJB-based enterprise application; namely, the way the code is written and the EAR deployment configuration. As WAS ND v7 supports the EJB 3.0 API (without the need for a special feature pack) this chapter will focus on some of the new aspects introduced by that version. Throughout this chapter, when the term EJB appears, it refers to version three of the API.

The EJB 3.0 API introduced the concept of annotations for conveying security configuration information. Therefore, the chapter will use this technique to show how security can be defined and enforced. In essence, there are two security mechanisms: declarative security and programmatic security.

Declarative security

In declarative security, security policies can be conveyed through XML entries in the deployment descriptor or through annotations. As stated earlier, this chapter will focus on the latter. The suite of annotations that can be used in EJB's is:

- **RolesAllowed** lists which roles are able to access a class or execute a method
- **PermitAll** indicates that the class or method is accessible to anyone
- **DenyAll** prevents access to a class or method
- **DeclareRoles** states, at the class level only, which roles will be referred in a class
- **RunAs** is a mechanism used at the bean level (therefore, only allowed to be declared at the class level) that allows an EJB to invoke another EJB using a different role

Programmatic security

In programmatic security, an EJB code will include calls to the security API in order to determine the identity of an authenticated user and set a specific course of action based on that information. The specification interface used for this purpose is `javax.ejb.EJBContext`. This interface provides a couple of methods that can be used in an EJB code:

- `getCallerPrincipal()` returns as a `java.security.Principal` Java object, the name of the authenticated caller
- `isCallerInRole`(String role) returns a *Boolean* value depending on whether or not the caller is in the stated *role*

EJB project design

The security EJB concepts mentioned in *EJB application security concepts* will be explored in the remainder of this chapter by using a mini-project.

EJB application du jour

The application to be presented, implements a very rudimentary portal application. In this application, the home page content is customized according to the group (mapped to a role) the user belongs to. The EJB will be the core of the application.

Objective—security

One of the purposes of the application is to demonstrate how security is applied to an EJB application. Although the code is short, the solution uses both declarative and programmatic security.

Objective—functional

From the functional perspective, the project works around the concept of a portal application. The intent is to present personalized content that is drawn from three distinct applications. Users will see only the content that their group membership allows them to access.

Project design—UI aspect

The idea behind this project is rather simple, however, it will help demonstrate how to use security on an EJB module. From the UI point of view, this project builds up on the previous chapter mini-project. In other words, this project will re-use three dynamic web applications (or modules), namely `allemp.war`, `hronly.war`, and `open.war`. Therefore, this project will access the existing modules in the same way, using the URI's `/allemp/`, `/hronly/`, and `/open/`.

The current mini-project will add a new home page, which will be available via the URI / (slash). This page will be tailored according to the role a user belongs to. From that page, which will be referred in the rest of the chapter as *the portal home page* (or simply *portal page*), users will be able to navigate to the **legacy** applications from the previous chapter. The following diagram depicts this simple architecture:

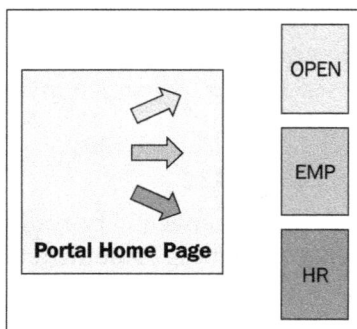

In the preceding figure, when a user requests the main URI /, (the full URL would be something similar to `https://<FQDN_hostname>:<IHS_port>/`) that user will be asked to log in (for example, authenticate). Upon successful authentication, the portal page will be presented to the user. In the diagram, the portal page is represented by the largest rectangle (gold) on the left. As stated previously, depending on the role associated with the user ID, the portal home would present a snippet of content (or functionality) *from* the legacy applications. For this project, the way the portal page will customize its content is by displaying an appropriate banner for each *portlet* and by providing a link to the legacy application the user is entitled to access. This fact is represented in the preceding diagram by the smaller rectangles on the right.

Depending on the user's role, the suitable number of arrows will be available on the portal home. Recalling from the previous chapter, some of the roles are *Employee Role* and *HR Role*. In addition, The HR Role is the category that provides the most access to the portal content. Thus, the preceding diagram would be a representation of the portal page for a user with the HR Role.

Furthermore, the following diagram offers a closer look at the UI architecture. Diagram a) shows a generic architecture for the portal page. It is made of four main components, namely: the portal body, the header, the footer, and the personalized page. The portal body is represented by the outer rectangle (yellow) labeled *Portal Home Page*, which in our case will be common to any authenticated user. The next two components, header and footer, represented by the two small rectangles (gold) at the top and bottom of the overall layout, could be used for many purposes, including customized navigation of a legacy application. For this mini-project (in order to keep things very simple) both header and footer will be common to any authenticated user in the same way as the main portal body. Finally, the personalization component, represented by the large square (purple) in diagram a), is the core of our project and it will customize its content according to the role a user is assigned. The remaining diagrams in the figure portrait possible scenarios for each of the roles.

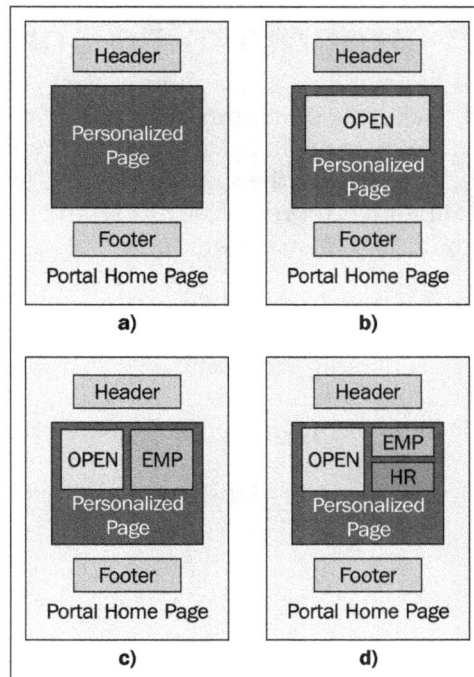

The preceding diagram b) illustrates the scenario for a registered visitor of the web site. The personalized component renders content appropriate for anybody who has registered and given a valid ID. This fact is represented by the rectangle labeled **OPEN** (orange) in the diagram. As stated earlier, the *content* of the personalized area includes a welcome message directed to visitors and a link to access the legacy *open* application.

Next, in diagram c), the scenario for a regular employee portal page is depicted. It contains the same components as the generic architecture shown in diagram a). The chief difference has to do with the personalized component of the portal page. In addition to the *OPEN* rectangle presented to any authenticated user, the personalized area adds a *portlet* with content/functionality of interest to a regular employee. This employee-oriented content is denoted by the rectangle labeled *EMP* (green).

Finally, diagram d) presents the most complex situation in this mini-project. This situation is related to the content personalization for members of the Human Resources department. In addition to the *OPEN* and *EMP* rectangles, the personalized area now includes an additional rectangle labeled *HR* (blue) that represents content exclusive for the Human Resources members. The *HR* area provides, similar to the previous cases, a link to the legacy application *hronly*.

Project design—programming component

In order to have a better understanding of the mini-project J2EE component architecture layout and the securing of its components, let's review the MVC paradigm in a visual way. Analyze the following diagram where the ovals represent the main components of the paradigm; the solid lines stand for remote functionality execution, whereas the dotted lines represent events taking place. Furthermore, in the classic MVC representation for an application:

- The **model** component (represented by the oval—blue—labeled **Model**) holds the application state and reveals the application functionality. One of the model component obligations is to *accept* application state inquiries (depicted by the full line—maroon—labeled *State Query*) from the view component. In addition, the model component must alert the view component when the application state changes by sending *event* notifications (shown as the dotted line—blue—labeled *Change notification*).

- The **view** component (represented by the oval—maroon—labeled '*View*') synthesizes the model according to a well-defined realm or context so users can interact with the application. For instance, a realm could be the rendering of the application suitable to be accessed by a smart phone device. Among its obligations, the view component *requests* the model (represented by the full line—maroon—labeled *State Query*) for changes in the application state. Moreover, the view broadcasts *event* notifications to the controller of user interactions with the view. These notifications are represented in the diagram by the dotted line (maroon) labeled *User response*.

- Last, but not least, the **controller** component declares the application functionality, *selects* the view to be displayed to users according to the well-defined context and translates user's *actions* to model updates.

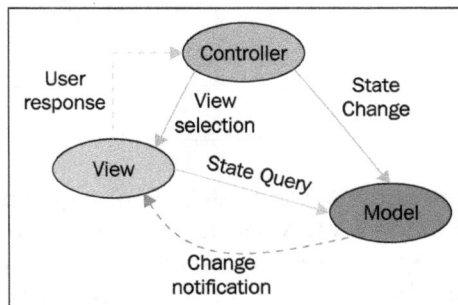

(Adapted from http://java.sun.com/blueprints/patterns/MVC-detailed.html)

In light of the MVC classic model, we can now depict how it can be implemented in a J2EE application. The following diagram shows the J2EE components and their associations and interactions. In a nutshell, the controller is carried out by the Servlet; the model is implemented by the EJB; and the view is instantiated by the JSP.

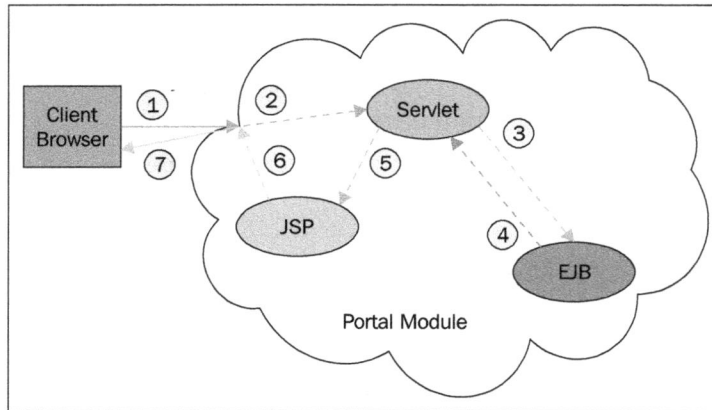

In the J2EE implementation of the MVC model, client requests (1) are intercepted by the controller (2), namely the Servlet. A Servlet, then, has two main jobs to carry out. On the one hand, it must map the user requests to the EJB functionality by making remote method invocations (3). Therefore, the EJB implements the model component. The EJB will then execute the request and return the result to the Servlet (4). On the other hand, based on the request, the Servlet must decide what protocol (for example, HTTP, WAP) and format (that is, WML, HTML) to use in order to select the appropriate JSP that would assemble the response to the user. Once selected or identified, the Servlet will pass the required information to the JSP (5). The specialized JSP will then use the information received to produce the result object in the appropriate format and sent using the corresponding protocol (6, 7).

In the last few paragraphs we have been focusing on the models and the J2EE components to instantiate such models. It is time now to turn our attention to what this book is all about. In particular for this chapter, the securing of the various J2EE components used to make up the mini-project. Let's proceed to the next subsection.

Project design–implementation phase

As we have experienced throughout this book, there is always more than way of either analyzing (viewing) or synthesizing (implementing) a problem. Our mini-project is not an exception. So, let's start by identifying the points of entry to the overall application.

Such points of entry to the application are normally identified or referred to as URIs. For the mini-project we have four:

- `/`: main point of entry to the overall site and access to the **portal** application (module)

- `/open/`: main entrance for all authenticated users to the **open** application

- `/allemp/`: access point to the **allemp** application available to all regular employees

- `/hronly/`: point of entry to the **hronly** application, an area restricted to members of the HR department

In the previous chapter, the securing of the last three applications shown previously was done by mapping each application to a role and then creating relationships between the roles defined by the applications and user groups defined in the security user registry used. The roles then were used to secure each of the applications.

The EJB v 3.0 model enables us to apply a more granular security schema by using different approaches such as declarative and programmatic security. For this mini-project, the declarative security will be used. Declarative security can be applied at the class and even at the method level.

As a result of this, the **portal** application will be secured by granting access to the application URI to all authenticated users and then tightening the security at the time when remote method invocation is performed against the EJB.

At this point, we can point out what the main implementation components of the mini-project are. Notice however, that on occasion the type of tool used may dictate a certain course of action. Our case was not the exception. The tool selected to develop, build, and package our project is *IBM Rational Application Developer Assembly and Deployment Features for WebSphere Software V7.5 for Multiplatforms* (a mouthful of a product name — please refer to the tip box at the end of this subsection for a brief description about this selection).

Therefore, the following major components make up this mini-project. All of the components will be brought together through the enterprise project:

- **chap6-EAR-miniproject** enterprise application project used as an umbrella to include all the modules needed. In other words, this would be the end-result of all of the components packaged together.

  Three of the components were created in *Chapter 5, Securing Web Applications* and will be reused in this chapter's project which are as follows.

- **chap6-allemp-webapp** dynamic web application project: It is made of the same components as **allemp.war** from *Chapter 5*. It uses group-role relationships to implement authorization security. Implements the /allemp/ application. The minor components are:

  - **HomePage** Servlet: Enforces access to the application and forwards request flow to JSP
  - empindex.jsp JSP: Displays employee-related content

- **chap6-hronly-webapp** dynamic web application project: It holds the same components and configuration as hronly.war from *Chapter 5*. As its legacy siblings do, it uses group-role relationships to implement authorization security of resources. It implements the /hronly/ application. Its component is: index.jsp JSP, which displays HR department related content

- **chap6-open-webapp** dynamic web project: It contains the same components as open.war from *Chapter 5*. As the previous legacy applications, it also keeps the same security configuration, using group-role relationships to implement resource authorization. It implements the /open/ application. Its component is: index.html web page, which displays content suitable to any authenticated user.

  Two new projects will supplement the previous modules and help us explore EJB security much closer.

- **chap6-portal-webapp** dynamic web application: It consists of five HTML files in addition to several JSP files and one Servlet class, **PortalHomeSelectorServlet**. A combination of these components added to the last module, **chap6-portal-ejbean** (cf. below), implement the portal application. As this is the point of entry to the multiple applications, there is not a formal context root. Therefore, the URI to access this module is / (slash). The details of this module will be provided in the following sections.

- **chap6-portal-ejbean** EJB project: It comprises an EJB class and three Java interfaces that provide the means of accessing the functionality offered by the EJB. The EJB class, named **PortalSelectorSessionBean**, is hidden from the user. Its main functionality is to provide the Servlet from chap6-portal-webapp (**PortalHomeSelectorServlet**) the parameters needed to assemble the introductory portal. The parameters are selected based on the role of the user that sent the request to the Servlet.

Selection of the IDE

Even though this book is not about writing code, in order to show how security can be applied to an EJB application, it was necessary to implement a very simple EJB that would behave differently according to the role of the user making the request. The tools used in the last chapter, specifically the AST and Eclipse, were not suitable for developing and packaging an EAR that contains EJBs. Several combinations were made to no avail. Therefore, the version of Rational Developer licensed with WebSphere Application Server Network Deploy v7 was selected for use in this chapter. If your company uses IBM's Passport Advantage to access your entitlements, you will need to download the five packages that are labeled *IBM Rational Application Developer Assembly and Deployment Features for WebSphere Software V7.5 for Multiplatform*. The packages identifiers are: C1KJ4ML (set up), C1KJ5ML (disk one), C1KJ6ML (disk two), C1KJ7ML (disk three), C1KJ8ML (disk four), and C1KJ9ML (disk five).

EJB project prerequisites and assumptions

In terms of assumptions and pre-requirements for this mini-project, they are very similar to the ones listed in *Chapter 5*. A summary of them will be given next.

Project assumptions

The assumptions for this mini-project are as follows:

- The global security for the WebSphere cell uses the built-in federated user registry. (Refer to Chapter 3, *Configuring User Authentication and Access* subsection *Configuring security domains based on global security*, for details).
- There are at least three distinct user groups defined in the user repository. (Please consult *Chapter 5*, section *Enterprise application architecture* and subsection *Application groups*).

- There are at least three different users defined in the federated user registry. (For details, kindly refer to *Chapter 5* section *Enterprise application architecture* and subsection *Application users*).

- There is an IHS installation that is integrated through the WebSphere Plug-in to the WebSphere Application Server v7 environment.

- You have completed the mini-project from *Chapter 5*. (Details can be found under the section *Creating the dynamic web application projects*.) Therefore, the following modules are available for use or for importing:

    ◦ `allemp.war`

    ◦ `hronly.war`

    ◦ `open.war`

- The users and groups are organized in the same way as in *Chapter 5*. The group-role mappings are also the same.

- You have access to the *IBM Rational Application Developer Assembly and Deployment Features for WebSphere Software V7.5* (which will be referred to as *IBM RAD* or just *RAD* in the rest of this chapter) or similar IDE which supports EJB v3.0 and it is capable of packaging EAR files compatible with WebSphere AS v7.0

- IBM RAD is installed on the same host as the WAS ND v7 Deployment Manager profile resides.

Project prerequisites

In order to get started with this chapter's mini-project, the following tasks must be completed. As such tasks are either not related directly to security but familiar enough to WebSphere administrators, or the task has been covered in the previous chapters and the reader should be able to perform it without detailed guidance.

Using the Integrated Solutions Console perform the following:

1. Create a new Application Server. The one used in this project is named **Chap6AppServer**.

2. Create a new virtual host. Name it `chap6_vh`. (If you decide to name it differently, you will have to use the custom value when references to **chap6_ vh** are made in the rest of this chapter.) Remove the default ports assigned to it and add:

   ○ `9445`: to be used as the JVM web container secure HTTP transport port; if yours is different, modify this value to match your Application Server `WC_defaulthost_secure` value.

   ○ `8445`: to be used as the IHS server listening port.

3. Create a new security domain. Make this security domain by copying the global security configuration. Name it `chapt6.yourcompany.com`. If so desired, please refer to *Chapter 3*, subsection *Configuring security domains based on global security*, for further details.

4. Assign domain. Customize domain.

5. After creating the enterprise project, you need to import the modules from the last chapter (which are mentioned in the previous section). They will be denoted as legacy applications in the rest of this chapter. When importing the legacy applications assign them to the chap6-EAR-miniproject project.

Creating an Enterprise Application Project

In order to get started, the IDE project must be created. As mentioned earlier, in this chapter, directions and screenshots will be taken from IBM Rational. The following excerpt was already mentioned previously. If you decide to get the WAS ND v7 version of Rational, please refer to the following information box. For further details, refer to the preceding subsection *Project design–Implementation phase*.

> If your company uses IBM's Passport Advantage to access your entitlements, you will need to download the five packages that are labeled *IBM Rational Application Developer Assembly and Deployment Features for WebSphere Software V7.5 for Multiplatform*. The packages identifiers are: C1KJ4ML (set up), C1KJ5ML (disk one), C1KJ6ML (disk two), C1KJ7ML (disk three), C1KJ8ML (disk four), and C1KJ9ML (disk five).

Creating the project workspace

It is desirable to start with a clean IDE workspace so no residual data from a previous project can introduce unforeseen elements. To start with a clean workspace environment, launch Rational or your selected IDE. Select a new clean directory. This will create the desired workspace.

Next, if not already open, select a **Java 2EE** perspective. Using the *Window* menu, navigate to: **Window | Open Perspective | Other**. An **Open Perspective** selector window opens. Select **Java 2EE**.

Enterprise application project requirements

For a successful project, there are two important attributes of an enterprise application project that need to be defined correctly. These attributes were the reason for selecting RAD as an IDE tool and are defined as follows.

EAR version

In order for the project to be able to host an EJB 3.0 component, the project's EAR version must be 5.0 or higher. This version is default when creating an enterprise application project (referred to as EAP in the rest of this chapter) with RAD. This selection will be given at the time of EAP creation.

Target runtime

In addition, to ensure that the code to be developed and deployed in WebSphere is compatible with it, a new RAD *Target Runtime* must be created. This target runtime will be configured to point at the root directory path of the WAS ND installation. Although we can create a target runtime in different ways, in this chapter it will be done while creating the EAP.

Creating the enterprise application project

This chapter's mini-project will include several J2EE components such as WARs and JARs. The best type of RAD project suitable for deploying in a WebSphere environment is the creation of an EAR. RAD calls EAR projects **Enterprise application projects**.

Selecting the project EAR version

Using the **File** menu, navigate to: **File | New | Enterprise Application Project**. A **New EAR Application Project** wizard opens. Name the project `chap6-EAR-miniproject`. Ensure that the **EAR version** selected is 5.0 or higher.

Creating a target runtime

While still on the first window of the wizard and under the *Target Runtime* section, perform the following:

1. Click the **New...** button. A **New Server Runtime Environment** wizard opens.

2. If necessary, expand the IBM folder.

3. Select **WebSphere Application Server v7.0**. Click the **Next** button.

4. Name the new runtime: `WebSphere Application Server 7.0 installation`.

5. Under the Installation directory field enter the location of your WAS ND v7 installation (for example, `/opt/IBM/WebSphere/AppServer` in SuSE Linux).

6. Click the **Finish** button.

Creating the deployment descriptor

Once the target runtime has been created, back on the New EAR wizard, click the **Next** button. Towards the bottom of the wizard window, click the **Generate Deployment Descriptor** check box. The next step is to fill the EAR content field with the value `EarContent`. Finally, click the **Finish** button to create the EAP.

RAD will point out errors and the appropriate icons are shown to reflect the fact that at the moment, there aren't any modules associated with the **chap6-EAR-miniproject** EAP. This is normal as we have yet to either create or import such modules. The reason that RAD displays such error(s) is because the current content of the deployment descriptor (`application.xml`) is missing the `<module>` directive, which is required for this version of EAR descriptor. Once the first module is associated with the EAP, the errors will disappear.

Creating the portal Dynamic Web Project

The procedure for creating a dynamic web project was reviewed in *Chapter 5* under the section **Securing a web application | Securing a J2EE web application | Creating the dynamic web application projects**. For this reason, the following description will not be very detailed. Only the aspects that are related to RAD and specifics about the EAR version will be pointed out. For simplicity, the term dynamic web project will be denoted as DWP in the rest of this chapter.

Creating the portal DWP

In RAD, using the **File** menu:

1. Follow the sequence: **File | New Dynamic Web Project**.
2. Name the project chap6-portal-webapp.
3. Ensure that the version for **Dynamic Web Module** is 2.5 or higher.
4. Under the section EAR membership, ensure that **Add project to an EAR** is checked and that **chap6-EAR-miniproject** is selected.
5. Click the **Next** button.

The properties to be provided on the last screen of the wizard are very important, so they are presented here as subsections to call attention to them.

Defining the DWP context root

The objective for this module is to become the main point of entry to the applications contained in the EAP. Therefore, the context root selected is / (slash). Enter this value under the field **Context Root**.

> Any URI used to access this chapter application that does not match the patterns /allemp/*, /hronly/*, or /open/* will be routed to the portal application.

Creating the DWP deployment descriptor

On the same screen in the wizard, at the bottom, click the **Generate deployment descriptor** check box so it appears checked. Leave the rest of the fields with their default values. Then click the **Finish** button to create the initial (empty) DWP.

> Notice how the errors that appeared on the **chap6-EAR-miniproject** have been fixed by adding a module to the EAP.

Configuring the portal DWP deployment descriptor

The next task is to further customize the newly created DWP. Aspects that will be customized are welcome file list and login information.

Defining the welcome pages suite

For the portal DWP we wish to reduce the welcome pages list to only index.html. In order to do so, in RAD, open the DWP deployment descriptor (web.xml). On the left pane, select the **Welcome File List** item. A list of built-in file names appears on the right-hand side. Delete all but the index.html file name.

Adding login information

In order to add log-in information, using RAD and working with the DWP deployment descriptor, click the **Add...** button. Select **Login Configuration** from the list presented in the **Add Item** selector dialog. Click the **OK** button.

Under **Properties for the login configuration** section, enter BASIC for **Authentication Method**. For the **Realm Name** field type Chapter 6 Mini-Project. Save the configuration changes.

Securing protected URI patterns and HTTP methods

In order to secure the URI patterns and the HTTP methods, two aspects need to be configured: security constraints and resource collections.

Defining security constraints

Continuing to edit the DWP deployment descriptor, click the **Add...** button once more. This time select the **Security Constraint** item. Enter Authenticated constraint in the **Display Name** field. Once the security constraint is defined, it is possible to add resource collections.

Defining resource collections

Expand the **Security Constraint icon** under **Web Application**. Select **Web Resource Collection**. The right-hand side of the editor adjusts accordingly. In the **HTTP method** section, click the **Add** button. Type GET. Repeat the steps but this time enter POST.

Go to the **URL Pattern** section. Click the **Add** button. Type /* as pattern. Moving lower, under **Web Resource Name**, enter the text Authenticated. Save the work.

Defining application roles

As the portal application needs to be accessed by all registered users (including registered visitors and employees) the Authenticated Role must be configured. In the application deployment descriptor editor, select once more **Web Application**. Add a Security Role. Enter Authenticated Role in the **Role name** field. Optionally, enter All authenticated users role as its description.

Defining the client-server transport type

In order to force the HTTPS protocol between the Application Server and the IHS/ Plug-in perform the following sequence. Select the **Security Constraint** icon under the **Web Application Structure** section. Under the **User Data Constraint** section at the bottom right-hand side, select **CONFIDENTIAL** from the **Transport Guarantee** pop-up menu. Save the changes to the file.

Mapping module to virtual host

The last piece needed is to map this module to the desired virtual host. In the editor, select the **Web Application** icon. From the list of links located at the bottom, on the right-hand side of the window, click the **Open WebSphere Bindings** link. A new editor tab opens (file name: ibm-web-bnd.xml). Replace the text **default_host** with **chap6_vh**.

This concludes the customization and configuration of the portal DWP, **chap6-EAR-miniproject**. In the next section, the content that makes up the application will be described.

Creating content for the portal DWP

Once the DWP has been configured, we can proceed to add the content that will implement the functionality of this module. We could just provide a list of the files that are part of the application, however, that would not help to understand how the application operates and how it is protected.

Location of files within the project

There are several HTML and JSP files used by the portal DWP. All of them are located in the **WebContent** directory as shown in the following screenshot. Furthermore, those files, which are components of a larger unit, are grouped under the templates directory.

The preceding screenshot also shows a Servlet class, the **PortalHomeSelectorServlet**. It is logically stored under the Java package **was7sec.chap6.web**. This Servlet is mapped to the URI /index.html, therefore, it is the first component invoked when the portal application is accessed.

Logical file organization

The files that were shown in the previous section fall neatly onto the portal home page. The following diagram depicts how each one of the files relates and fits within the portal home:

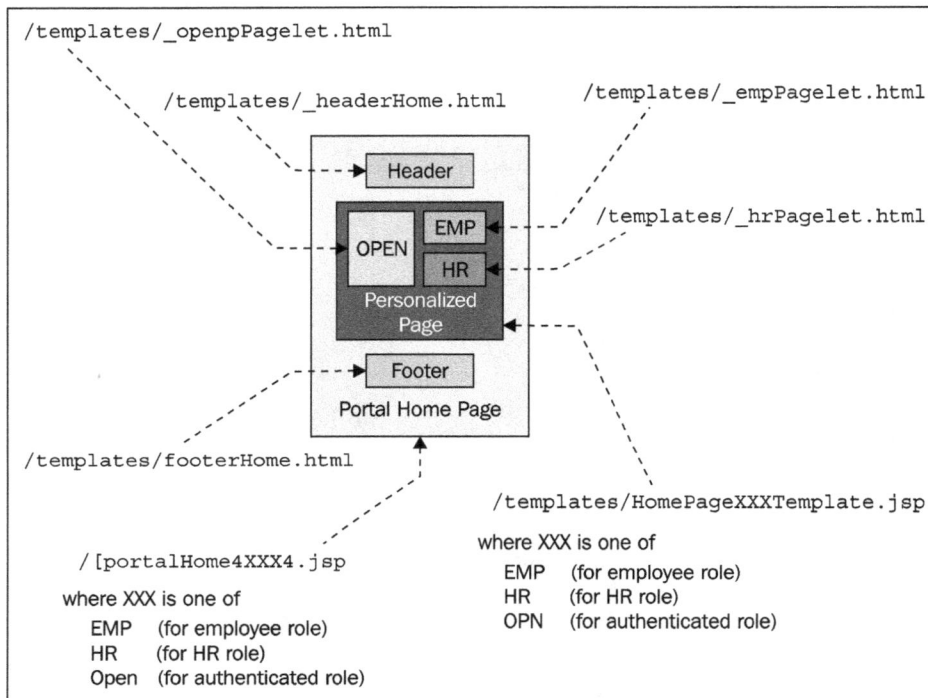

```
/templates/_openpPagelet.html

        /templates/_headerHome.html          /templates/_empPagelet.html

                    ┌──────────────────────┐
                    │      ┌─────────┐      │
                    │      │ Header  │      │
                    │   ┌──┴─────────┴──┐   │
                    │   │       ┌─────┐ │   │
                    │   │       │ EMP │ │◄─ ─ ─ /templates/_hrPagelet.html
                    │   │ OPEN  ├─────┤ │   │
                    │   │       │ HR  │◄┼ ─ ─
                    │   │ Personalized  │   │
                    │   │     Page      │◄─ ─ ─
                    │   └───────────────┘   │
                    │      ┌─────────┐      │
                    │      │ Footer  │      │
                    │      └─────────┘      │
                    │   Portal Home Page    │
                    └──────────────────────┘

/templates/footerHome.html

                                    /templates/HomePageXXXTemplate.jsp

                                    where XXX is one of
      /[portalHome4XXX4.jsp           EMP   (for employee role)
                                      HR    (for HR role)
      where XXX is one of             OPN   (for authenticated role)
         EMP   (for employee role)
         HR    (for HR role)
         Open  (for authenticated role)
```

Creating the common HTML files

In order to organize the files into the project as already described, create a folder named `templates` and place it under the directory `WebContent`.

It is now possible to add content files. Start by adding the `footerHome.html` and `headerHome.html` files. Give `footerHome.html` the content shown in the following screenshot:

```
headerHome.html ⊠
1<!DOCTYPE html PUBLIC "-//W3C//DTD HTML 4.01 Transitional//EN" "http:
2<html>
3<head>
4<meta http-equiv="Content-Type" content="text/html; charset=UTF-8">
5<title>YourCompany.COM INC</title>
6</head>
7<body>
8<H1 align="center">YourCompany.COM INC</H1>
9<PRE>
10
11
12
13</PRE>
14<FONT size="-2">Component: <em>headerHome.html</em></FONT>
15<hr>
16</body>
17</html>
18<!-- Component status: complete -->
```

In a similar way, give `headerHome.html` the content shown in the following screenshot:

```
footerHome.html ⊠
1<!DOCTYPE html PUBLIC "-//W3C//DTD HTML 4.01 Transitional//EN" "http:
2<html>
3<head>
4<meta http-equiv="Content-Type" content="text/html; charset=UTF-8">
5<title>Insert title here</title>
6</head>
7<body>
8<PRE>
9
10
11</PRE>
12<hr>
13<H5 align="right">That's all folks! (C) 2010 YourCompany.COM INC</H5>
14<PRE>
15
16
17
18</PRE>
19<FONT size="-2">Component: <em>footerHome.html</em></FONT>
20</body>
21</html>
22<!-- Component status: complete -->
```

The actual content of the file is basic HTML markup. The main purpose in this project is that the actual content helps us identify the component when it is rendered on the portal page. Thus, most of the HTML and JSP files include their name as part of their content. Cf. line 14 on the first of the screenshots and line 19 on the second screenshot.

Creating the custom HTML files

The next three HTML files (**_empPagelet.html** — mapped to the rectangle — green — labeled **EMP** in the preceding diagram, **_hrPagelet.html** — mapped to the rectangle — blue — labeled **HR**, and **_openPagelet.html** — mapped to the rectangle — orange — labeled **OPEN**) are the components that, from the UI point of view, *control* access to the legacy applications. In this sense, *control* is implemented by providing a link to the legacy application. The actual control is enforced by the EJB/Servlet/Domain security configuration settings. So, structurally, they are very similar in which they display some relevant content and links to applicable legacy application.

You can now create these three files and give them the content shown in the following screenshots. Start with **_empPagelet.html**, giving it the content shown in the next screenshot:

```
_empPagelet.html ⊠
1<TABLE width="300" height="325" bgcolor="#FFCC99">
2<TR><TD valign="top">
3<H5 align="center">Employee Highlights</H5>
4<PRE>
5
6
7</PRE>
8<A href="/allemp/index.html">Employee page</A>
9</TD></TR>
10</TABLE>
11<PRE>
12
13
14
15
16
17
18</PRE>
19<FONT size="-3">Component: <em>_empPagelet.html</em></FONT>
```

Continue with **_hrPagelet.html**, giving it the content shown in the next screenshot:

```
 _hrPagelet.html ⊠
 1 <H3 align="left">YourCompany.COM Highlights</H3>
 2 <TABLE width="300" height="325" bgcolor="#FFCC99">
 3     <TR>
 4         <TD valign="top">
 5         <H5 align="center">Employee Highlights</H5>
 6         <PRE>
 7
 8
 9 </PRE> <A href="/allemp/index.html">Employee page</A></TD>
 0     </TR>
 1     <TR>
 2         <TD valign="top">
 3         <H5 align="center">HR Department Information</H5>
 4         <PRE>
 5
 6
 7 </PRE> <A href="/hronly/index.jsp">HR page</A></TD>
 8     </TR>
 9 </TABLE>
 0 <PRE>
 1
 2
 3
 4
 5
 6
 7 </PRE>
 8 <FONT size="-3">Component: <em>_hrPagelet.html</em></FONT>
```

Conclude this portion by giving **_openPagelet.html** the content shown in the next screenshot:

```
 _openPagelet.html ⊠
 1 <H3 align="left">YourCompany.COM Highlights</H3>
 2 <pre>
 3
 4
 5
 6
 7
 8 </pre>
 9 <A href="/open/index.html">Start the OPEN page</A>
 0 <pre>
 1
 2
 3
 4
 5
 6 </pre>
 7 <FONT size="-3">Component: <em>_openPagelet.html</em></FONT>
```

As can be seen, there is not special code used in these files. There is a simple *H3* HTML directive plus the appropriate number of links, *A* directives, plus a page identifier at the bottom.

Creating the JSP files

The portal module uses two sets of JSP files. One set (represented by the rectangle--purple--labeled Personalized Page in the diagram in previous section *Logical file organization*) is used to select the number of Pagelets to display in the portal page. The second set (represented by the large rectangle--gold--labeled **Portal Home Page** in the same diagram) is used to select the appropriate portal page customized for a particular role.

Pagelet selector JSP files

Create, under the /templates directory, the JSP files: `HomePageEMPTemplate.jsp`, `HomePageHRTemplate.jsp`, and `HomePageOPNTemplate.jsp`. Give them the content shown in the next three screenshots. To the `HomePageEMPTemplate.jsp`, give it the content provided in the following screenshot:

```
HomePageEMPTemplate.jsp ⊠
1 <%@ page language="java" contentType="text/html; charset=ISO-8859-1"
2     pageEncoding="ISO-8859-1"%>
3 <!DOCTYPE html PUBLIC "-//W3C//DTD HTML 4.01 Transitional//EN" "http://www.
4 <html>
5 <head>
6 <meta http-equiv="Content-Type" content="text/html; charset=ISO-8859-1">
7 <title>HomePageTemplateEMP</title>
8 </head>
9 <body>
10 <%
11     String TpltID = "\n\n* * * * HomePageTemplateEMP:\n\t";
12     String openURITplt = (String) request
13         .getAttribute("customframe.openURI");
14     String allempURITplt = (String) request
15         .getAttribute("customframe.allempURI");
16 %>
17
18 <TABLE>
19     <TR>
20         <%-- Left hand-side: common to everybody = _openPagelet.html  --%>
21         <TD><jsp:include page="<%=openURITplt%>" /></TD>
22         <%--
23             Right-hand side: customized template per user.
24             Authenticated = none. Employee = _empPagelet.html
25             Human Resources = _hrPagelet.jsp
26         --%>
27         <TD><jsp:include page="<%=allempURITplt%>" /></TD>
28     </TR>
29 </TABLE>
30 <PRE>
31
32
33
34
35
36
37 </PRE>
38 <FONT size="-2">Component: <em>HomePageTemplateEMP.jsp</em></FONT>
39 </body>
40 </html>
```

In a similar way, to the `HomePageHRTemplate.jsp`, give the content shown in the following screenshot:

```
HomePageHRTemplate.jsp ⊠
1 <%@ page language="java" contentType="text/html; charset=ISO-8859-1"
2     pageEncoding="ISO-8859-1"%>
3 <!DOCTYPE html PUBLIC "-//W3C//DTD HTML 4.01 Transitional//EN" "http://www.\
4 <html>
5 <head>
6 <meta http-equiv="Content-Type" content="text/html; charset=ISO-8859-1">
7 <title>HomePageTemplateHR</title>
8 </head>
9 <body>
10 <%
11     String TpltID = "\n\n* * * * HomePageHRTemplate:\n\t";
12     String openURITplt = (String) request
13             .getAttribute("customframe.openURI");
14     String hronlyURITplt = (String) request
15             .getAttribute("customframe.hrURI");
16 %>
17
18 <TABLE>
19     <TR>
20         <%-- Left hand-side; common to everybody = _openPagelet.html   --%>
21         <TD><jsp:include page="<%=openURITplt%>" /></TD>
22         <%--
23             Right-hand side: customized template per user.
24             Authenticated = none. Employee = _empPagelet.html
25             Human Resources = _hrPagelet.jsp
26         --%>
27         <TD><jsp:include page="<%=hronlyURITplt%>" /></TD>
28     </TR>
29 </TABLE>
30 <PRE>
31
32
33
34
35
36
37 </PRE>
38 <FONT size="-2">Component: <em>HomePageHRTemplate.jsp</em></FONT>
39 </body>
40 </html>
```

Conclude this portion by giving `HomePageOPNTemplate.jsp`, the content provided in the following screenshot:

```
HomePageOPNTemplate.jsp 

 1<%@ page language="java" contentType="text/html; charset=ISO-8859-1"
 2     pageEncoding="ISO-8859-1"%>
 3<!DOCTYPE html PUBLIC "-//W3C//DTD HTML 4.01 Transitional//EN" "http://www.
 4<html>
 5<head>
 6<meta http-equiv="Content-Type" content="text/html; charset=ISO-8859-1">
 7<title>HomePageTemplateOPN</title>
 8</head>
 9<body>
10<%
11     String TpltID = "\n\n* * * * HomePageTemplateOPN:\n\t";
12     String openURITplt = (String) request
13          .getAttribute("customframe.openURI");
14%>
15
16<TABLE>
17   <TR>
18      <%-- Left hand-side; common to everybody = _openPagelet.html   --%>
19      <TD><jsp:include page="<%=openURITplt%>" /></TD>
20      <%--
21          Right-hand side: customized template per user.
22          Authenticated = none. Employee = _empPagelet.html
23          Human Resources = _hrPagelet.jsp
24       --%>
25   </TR>
26</TABLE>
27<PRE>
28
29
30
31
32
33
34</PRE>
35<FONT size="-2">Component: <em>HomePageOPNTemplate.jsp</em></FONT>
36</body>
37</html>
```

The analysis for the files `HomePageEMPTemplate.jsp`, `HomePageHRTemplate.jsp`, and `HomePageOPNTemplate.jsp` is as follows. **Lines 1-9** are basic JSP document type declarations (1-3) and standard HTML document introduction statements (4-9). **Lines 10-16** (for EMP and HR template files) and **10-14** (for OPN template file) are JSP Scriptlets for variable assignment. *Line 11* defines the page identifier. The function of this variable, **TpltID** is to help us track the flow of processing. If interested in performing this tracking, as an additional exercise, add JSP code after line 16 (for EMP and HR) and 14 (for OPN), which prints a message to the `SystemOut.log` file identifying that the JSP was executed. (Use the method `System.out.print` and `System.out.println` to write to the standard output; cf. any of the portal home JSP files). *Lines 12-15* (for EMP and HR template files) and Lines 12-13 (for OPN template file) define and assign values to JSP variables needed to fill in the customization areas in the templates.

For all template files, `openURITplt` will hold the value of the URI to the **open** application Pagelet. The value is stored as an attribute `customframe.OpenURI` in the HTTP request object. For the EMP template, the JSP variable `allempURITplt` will hold the value of the URI to the **allemp** application Pagelet. This value will be obtained from the `customframe.allempURI` HTTP request object attribute. Finally, for the HR template, the variable `hronlyUIRTplt` will hold the value of the URI to the **hronly** application Pagelet. This value may be obtained from the `customframe.hrURI` attribute in the HTTP request object.

> **Passing values between J2EE components: Servlet to JSP**
>
> In this project, the *HTTPServletRequest* Java class object *attribute* was used to pass various parameters from the Servlet to a JSP. In this model, JSP files know what attributes from the HTTPServletRequest are needed; whereas the Servlet will collect both attribute name and value from the EJB. **PortalHomeSelectorServlet** does not know which particular attributes are needed by a particular JSP. The Servlet requests from **PortalSelectionSessionBean** a custom object (**HomeComponents**, which implements a Hashtable Java class) that contains the information. Cf. *Creating an EJB project* for further details.

The remaining lines (**Lines 18-38** for EMP and HR templates and **Lines 16-35** for the OPN template) include a mix of HTML code and JSP include directives used to embed the corresponding Pagelet. Refer to the comments in the JSP files for further details.

Portal home selector JSP files

Create, under the `WebContent` folder, the JSP files: `PortalHome4EMP.jsp`, `PortalHome4HR.jsp` and `PortalHome4Open.jsp`. Give them the content as shown in the next screenshot, except as noted:

```
  PortalHome4EMP.jsp ⊠
 1 <%@ page language="java" contentType="text/html; charset=ISO-8859-1"
 2     pageEncoding="ISO-8859-1"%>
 3 <!DOCTYPE html PUBLIC "-//W3C//DTD HTML 4.01 Transitional//EN" "http://www.w3.org
 4 <html>
 5 <head>
 6 <meta http-equiv="Content-Type" content="text/html; charset=ISO-8859-1">
 7 <meta name="project-id" content="chapter 6.01">
 8
 9 <% String homepageTitle = (String) request.getAttribute("homepage.title");
10    String homepageBodytplt = (String) request.getAttribute("homepage.bodytplt");
11    String MyID = "\n\n* * * * PortalHomePage:\n\t"; %>
12
13 <% System.out.print( MyID );
14    System.out.print("Received attribute homepage.title with value ");
15    System.out.println( homepageTitle );
16    System.out.print(MyID);
17    System.out.print("Received attribute homepage.bodytplt with value ");
18    System.out.println( homepageBodytplt ); %>
19 <title><%= homepageTitle %></title>
20 </head>
21 <body>
22
23 <TABLE>
24 <TR><TD> <%@ include file="templates/headerHome.html"; %> </TD></TR>
25 <TR><TD> <jsp:include page="<%= homepageBodytplt %>" /> </TD></TR>
26 <TR><TD> <%@ include file="templates/footerHome.html"; %> </TD></TR>
27 </TABLE>
28 <PRE>
29
30
31
32
33
34
35 </PRE>
36 <FONT size="-2">Component: <em>PortalHome[4EMP].jsp</em></FONT>
37 </body>
38 </html>
```

The content of the JSP files `PortalHome4EMP.jsp`, `PortalHome4HR.jsp`, and `PortalHome4Open.jsp` is the same, except for line 36, which identifies the JSP file. The reason for having three JSP files instead of a single one has to do with security. Having a single JSP caused to cache its complied Java class the first time the application was invoked. So if a member from the HR department was the first user to access the application, the value for homepageBodyTplt would contain `HomePageHRTemplate.jsp` in its value. This value would then be cached in the compiled JSP. If another user, say external to the company but registered attempted to access the application, the common home JSP file would attempt to return the same HTML code as for the user form HR. This would cause many authorization (403) HTTP errors, something not desirable. A quick solution was to have three different JSP files from which to select according to the role of the user. (As stated before, the author is not a developer, so there may be better ways to code the JSP file to avoid the caching side effects.)

The analysis for these JSP files is as follows. **Lines 1-8** are standard JSP and HTML document definition. **Lines 9-18** make up a Scriptlet in Java. Lines 9-10 are the only lines that are essential to the JSP as they declare the JSP variables needed in the main body of the document, namely **homepageTitle** and **homepageBodyTplt**. Lines 11-18 are used to track the flow of processing. **Lines 19-38** are a combination of simple HTML code and a couple of JSP directives. The HTML code provides the frame for the portal page. In line 19, the title of the page is added by using a reference to the JSP variable **homepageTitle** defined in line 9. In line 25, a JSP directive to include an external file uses the variable **homepageBodyTplt** defined in line 20 to extract the path to the file.

Creating the Servlet PortalHomeSelectorServlet

The Servlet to be created in this section will be placed in its own package. So the next major tasks are to create the Java package and then create a Servlet in that package.

Creating a Java package

In RAD, select the `src` folder of the portal DWP. Right-click and follow the sequence **New | Package**. Name the package: `was7sec.chap6.web`.

Creating the Servlet

Again in RAD, select the newly created package. Right-click and follow the sequence **New | Servlet**. Give it the name `PortalHomeSelectorServlet`. Ensure that all the values shown match for the DWP. Ensure that a new Servlet mapping is created, `/index.html` (second screen).

Creating the code for PortalHomeSelectorServlet

As the source file for the Servlet contains 203 lines of code, this section will break the contents down by logical definitions (that is, variables, methods, and so on). The subsections that follow describe the most important definitions.

Package definition and import statements

The following screenshot shows the declaration of the Java package in **Line 1**. **Lines 3-13** declare the import packages or classes that the Servlet would refer to:

```
PortalHomeSelectorServlet.java ⊠

  chap6-portal-webapp  ▸   src  ▸   was7sec.chap6.web  ▸

 1  package was7sec.chap6.web;
 2
 3⊜import java.io.IOException;
 4  import javax.servlet.ServletException;
 5  import javax.servlet.http.HttpServlet;
 6  import javax.servlet.http.HttpServletRequest;
 7  import javax.servlet.http.HttpServletResponse;
 8  import javax.servlet.RequestDispatcher;
 9  import javax.naming.InitialContext;
10  import javax.naming.NamingException;
11  import java.util.Hashtable;
12  import java.util.Enumeration;
13  import was7sec.chap6.ejbclient.*;
```

Declaration of class constants and variables

Among the class constants only **serialVersionUID** is required in Line 31. The variable of interest to the project is **nextJSP**, which will hold the value of the JSP to be used as portal home.

```
30  public class PortalHomeSelectorServlet extends HttpServlet {
31      private static final long serialVersionUID = 1L;
32      private static final String MyBanner = "\n\n* * * *\n*\r
33      private static final String MyFooter = "*\n*\n*\n*\n* Port
35⊕    * Servlet ID for debugging purposes
37      private static final String MyID = "\n\n* * * *\n*\n* Po
38      private String nextJSP = null;
```

HTTP methods

Both `doGet` and `doPut` methods are identical. The only call of relevance in that method is:

```
getParamAndForward(request, response);
```

The rest of the code is for process tracking purposes and can be ignored.

Getting parameters

The method `getParamAndForward` objective is to trigger the action to populate the HTML-related values that will be needed by other components down the chain (for example, JSP files). That is achieved by invoking the method `collectHTMLComponents`, as shown in **Line 160**.

```
148   private void getParamAndForward(final HttpServletRequest req,
149       final HttpServletResponse resp) throws IOException,
150       ServletException {
151       /**
152        * 1. Identify the request protocol (browser type: HTML, WAP, XML, etc.)
153        * 2. Base on protocol, invoke the protocol-friendly private method 3.
154        * NOTE: Information is passed in the form of dictionary entries (pairs)
155        * Such pairs will be added to the request object as attribute-parameter
156        **/
157       System.out.println(MyID + "Method getParamAndForward ... entering");
158       context = req.getContextPath();
159       String uri;
160       collectHTMLComponents(req);
161       if (!context.isEmpty()) {
162           uri = context + "/" + nextJSP;
163       } else {
164           uri = "/" + nextJSP;
165       }
166       System.out.println(MyID + "getParamAndForward: uri <-- '" + uri + "'");
167       System.out
168               .println(MyID
169                   + "Method getParamAndForward: forwarding to URI: '"
170                   + uri + "'");
171       forwardToPage(req, resp, uri);
172       System.out.println(MyID + "Method getParamAndForward ... exiting");
173   }
```

Once the values needed by the JSP files have been gathered, **Lines 161-165** compute the URI to the portal home JSP to be used. When all of the required values are accounted for, control is passed to the **forwardToPage** method, as shown in **Line 171**.

Communicating with EJB

The method `collectHTMLComponents` main objective is twofold. On the first hand, it communicates with the EJB using RMI and the EJB remote interface in order to retrieve a Hashtable object that contains the values to propagate down the chain. On the other hand, it populates the request object with the values retrieved from the EJB in the form of attribute-value pairs.

The analysis of the code is as follows. In **Lines 105-119** an attempt to identify the EJB remote interface object is made (specifically *Lines 106-108*). If successful, the code requests the Hashtable containing the values to be used as attributes (*Line 113*). Lines **122-131** present the code that takes the pairs found in the Hashtable object retrieved in line 113 and inject them as attributes of the request object (*Lines 126-130*).

A special case of retrieved value is the Hashtable key `controller.nextjsp`. This pair is extracted and removed from the Hashtable prior to populating the request object attributes (*Line 125*).

```
97-   @SuppressWarnings("unchecked")
98    private void collectHTMLComponents(final HttpServletRequest req)
99          throws IOException, ServletException {
100       System.out.println(MyID + "Method collectHTMLComponents ... entering");
101       Hashtable portalComponents = null;
102       System.out
103             .println(MyID
104                   + "Method collectHTMLComponents ... creating an InitialContext");
105       try {
106           InitialContext ctx = new InitialContext();
107           PortalSelectorRemote selectorBean = (PortalSelectorRemote) ctx
108                 .lookup("was7sec.chap6.ejbclient.PortalSelectorRemote");
109           System.out
110                 .println("*\t... possibly found PortalSelectorBeanRemote");
111           System.out
112                 .println("*\t... invoking remote method getHomeComponents");
113           portalComponents = selectorBean.getHomeComponents();
114           System.out.println("*\t... back from getHomeComponents");
115       } catch (NamingException ne) {
116           ne.printStackTrace();
117       } catch (Exception e) {
118           e.printStackTrace();
119       }
120       System.out
121             .println("*\t... attempting to extract attributes and values");
122       if (!portalComponents.isEmpty()) {
123           Enumeration attrs = null;
124           attrs = portalComponents.keys();
125           nextJSP = (String) portalComponents.remove("controller.nextjsp");
126           while (attrs.hasMoreElements()) {
127               String attribute = (String) attrs.nextElement();
128               String value = (String) portalComponents.get(attribute);
129               req.setAttribute(attribute, value);
130           }
131       }
132       System.out.println(MyID + "Method collectHTMLComponents ... exiting");
133   }
```

Forwarding control to another component

The method `forwardToPage` is used to cede control to the next J2EE element down the chain. In this particular case, control is given to the corresponding portal home JSP file. As this method is the same in essence as the used for the Servlet *HomePage* from *Chapter 5*, its content will not be included in this chapter. There are only two aspects to be highlighted.

The first one is that the **forwardToPage** method uses the Servlet context object to retrieve the RequestDispatcher object. In other words:

```
RequestDispatcher dispatcher = getServletContext().
getRequestDispatcher();
```

The second aspect to stress is that the `forwardToPage` method uses the `RequestDispatcher` object method **forward** to cede control.

Creating an EJB project

Once the portal DWP is completed, we can turn our attention to the final component of this mini-project, the EJB. This project is made of a session EJB and three interfaces. One of the interfaces is used as a common interface where the exposed EJB methods are declared. In addition the security annotations from the EJB are declared in this interface as well. The other two interfaces extend the common interface and perform the function of local and remote interface to the EJB. The project is organized in two Java packages. One package will hold the EJB and the other package will hold the interfaces.

Creating the initial project

Using RAD to create an EJB project is very similar in principle to creating other projects. From the **File** menu, select to create an EJB project. Give it the name `chap6-portal-ejbean`. Ensure that EJB Module version is set to 3.0 or higher. In addition, make sure to associate this new project with the mini-project's EAR project (**chap6-EAR-miniproject**). On the second screen of the wizard, deselect the **Create an EJB Client JAR...** option. We will create those interfaces manually and will include them as part of this project. Click the **Generate deployment descriptor** check box so it is selected.

Creating the Java packages

By now, you should have experience in creating Java packages. Expand the **chap6-portal-ejbean** project and locate the **ejbModule** icon. From the **File** menu, select **New | Other | Java | Package** to create a Java package. Ensure that its parent directory (identified as **Source folder**) is the **ejbModule** item that you selected. Give it the name `was7sec.chap6.ejb`. Repeat the process and create the Java package **was7sec.chap6.ejbclient**.

Creating the EJB interfaces

As stated earlier, this project contains three interfaces. For all of them, select the last Java package created, that is, **was7sec.chap6.ejbclient**.

Creating IPortalSelectorSessionBean interface

From the **File** menu, follow the sequence **New | Interface**. Ensure that source folder and package are correct. Give it the name `IPortalSelectorSessionBean`. The Java editor opens with the newly created interface.

In order to complete the code, make this interface an extension of *Serializable* (cf. **Line 13**). Therefore, importing the class `java.io.Serializable` is required (cf. **Line 6**). It is now time to declare the lone method that will be exposed from the upcoming EJB. Declare a method named `getHomeComponents` without any arguments. The method returns an object of the *Hashtable* class. (Cf. **Line 16**). Due to this, it is necessary to import the `java.util.`*Hashtable* class (cf. **Line 7**). The code for this interface is shown in the following screenshot:

```
4 package was7sec.chap6.ejbclient;
5
6 import java.io.Serializable;
7 import java.util.Hashtable;
8
10  * @author ops
13 public interface IPortalSelectorSessionBean extends Serializable {
14
15     @SuppressWarnings("unchecked")
16     public Hashtable getHomeComponents();
17
18 }
```

Creating the local and remote EJB interfaces

In a similar way in which `IPortalSelectorSessionBean` was created, create the following two interfaces. Give the first one the name `PortalSelectorLocal` and the second `PortalSelectorRemote`. Each interface must extend the `IPortalSelectorSessionBean` interface. (Cf. **Line 13**). For the local interface, add a directive to import the `javax.ejb.Local` class. Similarly add a directive to the remote interface to import the `javax.ejb.Remote` class (cf. **Line 6**). Finally, in the local interface, the class declaration must be annotated with `@Local`. In a similar way, the remote class declaration must be preceded with the `@Remote` annotation. (Cf. **Line 12**).

The remote interface **PortalSelectorRemote** is shown in the following screenshot. The code for the local interface is very similar, changing only what was stated previously.

```
4 package was7sec.chap6.ejbclient;
5
6 import javax.ejb.Remote;
7
9  * @author ops
12 @Remote
13 public interface PortalSelectorRemote extends IPortalSelectorSessionBean {
14
15 }
```

Creating the EJB

Creating an EJB is similar to creating other J2EE components. Using the
sequence **File | New | Session Bean**. In the wizard, give it the name
PortalSelectorSessionBean. Ensure that the source folder is that of the EJBP. In
addition, make sure that the package **was7sec.chap6.ejb** is selected. Under the field
superclass, enter java.lang.Object. Ensure that none of the business interfaces are
selected. Leave the other values as they appear.

Creating the code for
PortalSelectorSessionBean

The same technique used in analyzing the code for the Servlet will be employed in
this section, that is, breaking the code into logical segments and highlighting those
sections that convey security concepts or that are essential for the understanding
of the EJB.

Package definition and import statements

Line 1 defines the package to which the EJB belongs. **Lines 3-9** show the external
classes and packages needed by the EJB. The imported classes that are relevant to EJB
security are shown in the following screenshot:

```
6 import javax.annotation.Resource;
7 import javax.annotation.security.RolesAllowed;
8 import javax.ejb.SessionContext;
```

Class definition

Lines 15-17 show the class definition. It is defined as a Stateless class (line 15). In
addition, it extends the Object class (line 16) and implements our two interfaces,
namely **PortalSelectorRemote** and **PortalSelectorLocal** (line 17).

Instance variables

Line 33 declares the instance variable **HomeComponents**, which is an instance of the
Java class Hashtable. This is the object that will be created and then populated with
the values needed for assembling the portal page.

Linking to the user context

Lines 37-38 show how the user context is accessed by the EJB. Using the Java class `javax.annotation.Resource` the EJB is able to retrieve the user context. Line 37 shows the annotation used whereas line 38 shows the use of the resource SessionContext to achieve the EJB's purpose.

Programmatic security

Lines 115-143 contain how programmatic security is used by the method `getHomeComponents`, the only exposed method of the EJB. The following screenshot shows the content of the method's lines:

```
115    @RolesAllowed("Authenticated Role")
116    public Hashtable getHomeComponents() {
117        System.out.println(MyID + "Method getHomeComponents ... entering");
118        try {
119            if (userCtx.isCallerInRole("HR Role")) {
120                System.out.println(MyID
121                    + "getHomeComponents: processing for 'HR Role'");
122                getComponentsForHRRole();
123            } else if (userCtx.isCallerInRole("Employee Role")) {
124                System.out.println(MyID
125                    + "getHomeComponents: processing for 'EMPLOYEE Role'");
126                getComponentsForHRRole();
127                getComponentsForEmployeeRole();
128            } else if (userCtx.isCallerInRole("Authenticated Role")) {
129                System.out
130                    .println(MyID
131                        + "getHomeComponents: processing for 'AUTHENTICATED Role'");
132                getComponentsForHRRole();
133                getComponentsForAuthenticatedRole();
134            } else {
135                initHomeComponents();
136            }
137        } catch (Exception e) {
138            System.out.println(MyID + "Method getHomeComponents ... OOPS!");
139            e.printStackTrace();
140        }
141        System.out.println(MyID + "Method getHomeComponents ... exiting");
142        return HomeComponents;
143    }
```

Line 115 contains the annotation for roles allowed to execute (remotely invoke) the method. For our purposes, we wish to allow anyone that has authenticated access to this method. (Cf. how users and groups have been assigned as members of other groups and how groups and roles are mapped in *Chapter 5*).

Lines 119-136 are the locations where programmatic security is used. The method uses the `SessionContext` method `isCallerInRole`, which takes as an argument the name of a role in the form of a String. This method is used in lines 119, 123, and 128. The method first checks if the caller is in the role of highest security, HR Role, (line 119). If the caller is in the role, a method that only can be invoked by the HR Role is invoked, (cf. line 122). However, if the user is not in that role it checks to see if the caller is in the role next in security hierarchy, Employee Role, (line 123). If the caller is in that role, a method only available to members of the Employee Role is invoked, (line 126). If the caller is not in any of the previous roles, the method checks for the caller role membership against the next role in the security hierarchy, Authenticated Role, (line 128). If the caller membership matches the desired role, a method that only those callers in the Authenticated Role can invoke is called, (cf. line 132). If the caller does not belong to any of the stated groups, `getHomeComponents` would return an empty HomeComponents Hashtable object. However, as `getHomeComponents` can only be invoked in a context where the caller is in the role Authenticated Role, this case should not happen. It is included for completeness sake in case that an unforeseen change external to the EJB would break its security behavior. Therefore, the else clause in lines 134-136 ensure that no information be retrieved.

Summing-up this section, the method isCallerInRole is that element of the security API that helps developers to enforce security policies in their code.

Declarative security

Finally, although already observed previously, our bean PortalSelectorSessionBean uses declarative security in the form of annotations to impose security policies. The specific security annotation used is `@RolesAllowed`. The methods that use this mechanism are `getComponentsforHRRole`, `getComponentsforEmployeeRole`, and `getComponentsforAuthenticatedRole`. As their name implies, these methods can only be invoked by callers in the role that is mentioned as part of the method's name. For instance, the method `getComponentsforEmployeeRole` can only be invoked by callers in the Employee Role, as shown in the following screenshot (cf. line 84). The same goes for the other two methods.

```
84    @RolesAllowed("Employee Role")
85    private void getComponentsForEmployeeRole() {
86        if (!HomeComponents.isEmpty())
87            initHomeComponents();
88        setComponents("controller.nextjsp", "PortalHome4EMP.jsp");
89        setComponents("homepage.title", "EMPLOYEE TITLE");
90        setComponents("homepage.bodytplt", "/templates/HomePageEMPTemplate.jsp");
91        setComponents("customframe.openURI", "/templates/_openPagelet.html");
92        setComponents("customframe.allempURI", "/templates/_empPagelet.html");
93    }
```

As can be observed, all the work these methods do is to populate the HomeComponents Hashtable with the appropriate values (as called by the security policies for each of the roles) that will help the other J2EE components to build a customized portal home.

This example is very primitive but helps to show the point as to how to use security for an EJB application. You are highly discouraged from using this type of solution in a production environment. Many improvements need to be made in order to make this simple and rudimentary portal application scalable and easy to maintain. One improvement that comes to mind is to store the values that are to be passed from the EJB to the other J2EE elements in a database. That will improve maintenance and add flexibility. In order to improve scalability, a much better algorithm to identify the role of a caller must be used. Doing so will improve performance and scalability.

The grand finale

Once that you have completed the previous sections you are in a position to finish this mini-project.

Packaging the enterprise project as an EAR

Using RAD, once all of the deployment descriptors are configured based on instructions throughout this chapter and the references to *Chapter 5*, export the **chap6-EAR-miniproject** enterprise project as an EAR file. If RAD complains about any of the modules, the error messages are very intuitive and will help you identify any possible problem.

Deploying the EAR

In order to proceed with the deployment, the only thing to consider is to do it the same way in which you have deployed EJB applications. If you do not have much experience with this type of EAR, the only thing to pay close attention to is that on the step number two. Make sure to indicate to deploy EJBs, which by default is not selected. In addition, when appropriate select the application server **Chap6AppServer** for deployment of all the modules. Ensure that the virtual host is **chap6_vh**. The other point that may need close attention is when you get to the Groups and Roles step. If you do not see the correct mapping, make the changes so there is a one-to-one correspondence between groups and roles. That should be it. Easy, don't you think?

Testing the application

Once your EAR has been deployed, start the application server **Chap6AppServer**. Monitor its `SystemOut.log` file. You should see towards the end when your application and modules start. Using a browser access the main URL (`https://<your_hostname_FQDN>:<VH_Port>/`). Ensure that you use the same value as the host name that was defined when creating the virtual host `chap6_vh`.

First, log in as the user in the Authenticated group, `sam_visitor`. Observe the portal home displayed. It should contain only one link, to the /open/ legacy application. With the same browser, attempt to manually enter the URLs for /allemp/ and /hronly/. You should get authorization errors (403). Next, using a different browser, do the same for the member of the Employee group, **ravi**. Observe the differences in the portal home page. Finally, also using a new browser, login as **lola** who is Ms HR and observe and compare her portal home with the others'. Well done!

Summary

In this chapter, you have learned quite a bit. You can now show off with colleagues and tell them that you know all about:

- The two main mechanisms to apply security to EJB 3.0 applications
  - Declarative security using annotations
  - Programmatic security using the `javax.ejb.SessionContext` class and in particular its method `isCallerInRole`(String)
- How to create EJB projects
- How to deploy secured EJB applications

You can also brag about having written a simple, very simple portal application. Hmm, what do you think, why not go now and ask for a raise!

7
Securing Back-end Communication

Almost no entity is completely independent in order to perform its designed purpose. Plants in order to be plants at the very least require the sun and water; animals, similarly, require nutrients to *be* animals. WebSphere enterprise applications are no different; they probably require external resources (for example, a back-end database) in order to provide their service.

Let's expand a little on the entity-purpose concept. For this, let's use a house as an analogy. In most cases, for a house to be functional it requires different types of services such as power, water, perhaps a source of natural gas. In more sophisticated instances, a resident of a house may perceive as a need the addition of a telephone line, cable television, and high-speed Internet. All of these 'connections' form a type of backbone for that particular residence to provide the set of services expected by the owners and possible guests.

For many or all of these connections/services, the person in charge of the house would have to establish a contract with the company providing such services, possibly agreeing as to how the consumer is to pay for the service, that is, whether a billing period must be paid in advance or after the service is received. In any event, for this analogy it will be considered that the establishment of an account would be equivalent to the authentication aspect in WebSphere.

In addition, some of the services, such as telephone and cable television, place an additional security component to the location in which their infrastructure interface connects at the house; mostly in the form of a locked container that only personnel authorized by the service provider can access (for example, cable box). Stretching this analogy, this could be compared to the encryption of the service channel; the information in such a container can only be accessed with a special key; without it, it is practically impossible to access whatever may be inside the container. In other words, it's like securing a service channel in the WebSphere world using encryption in a way that the information can be accessed only with certain keys. So, this chapter presents possible methods to secure some of the communication channels to infrastructure resources, such as using LDAP for authentication, that enable a WebSphere enterprise application (EAR) accomplish its purpose for the intended audience (that is, authenticated users).

The following diagram helps illustrate where this chapter belongs in our security roadmap. Represented by the rectangle (light silver) labeled 'Back-End Security', this chapter borrows from its predecessors and applies in new ways the concept of *authentication*, which had been mostly applied to interactions of users with applications. In addition, the chapter continues to build on the concept of *data encryption*.

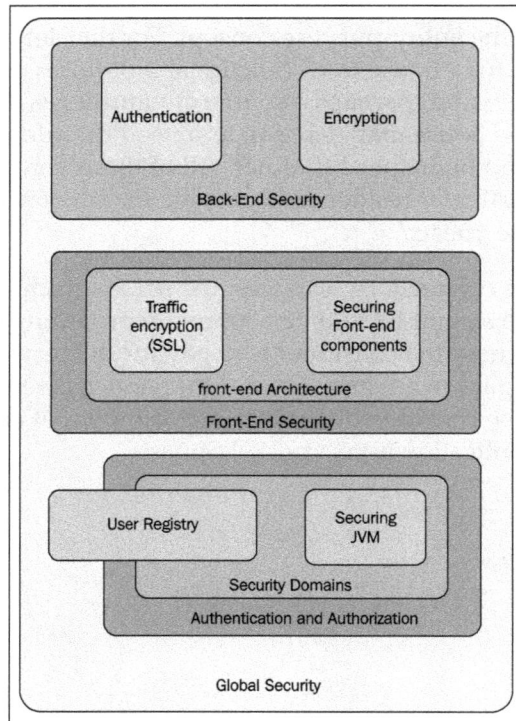

The focus of the chapter is then summarized in two concepts:

- **Authentication**: The JDBC back channel will be used to illustrate how authentication can be used by back-end services to remove the need for applications to deal with user IDs and passwords, instead leaving to the WebSphere infrastructure to be responsible for that aspect.

- **Data encryption**: The LDAP back channel will be used to show how a clear text channel can be made safer by using an SSL transport to encrypt its data. The chapter also shows how to create an additional layer of security isolation by creating a complete new set of stores and configuration settings.

LDAP: Uses of encryption

The LDAP protocol (denoted as just LDAP in this chapter) is the back-end channel used by the WebSphere infrastructure to obtain information about users and groups. There are mainly two uses in a WebSphere Application Server infrastructure for this type of information: **authentication** and **authorization**, as reviewed in *Chapter 3, Configuring User Authentication and Access*. Usually, the data transmitted between the WebSphere infrastructure and an LDAP server is very sensitive in nature as it may contain user credentials information among other things. Therefore, this section will highlight the aspects that allow securing the WebSphere-LDAP communication channel.

Securing the LDAP channel

The next three subsections will briefly describe the importance of securing the WebSphere-LDAP channel. In addition, these sections point out the choices that the WebSphere Application Server ND v7 offers for securing the WebSphere-LDAP channel.

Protocol: LDAP and the Internet Protocol Suite

If you recall, in Chapter 4 under the *SSL configuration and management* section, and subsection, the protocol combination HTTP/SSL was placed within the Internet Protocol Suite model. The following diagram depicts how LDAP is related to the model. As it can be observed, LDAP falls in the same category as the HTTP protocol, that is, they belong to the **Application Layer** family of protocols. This is represented in the diagram as the rectangle labeled with the text **LDAP**. Thus, LDAP is a clear-text type of protocol. In other words, the information exchanged between an LDAP server and, in this case, the WebSphere infrastructure, is not encrypted by default since it is transported using the TCP transport layer protocol.

> Additional information about the Internet Protocol Suite can be found in RFC 1122, available online at `http://tools.ietf.org/html/rfc1122`.

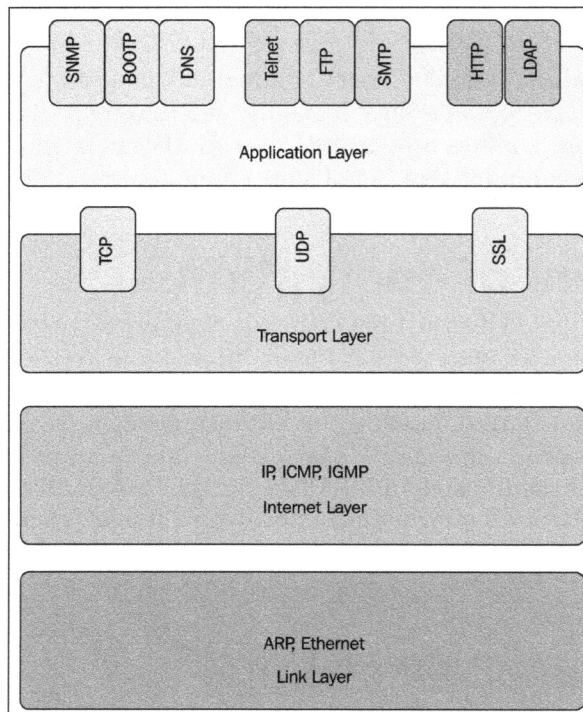

The importance of securing the LDAP channel

As mentioned earlier, the transfer of data between the WebSphere infrastructure and LDAP is rather sensitive; for instance it may include service accounts (that is, administrative) passwords that are used to bind to the LDAP server, that is to establish the initial communication between WebSphere and LDAP that will create a trusted channel between them. It may also include sensitive information about users, depending on what type of data the hosted application may require. Depending on the local laws where the application is hosted, there may be security policies that may need to be applied to the WebSphere-LDAP communication channel. Therefore, it is not only important that the authorization aspect of the communication is enforced, but also that the data flowing through the channel is encrypted.

Choices in securing the LDAP channel

From the previous diagram, the choices for a transport layer protocol are TCP, UDP, and SSL. The only two suitable to be used for LDAP are TCP and SSL. As such, WebSphere Network Deploy V7 provides two ways of accessing an LDAP server: using the LDAP protocol over the TCP transport layer or using the LDAP protocol over the SSL transport layer. Of the two transport layers, by design, only the SSL layer can be encrypted. Therefore, the only choice to secure the LDAP channel is to encrypt the communication by using the LDAP/SSL transport-application layers combination. In the previous diagram, this selection would be represented by the rectangle labeled **LDAP** (located at the application layer level) and the small rectangle labeled **SSL** (located at the transport layer level).

Enabling SSL for LDAP

As the LDAP/SSL combination is the only choice offered by WebSphere to protect the data from prying eyes, this section and its subsections that follow highlight the procedure to enable and enforce SSL to communicate with the LDAP server. However, Chapter 2 under its section *Enabling security* and subsection *Configuring the user registry* has already covered how to do the basic configuration for LDAP. That aspect of the configuration will not be repeated here. The reader is encouraged to refer to that chapter for further details.

There are two major components to configuring SSL for LDAP:

* The first and most simple is to set the flag to enable SSL
* The second is to configure the SSL certificates between WebSphere and LDAP server

The second component (that is, SSL certificates) was also reviewed in Chapter 2, thus the following subsections only highlight the process that needs to be followed. Furthermore, this same methodology can be applied to secure via encryption other service channels that the WebSphere Application Server may employ, such as Messaging (JMS) and Web Services.

Best practice: Use a separate key ring for an LDAP SSL configuration

In order to avoid possible confusion with other channels and, more importantly, to provide another level of isolation, it is best practice to use a brand new key ring and SSL configuration for LDAP or other back-end channels being secured through encryption. The creation of an SSL configuration requires both a key store and a trust store.

Therefore, the way in which the next subsections present the SSL configuration stages, will be done in a manner that it can be applied to additional back-end communication conduits other than the LDAP channel. The high level procedure to be followed is as given here:

- Create a key ring (create a file)
- Create a trust db file (create a file)
- Create a key store (associate store with file)
- Create a trust store (associate store to file)
- Create an SSL configuration
- Import LDAP (or back-end server) signer certificate

Creating a key ring for storing key stores

As mentioned in Chapter 4 under the subsection *Creating the SSL system component*, a new directory should be created in which all of the files associated with the LDAP key store will be kept. The location of this directory should match the scope for the LDAP configuration. For our purposes, we will assume that the WebSphere environment uses this LDAP registry as its global security user registry. Therefore, place it under the `<DeploymentManager_Profile_Root>/config/cells<cell_name>/` directory and give it a meaningful name that matches your organization standards. For instance, we will use the name `ldapts` (that is, LDAP Trust Store).

We are now in position to create the key ring file suite. In Chapter 4, the `gsk7capicmd` tool was used. We will use the `ikeyman.sh` graphical interface provided by WebSphere. Execute the command:

<DeploymentManager_Profile_Root>/bin/ikeyman.sh &

Select the **New...** option from the **Key Database File** menu. Select the type **PKCS12** as shown in the following screenshot, ensuring that the location is the desired one. We use, `<DeploymentManager_Profile_Root>/config/cells<cell_name>/ldapts`.

For the key ring file name, provide one that follows your corporate standards. We use, `ldap_key.p12`.

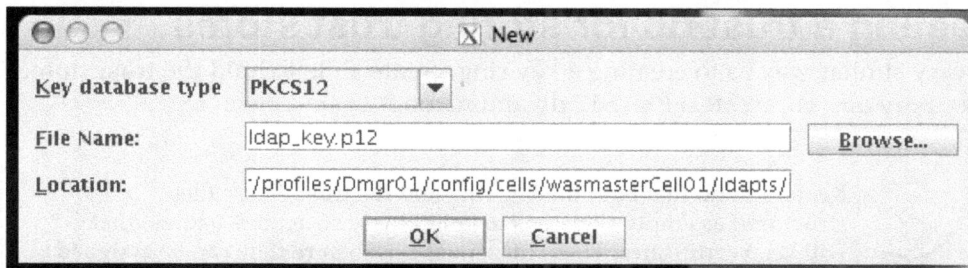

If there is an error stating that there is a problem with the policy files, perform the steps indicated next, in the subsection "JCE Policy files"; otherwise, enter a password for the file and terminate the `ikeyman` utility. The key ring creation is now completed. The file `<DeploymentManager_Profile_Root>/config/cells<cell_name>/ldapts/ldap_key.p12` must now exist.

JCE Policy files

JCE stands for **Java Cryptographic Extension**. By default, WebSphere includes a restricted or limited-size encryption keys policy files. If you get an error message indicating that the WebSphere JRE is using restricted policy files, it is necessary to apply a manual patch to use an unrestricted JCE set of policy files. What this really means is that the current set of policies do not allow the WebSphere JRE to handle long encryption keys, which is something desirable. In order to get the patch, use your corporate account to access the URL:

```
https://www14.software.ibm.com/webapp/iwm/web/reg/pick.
do?source=jcesdk&lang=en_US
```

Once you have logged in, select and download the JCE policy files for version 1.4.2+ as shown in the following screenshot:

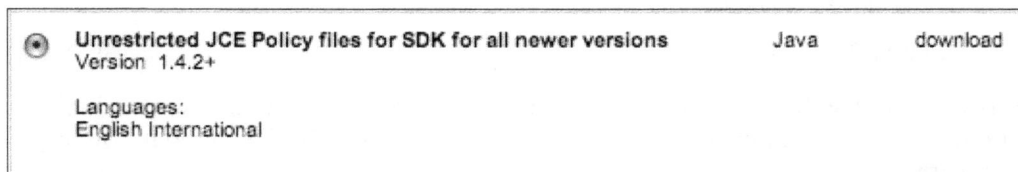

Un-archive the file. Backup the original JCE files (`US_export_policy.jar` and `local_policy.jar`), which are located in the directory `<WAS_Root>/java/jre/lib/security`. Copy the files that were just extracted with the same names in the security directory. Once completed, restart the `ikeyman` utility and continue creating the key ring.

Creating a trust db for storing trust stores

In a very similar way as to creating a key ring, create a file to hold the trust store. Using `ikeyman.sh`, create a PKCS12 db and name it `ldap_trust.p12`.

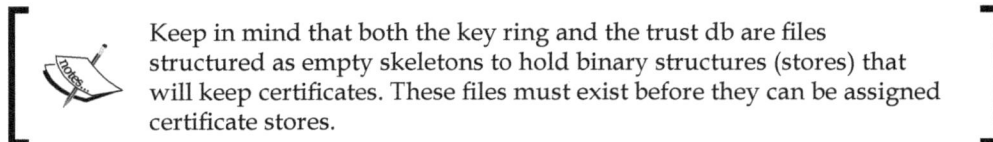

> Keep in mind that both the key ring and the trust db are files structured as empty skeletons to hold binary structures (stores) that will keep certificates. These files must exist before they can be assigned certificate stores.

Creating a key store for use with LDAP

During this step, we are telling WebSphere to use the key ring file as the OS component to be used as a certificate store. Using the Deployment Manager Console, follow the breadcrumb **Security | SSL certificate and key management | Key stores and certificates | New**.

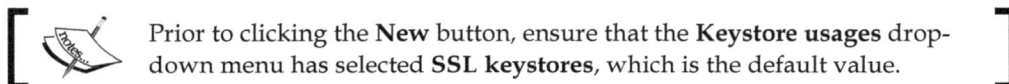

> Prior to clicking the **New** button, ensure that the **Keystore usages** drop-down menu has selected **SSL keystores**, which is the default value.

Enter the values for the following (values used in our environment are indicated in parenthesis):

- Name (**LDAPKeystore**)
- Description (**Keystore for the LDAP SSL encrypted channel**)
- Management scope (**cell**)
- Path (`${USER_INSTALL_ROOT}/config/cells/${WAS_CELL_NAME}/ldapts/ldap_key.p12`)
- Type (PKCS12)

For password, use the one utilized when the key ring was created. After the key store has been created, its configuration page should look similar to the following screenshot:

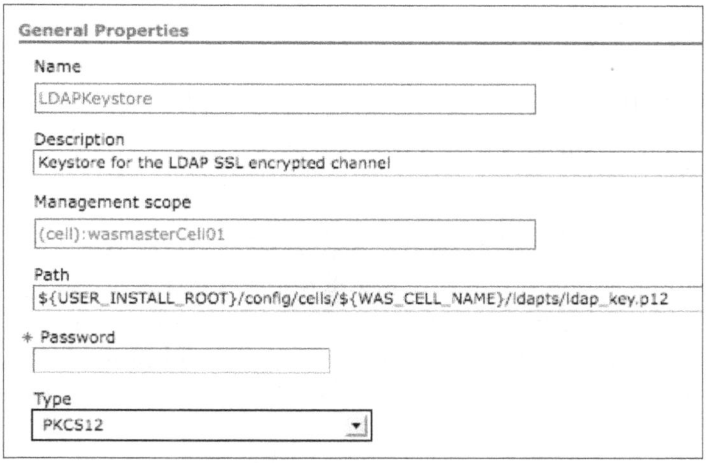

General Properties

Name

LDAPKeystore

Description

Keystore for the LDAP SSL encrypted channel

Management scope

(cell):wasmasterCell01

Path

${USER_INSTALL_ROOT}/config/cells/${WAS_CELL_NAME}/ldapts/ldap_key.p12

✴ Password

Type

PKCS12

Creating a trust store to use with LDAP

The procedure to create a trust store is the same as that used for creating a key store. As such, we are telling WebSphere to use the trust db as the OS component to be used as certificate store. Create a trust store, so that it is similar to the screenshot shown next:

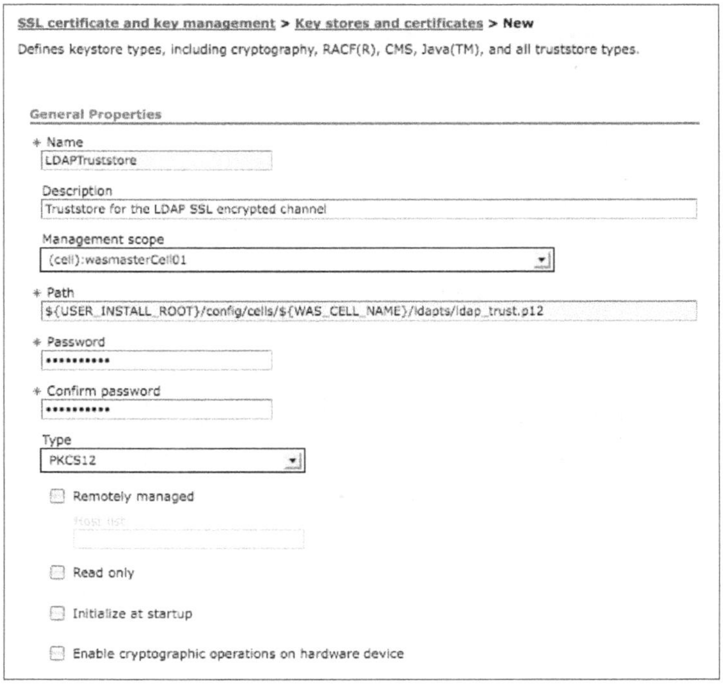

SSL certificate and key management > Key stores and certificates > **New**

Defines keystore types, including cryptography, RACF(R), CMS, Java(TM), and all truststore types.

General Properties

✴ Name

LDAPTruststore

Description

Truststore for the LDAP SSL encrypted channel

Management scope

(cell):wasmasterCell01

✴ Path

${USER_INSTALL_ROOT}/config/cells/${WAS_CELL_NAME}/ldapts/ldap_trust.p12

✴ Password

••••••••••

✴ Confirm password

••••••••••

Type

PKCS12

☐ Remotely managed

☐ Read only

☐ Initialize at startup

☐ Enable cryptographic operations on hardware device

> **Key and Trust Stores passwords**
>
> As the creation of a certificate store is in essence the mapping of the store binary structure to an OS file created with `ikeyman`, the passwords used while creating the key and trust stores must match the password of the key ring and trust db accordingly.

Creating an SSL configuration for LDAP

After completing the key store, we can create the SSL configuration component. Follow the breadcrumb: **Security | SSL certificate and key management | SSL configurations | New**. Create the `LDAPSSLSettings` configuration using the `keystore` and `truststore` just created, as shown in the following screenshot:

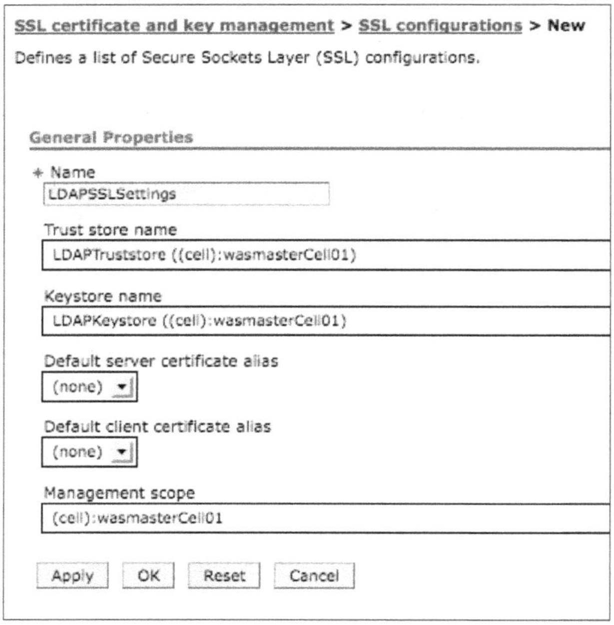

Obtaining the LDAP server SSL certificate

There are a couple of ways to import the LDAP server signer certificate:

- One would be requesting from the LDAP server administration team to provide an export of the signer certificate
- The other is to directly download the signer certificate using the Deployment Manager Console
- We will demonstrate the latter

Using the Deployment Manager Console, follow the breadcrumb **Security | SSL certificate and key management | SSL configurations | LDAPSSLSettings | Key stores and certificates | LDAPTruststore | Signer certificates | Retrieve from port**. Provide the SSL server information, including IP and SSL port. The following screenshot shows an example of this configuration:

This procedure will also work with other types of servers that use SSL, not only LDAP. For example, this method could be used between the WebSphere Plugin loaded in an HTTP server such as IHS and the WebSphere infrastructure when SSL is enabled between Plugin and WebSphere. The reason is that WebSphere will extract the server certificate during the initial handshake and place it in its trust store.

Configuring LDAP for SSL

The final step in this process is to enable SSL for LDAP. Using the Deployment Manager Console, open the page for configuring LDAP. Once there, change the LDAP server port to the server SSL port. Scroll down and check the box for **SSL enabled**. Save the changes. Perform a test connection. When successful, restart the Deployment manager and node agents for the changes to take effect.

JDBC: WebSphere-managed authentication

The next service pipeline (or back-end resource provider) that is going to be discussed is probably the most common resource for gathering and storing application data. WebSphere includes this resource under the generic term *data access resources*. The chief among them is the connectivity to application databases. Because each brand of database supported by WebSphere varies a great deal in terms of its configuration due to the database implementation by the vendor, this section will present brief general descriptions of a concept, followed by an example using one or two of the most popular databases used in a WebSphere v7 environment.

Protocol(s)

The protocol used to communicate with application databases that will be reviewed in this section is the **Java Database Connectivity (JDBC)**, which is an *API* and an Application Layer transfer protocol:

- The API aspect of it provides a layer of independence for accessing databases. This layer offers well-defined Java-oriented mechanisms for performing a variety of operations on relational databases.

- The Application layer aspect is implemented as modules implemented by vendor-specific drivers used to communicate with their database.

Let's look into this architecture more closely.

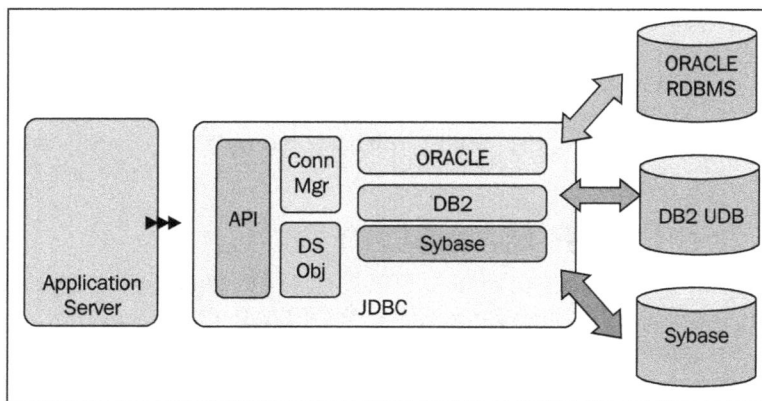

The JDBC API

The previous diagram depicts the *JDBC architecture* from the point of view of a WebSphere environment. The **JDBC** implementation in WebSphere is shown by the large rectangle, which is made up of several high-level components. As stated above, JDBC, on the one hand, is an API. The API component is represented in the diagram by the tall rectangle labeled **API**. The API provides the developer a suite of Java Objects and methods to interact with a database. The Java packages in which these Objects and methods are defined are the java.sql and javax.sql packages.

Connection/Driver Manager and Data Source/JDBC provider

Furthermore, these packages provide different approaches to establish a connection with a database. The two most commonly used in WebSphere J2EE applications are the **Connection/Driver Manager** method, illustrated by the small rectangle labeled **Conn Mgr**, and the **Data Source** Object technique, pictured by the small rectangle labeled **DS Obj**. The main difference between those two methodologies from the security point of view is that the former requires that the code include a database user and access password, whereas the latter does not require it in the code. From the WebSphere point of view, the authentication information is provided at the environment configuration, that is, when a Data Source is first defined.

The JDBC Application Layer

On the other hand, JDBC is a proprietary Application Layer transfer protocol implemented within the *Connection/Driver Manager* and the *Data Source/JDBC Provider* by each database vendor. In addition, WebSphere ND v7 supports several databases that can be used as an application database. Moreover, three of the most popular vendor databases are included in the diagram above and are represented by the long and short rectangles labeled **ORACLE**, **DB2**, and **Sybase**.

For an up-to-date list of databases and their versions that are supported by WebSphere please refer to IBM's page http://www-01.ibm.com/support/docview.wss?rs=180&uid=swg27012369, an entry port to the supported software for WebSphere ND v7. From that page, you would need to drill down, depending on your OS to find out the list of supported databases. For instance, for a system running Solaris on a SPARC architecture, the list of software (including databases) can be accessed at http://www-01.ibm.com/support/docview.wss?rs=180&uid=swg27012419.

Choices to secure the database channel

In terms of the approach or approaches to secure the JDBC channel, it is a sector dependent upon the proprietary vendor choices and many of which do not yet support encryption. In addition, currently in WebSphere ND v7 there is no mechanism to encrypt the link between WAS and the back-end database. If the back-end data is of a very sensitive nature, it is recommended to use virtual private network techniques to encrypt the channel. That, however, is a realm that normally would fall under the jurisdiction of a networks group within a corporation; therefore the advice given here is to work with the DBA and Network groups in your organization to implement a VPN channel between WAS and the database server.

In order to learn more about VPN, from some of the leaders in the field, refer to the white papers at http://www.vpnc.org/white-papers.html. In addition, if there is a desire to get some hands-on experience with this technology, an article that appeared on Network World Online can be useful. (How to set up a Virtual Private Network: http://www.networkworld.com/news/2010/060410-how-to-set-up-a.html). Its content, however, should not be the basis for a production-level environment implementation. Check with your network group.

Nevertheless, there are a few things that can be done to tighten the security of accessing back-end connections to databases. One of them is selecting the **Data Source** mechanism to communicate back and forth with a back-end application database. The main reason for this selection, in terms of the security of the database link, is to centralize the handling and management of authentication data at the administration level. In other words, developers would not need to concern about users and passwords to gain access to databases.

Examples of securing the JDBC connection

In order to use a **Data Source** there are two configuration stages that need to take place:

- On one hand, it is necessary to define a **JDBC Provider**, that is, it is required to indicate to WebSphere which is the Java class supplied by the vendor that implements the JDBC functionality to communicate with a specific database in addition to some vendor-specific parameters.

- On the other hand, the second configuration stage is the creation of the actual Data Source configuration. WebSphere indicates which are the required parameters for the particular provider. Among those parameters we may have the values needed to fully configure a data source such as:
  - ° Database server
  - ° Database port
  - ° Authorization information

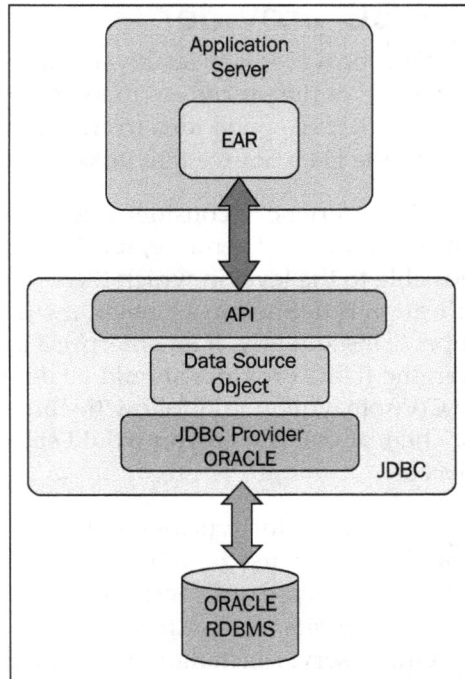

Let's look at this more closely. In the previous diagram, an enterprise application (represented by the rectangle labeled **EAR**) will connect to an Oracle database (illustrated in the diagram by the cylinder labeled **ORACLE RDBMS**) using the JDBC API (in turn, depicted in the diagram by the rectangle labeled **API**. The application will employ a subset of the API that invokes the use of a Data Source (`javax.sql.DataSource` Java class), which is shown in the diagram above by the rectangle labeled **Data Source Object**. The internals of the Java class will be implemented by the vendor's **database driver** (also known in the WebSphere world as the **JDBC Provider**). The database driver is pictured as a rectangle labeled **JDBC Provider – ORACLE**. It is the driver that actually creates the connection to the database (Oracle, in this example) and uses the vendor's proprietary protocol to enable the communication between the EAR and Oracle.

[✎ Database drivers are referred as JDBC providers in WebSphere.]

The next sub-sections will briefly indicate the procedure to be followed in WebSphere to define a JDBC provider and to create and configure a Data Source that uses the provider.

Defining a new JDBC provider

The procedure to define a JDBC provider is probably already familiar to you. This section will just highlight aspects of the procedure to increase the level of security of your environment. In addition, it is a good idea to create a one-to-one mapping between a JDBC Provider and the Data Source that talks to the database.

With that in mind, the first characteristic to consider is the scope of the definition and area of influence of the data source. Therefore, it is best to define the JDBC components as close as possible to the level in which the enterprise application executes. Thus, if the application is defined in a cluster, the JDBC provider should be defined at that cluster scope. Consequently, if an enterprise application is hosted in a single Application Server, the JDBC Provider should be defined at that scope also. Using the Administrative Console, you would follow the breadcrumb **Resources | JDBC | JDBC Providers**. Then, at that screen you would select the desired scope **Cluster** or **Application Server**.

The next step in the process is to select the type of database. This will be dictated by what brand of the actual database is used. For instance, select Oracle. It follows now to select the *provider type*; in the case of Oracle select the **Oracle JDBC Driver**. After that, select the desired *implementation type* for the driver. The Oracle client installation and that of the Oracle server installation will dictate the implementation type. In our example the **Connection pool data source** will be selected. The rest of the values will be driven by how the environment is set up. Complete the creation of the data source. In the data source screen it will be noticed that the implementation class name used is `oracle.jdbc.pool.OracleConnectionPoolDataSource`. For a DB2 connection pool based JDBC provided, this class would be `com.ibm.db2.jcc.DB2ConnectionPoolDataSource`.

Defining a new Data Source

The process of defining a Data Source should be familiar to you as one was already created in Chapter 3. (Refer to the section *Protecting application servers*, subsection *Create application JDBC Provider and DataSource*). Therefore, only a very brief summary will be given in this section.

> Details of creating a Data Source can be found in the WASND7 information center article *Configuring a data source using the administrative console*. (http://publib.boulder.ibm.com/ infocenter/wasinfo/v7r0/topic/com.ibm.websphere. nd.doc/info/ae/ae/tdat_ccrtpds.html)

The easiest way is to go to the recently created Data Source and in that screen select the **Data sources** link from under the **Additional Properties** section. Create the Data Source that matches your environment. The characteristics of the data source being created are the following. The JNDI name given to invoke it from the Context class: this value would probably be available from the application development team. The following screenshot shows an example of a DB2 data source:

General Properties

* Scope

    cells:wasmasterCell01

* Provider

    Chap7 DB2 Universal JDBC Driver Provider

* Name

    Chap7 DB2 UDB Datasource

    JNDI name

    jdbc/chap7/db2DS1

    ☑ Use this data source in container managed persistence (CMP)

    Description

    DB2 Universal Driver Datasource

The other aspect to highlight is to select a container managed authentication alias. If the alias has not been created, it can be defined by clicking the **JASS- J2C** authentication data link under the **Related Items** area on the right-hand side of the page. Creating a JASS-JC2 authentication alias requires of three values:

- **Alias**: The name to be used by the Data Source
- **User ID**: Database user

- **Password**: Database user's password

The following screenshot depicts an example of the security aspects of a data source configuration:

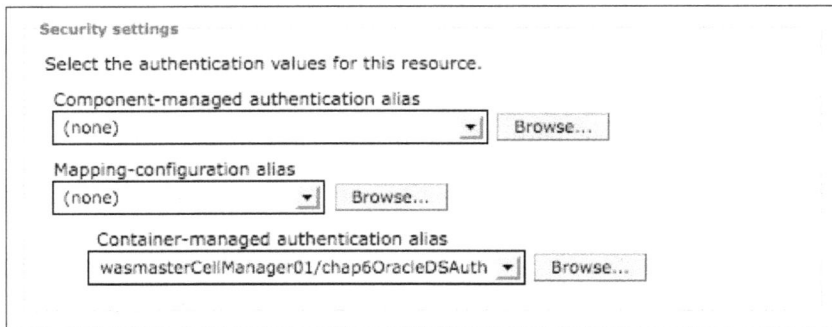

Security settings

Select the authentication values for this resource.

Component-managed authentication alias

| (none) | ▼ | | Browse... |

Mapping-configuration alias

| (none) | ▼ | | Browse... |

Container-managed authentication alias

| wasmasterCellManager01/chap6OracleDSAuth | ▼ | | Browse... |

If needed, provide the alias name, user ID, and database password. Finally, back in the data source screen, be sure to select the "Use this data source in container managed persistence". After restarting the node where the data source has been created, you can test the connectivity to it using the Administrative Console.

Summary

This chapter covered two powerful concepts that will enable you to add security to your WebSphere environment. They are authentication as applied to resources and data encryption:

- Whenever possible, move the authentication to resources aspect out of the application. Create JASS-J2C aliases at the resource level to provide the credentials needed to access the back-end resource. This technique can be easily applied to JDBC Data Sources and to JMS Queues.

- If the nature of the data exchanged with a back-end resource is sensitive, apply encryption to the channel. The preferred form is to use SSL communication. If that is not possible, research other alternatives such as VPNs.

I feel full of energy; I am not sure about you. This chapter seemed short in comparison with the previous one. Perhaps I miss having a mini project. So go get a cup of tea and let's move onto the next chapter, *WebSphere default installation hardening*. What do you say?

8
Secure Enterprise Infrastructure Architectures

This chapter describes areas that will enable an enterprise application hosted in a **WebSphere Application Server ND v7 (WAS ND7)** environment to interact with possibly other applications, resources, and services available in a corporation infrastructure. An example of such external application would be an application running under Domino. The two main areas are indicated as follows:

- Describe the mechanisms used to enable WAS infrastructure components intercommunication. Moreover:
  - ° Explain an additional way in which the same mechanisms can be used to enable WAS infrastructure components communication with external (IBM products) servers, services, and resources.

- Discuss the techniques that will enable users access to SSO across multiple applications in a corporation.

Furthermore, this chapter also covers the following topics that help to round up securing the enterprise infrastructure architecture:

- At the HTTP server level: external security policy manager
- At the Application Server level: trust association interceptor

The chapter will now introduce this book's definition of *enterprise infrastructure* centered on services provided by a WebSphere Application Server ND v7 environment.

The enterprise infrastructure

In this chapter, we define **enterprise infrastructure architecture** or simply *enterprise infrastructure* as that collection of technologies used in corporate IT environments that perform a very specific job and take a well-defined role among all of the other infrastructure members with the overall objective to supplement each other's part in carrying out a corporation's mission. (Well, that was quite a mouthful). As is expected, a WAS ND7 environment (be it a full WAS ND7 cell or just an enterprise application) is only a small piece of the whole enterprise infrastructure puzzle. Nevertheless, in order for that WAS ND 7 environment to accomplish its purpose, very likely it will depend on various pieces of information that may be logically scattered across multiple technologies supported by the enterprise infrastructure.

An Enterprise Application in relation to an Application Server

Consider the drawing in the following diagram. It is centered around the **Enterprise Application (EA)**. We can distinguish two areas of an Application Server that will interact with the EA: that related to the EA and its data and that of the EA and the environment *administrative* and *support* services.

On the one hand, an EA would probably require external data to carry out its function. For example, patient ID to pull medical history, or employee number in order to process pay roll information, and so on. The *container* capabilities will help the EA obtain any given data needed; be it from a back-end database or from a back-end process

In the diagram, an EA, represented by the solid gold rectangle labeled *Enterprise Application*, sits on the Web Container (blue rectangle) and the EJB Container (light green rectangle). In addition, several of the major components that may support that particular EA are also shown. For instance, inside the Web Container the EA could require the services of a Portlet Container (tiny red rectangle); or perhaps if the application were involved in some sort of streaming, it could use the services of the SIP Container (tiny orange rectangle). Therefore, the EA should concentrate on its function and data and let the containers supply the means to obtain and save data as well as the mechanisms (such as Java libraries) needed to process the data.

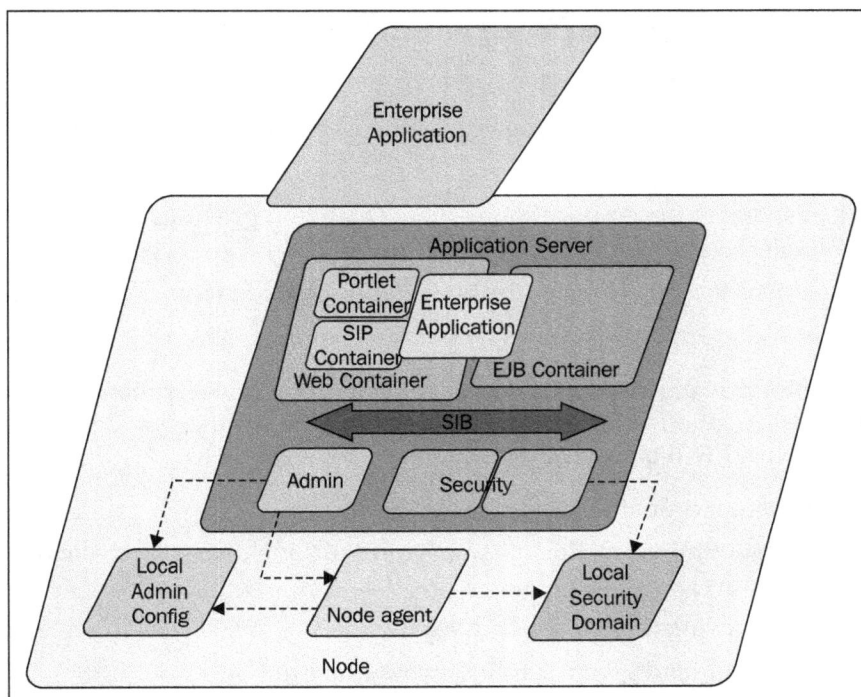

On the other hand, the second form in which an EA will interact with the Application Server is for administrative and support service purposes. The Application Server architecture provides components to supply specific support services such as user registry in which approved user lists reside. This type of information will be *defined* by the security domain in place; portrayed in the preceding diagram by the rectangle(gray rectangle). In addition, such information would be enforced by the Application Server security components (maroon rectangles).

Furthermore, any configuration changes to the overall WebSphere environment would be handled by the administration interface (orange rectangle), which would keep a copy of the overall environment configuration locally (small green rectangle). The node agent (small dark teal rectangle) is the runtime component that helps Application server members interact with other runtime entities of the WebSphere environment. For instance, if you were using the file-based built-in federated repository as the user registry of your environment and would make a modification such as adding a new member while monitoring the SystemOut.log file of the node agent, you would see that it would be reported the addition of a user. So the WebSphere security infrastructure would alert members to such changes. Let's do a simple observation exercise.

WAS infrastructure and EA's application server interactions

For this simple exercise the following requirements are assumed to be in place and available:

- At least one of the Application Servers created in previous chapters is available
- The global security is using the built-in file-based federated user registry
- Users and groups still exist as defined in prior chapters

Once you insure that the assumption-requirements are in place, proceed to complete the steps given as follows. In this exercise, the Application Server SecureAppServer01 will be used:

1. Open three terminal sessions to your host.
2. In the first terminal session, change your working directory to the node agent logs directory.
3. Start monitoring the **SystemOut.log** file.

   The **tail** command given as follows could be used:

   ```
   tail -f SystemOut.log
   ```

4. In the second terminal session, change your working directory to the SecureAppServer01 logs directory.
5. Start monitoring the SystemOut.log file of the SecureAppServer01 server.

   As in step 3, the **tail** command can be used in the same way.

   If needed, that is if the deployment manager or the node agent processes are not running, perform steps 6-X, as necessary.

6. Change your working directory to the bin directory of the appropriate profile, Deployment Manager, to start the dmgr process or to the Application Server profile to start the nodeagent process.
7. Use the adequate start script to start the dmgr or nodeagent process.

   For the dmgr, use the command:

   ```
   startManager.sh [ -nowait ]
   ```

   Using the -nowait flag will free up your terminal faster in case you also need to start the nodeagent process.

   For the nodeagent, use the command:

   ```
   startNode.sh [ -nowait ]
   ```

8. Return focus to terminals one and two.

9. Using a browser, connect to the Deployment Manager Console.

10. Follow the breadcrumb shown to navigate to the *Manage Users* screen:

    Users and groups | Manage Users

11. Optionally, perform a search for users to see currently defined users.

12. Enter data to create a new user.

13. Click the **Create...** button. For *User ID* enter the value **hassan**. Type `Hassan` in the **First name:** field. Type `Employee` in the **Last name** field. Use the string hassan for password. Then click the **Create** button.

14. If desired, enter a couple of blank lines in terminals one and two.

    In order to isolate the log data from the upcoming messages (as they are just a long line per screen), you can press *Enter* return a couple of times while the tail command is running. If desired, do this on both terminals.

15. Back in the browser, create the User ID `hassan`.

    Return focus to the browser and click the Create button. Immediately observe the output on terminals one and two. You should see almost identical messages on both log files monitors.

```
[7/1/10 8:07:54:164 EDT] 00000017 UserManagerMB I com.ibm.ws.wim.management.User
ManagerMBean processEvent CWWIM6008I  Received event 'websphere.usermanager.file
registry.change' from the deployment manager.
[7/1/10 8:08:30:754 EDT] 0000003b NodeSyncTask A  ADMS0003I: The configuration
 synchronization completed successfully.
```

The preceding screenshot is the output captured from the nodeagent's `SystemOut.log` file. The first line displays a notification that a user registry change event has taken place. This notification has been sent by the dmgr process to be broadcast by the administrative/security elements as needed. Furthermore, the nodeagent forwards this event notification to Application Servers members of the node.

The next screenshot is practically identical to the first screenshot. This one shows log messages from the SecureAppServer01 and it displays the portion in which the event related to the creation of a new user in the federated registry is received.

```
[7/1/10 8:05:20:720 EDT] 0000002c DiscoveryMBea I  ADMD0023I: The system discov
ered process (name: nodeagent, type: NodeAgent, pid: 3038)
[7/1/10 8:07:54:069 EDT] 00000024 UserManagerMB I com.ibm.ws.wim.management.User
ManagerMBean processEvent CWWIM6008I  Received event 'websphere.usermanager.file
registry.change' from the deployment manager.
```

> By default, the location of the process log files can be found
> under the path `<WAS_Profile_Root_Directory>/`
> `logs/<Process>`. Here, `<Process>` could represent an
> application server name or the process nodeagent.

Securing the enterprise infrastructure using LTPA

The first area mentioned in the introduction of the chapter is the use of an IBM proprietary security protocol named **LTPA**, which stands for **Lightweight Third-Party Authentication**. You may have already discovered that when, in *Chapter 2*, the administrative (that is, global) security was enabled, the LTPA authentication mechanism was selected as the default authentication using default trust stores and other encryption components.

In order to visualize this, log in to the Administrative Console and follow the breadcrumb **Security | Global Security** and review the authentication section, which can be found on the right-hand side of the page. It should look similar to the screenshot shown as follows:

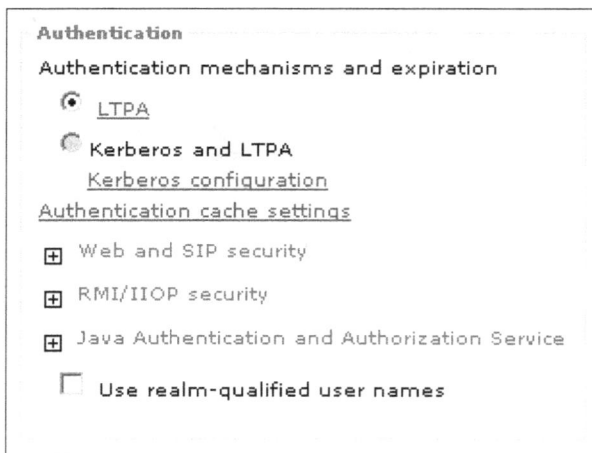

```
Authentication

Authentication mechanisms and expiration

    ⦿  LTPA

    ○  Kerberos and LTPA
       Kerberos configuration
Authentication cache settings

    ⊞  Web and SIP security

    ⊞  RMI/IIOP security

    ⊞  Java Authentication and Authorization Service

    ☐  Use realm-qualified user names
```

Why use the LTPA mechanism

So the question that might arise is, why do we have to bother with the LTPA authentication mechanism? However, perhaps a better question might be, when do we have to pay attention as to how LTPA is configured in a WebSphere Application Server ND v7 environment? The LTPA mechanism empowers a WAS ND v7 installation to send security-related, mainly authentication, information in an encrypted and safe way between itself and:

- Other WebSphere Application Server cell members executing on a remote OS host to the Deployment Manager OS host.
- Other WebSphere Application Server environments (for example, different cells).
- Other IBM products that support the LTPA-based security communication, such as products under the Lotus brand (for example, Domino, WebSphere Portal, Lotus WCM, and so on); products under the WebSphere brand (for example, MQ, EBS, Process Server, and so on) to name some.

In other words, a WAS ND v7 environment can be configured with a particular LTPA set of encryption keys. These signer keys can then be shared with other products that support the LTPA authentication mechanism and for which it is desired to allow them to be trusted. Let's review this concept in more detail.

How the LTPA authentication mechanism works

Once that such products have also been configured with the same set of keys, a trusted communication of security data (that is, authentication) can take place between them and the WAS ND v7 installation. One of the components, say a Lotus Domino application, would encrypt and sign the authentication information required by the target WSA ND v7. Upon receiving the encrypted information, WAS would use its LTPA key to decrypt and verify the identity of the Domino application. After completing the verification WAS would then allow the intercommunication with the Domino application in a trusted fashion.

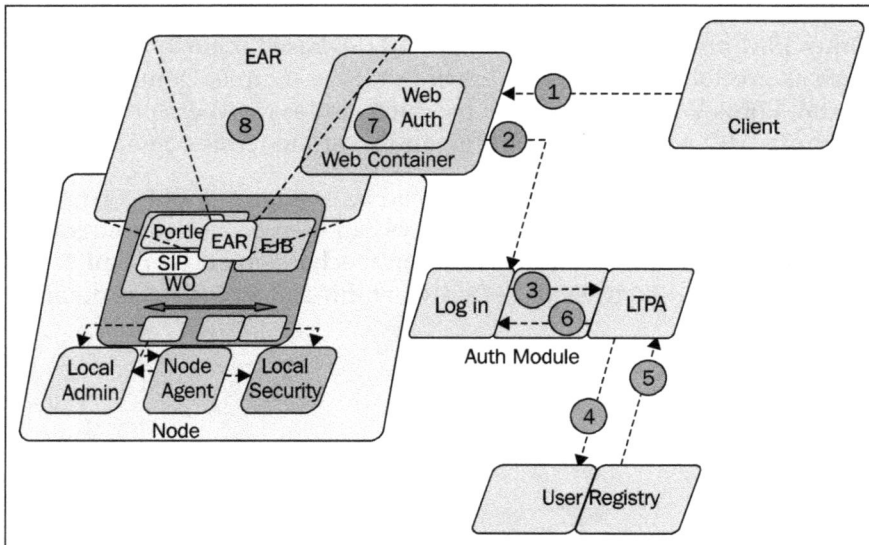

An alternative way of seeing how this mechanism works is depicted in the diagram above. Using a variant of the EAR—Application Server diagram presented at the beginning of this chapter, this new diagram blows up the EJB container and the authentication module component of the security functionality. In this scenario, a user has been authenticated and he/she uses those credentials to request a specific resource. Moreover, the data flow sequence is as follows:

1. An authenticated request is received in one of the inbound Container Transports. In the diagram, we can see a Web Container Transport Chain.

2. The request goes through the authentication modules, that is, Web authenticator and the login module.

3. The request and credentials are validated at the LTPA section of the diagram. Using the default trust association interceptor for LTPA, the authorization components verify if the credentials presented are entitled to the requested resource and if so, the credentials are deemed certified.

4. The LTPA/TAI component requests the required information about the user from the registry.

5. If found, a trusted token is created and stamped with the LTPA signer key. The new token is encrypted and only entities that share the same signer keys would be able to assert the authenticity of the credentials.

6. The new credentials are then sent to the Web Container.

7. With the new certified credentials, the request is given a green light to move forward.

8. The EA now is ready to process the request. The result will be added to the new token credentials to be passed to possibly other J2EE modules or back to the requestor.

The main use for LTPA in a WebSphere environment

Once we have reviewed how LTPA works in general terms, it's time to bring up that one of the main jobs of the LTPA infrastructure is to make attainable a highly desired functionality between web applications: allow SSO.

As covered in *Chapter 2, Securing the Administrative Interface*, **SSO** stands for **Single Sign-On**. It is a mechanism that establishes trust across two or more applications located on different OS hosts such that when a user, for example, US2, authenticates against one enterprise application, for example, EAi, US2 is guaranteed to access, *without having to re-authenticate*, a different enterprise application, for example, EAii, for which US2 has authorization to access — given that EAi and EAii share the same LTPA keys and their realm is the same. (What? No smart-alec remark? How disappointing!)

Securely enhancing the user experience with SSO

In a simplified way, the diagram that follows depicts the way in which the authentication and authorization take place. For this scenario, it is assumed that the browser utilized is a brand new browser process; that is, no cookies from a previous session are active/stored.

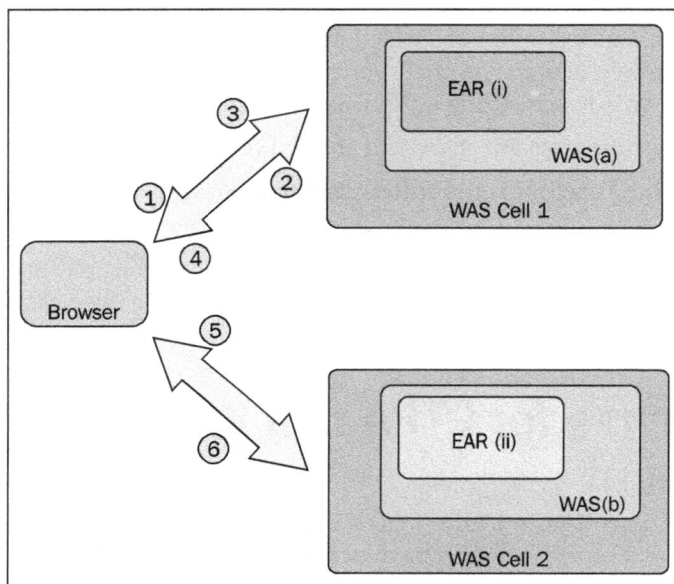

The following steps briefly describe requesting secured resources from two applications that share the same LTPA signers:

1. A user through a browser BR would request a page from EAi. The request won't include any session-related cookies.

2. The environment in which EAi is hosted would receive the request and it would be determined that BR must authenticate and, upon successfully doing so, BR must include the corresponding credentials to access the resource hosted by EAi.

3. EAi answers BR's requests by asking for a validation token. BR might be redirected to a generic authentication form and it is assumed that successfully would enter the required information and would receive an LTPA-encrypted token that includes the information about the user needed to validate her identity.

4. BR, at this point would send the request sent in one but the headers of the HTTP request would include a cookie that holds the LTPA-encrypted token received from the log in page. EAi would then accept the request after analyzing and validating the LTPA token.

   It could be possible that at one point EAi would include a link on one of its pages that would redirect a user to a *sister* application EAii. Or, on the other hand, after finishing her interactions with EAi, BR's user may decide to access EAii. In any case, the following scenario would take place:

5. BR would request a page from application EAii. The request would include the same credentials used with EAi because both enterprise applications belong to the same realm (or cookie domain).

6. EAii would receive the request from BR. Given that EAii and EAi share the same LTPA key set, EAii could decode the types of information shown in the following list. EAii would not have to make further demands from BR. All the information would be included in the token. So at this point EAii would process the BR request:

   ° The identity of the EAi application, certifying the validity of the token

   ° User-related so the identity of BR would be guaranteed

   ° User-related so the authorization of BR could be determined

> Due to the sensitivity of the information contained in an LTPA-encrypted token, tokens have an expiration time. After a token has expired, users would be requested to re-authenticate.

Required conditions to implement SSO

Most corporations use more than one type of applications. In addition, there may also be multiple independent WAS ND7 environments that may need to share a common login structure. The obvious solution is the implementation of SSO among such applications.

There are a couple of conditions that must be met so an environment is SSO-able. They are listed as follows. In such list, the term **SSO cluster** will be used to denote the group of infrastructure components in which applications are hosted. It is not an official term used in the WebSphere world.

• The OS servers that host the EAs that are to be in the same SSO cluster or group must belong to the same DNS domain.

- The application environments (for example, WAS ND7, a Lotus Domino server, and so on) must use the same user registry. Therefore, it is very important to select the type and brand of user registry that is supported by all of the application environments involved in the SSO cluster.

- In addition, verify if the products that will be involved in the SSO cluster have the capability to use multiple user registries of the type LDAP. If that is not the case, your SSO cluster will be restricted to using only one LDAP.

Implementing SSO in WebSphere

As you already have the experience of configuring SSO from *Chapter 2 (Setting the domain name)* this section will just briefly describe the possible parameters that can be used in configuring SSO. The following screenshot displays the SSO configuration page. As you may recall, in order to get to this page the following breadcrumb needs to be followed:

Global Security | Single sign-on (sso) (under sections **Authentication | Web and SIP security**)

Cell=wasmasterCell01, Profile=Dmgr01

Global security

Global security > **Single sign-on (SSO)**

Specifies the configuration values for single sign-on.

General Properties

☑ Enabled

☐ Requires SSL

Domain name
yourcompany.com

☐ Interoperability Mode

☑ Web inbound security attribute propagation

Apply   OK   Reset   Cancel

The preceding screenshot is the actual configuration that has been used for the exercises and mini projects from previous chapters. Several of the parameters are self-explanatory. Let's take a look.

[⟨note icon⟩ Remember: in order to enable SSO, global security must also be enabled.]

The **Enabled** check box is used to turn on SSO. If you wish to disable SSO either permanent or for troubleshooting purposes, this configuration box can be used for that purpose.

The next check box, **Requires SSL**, indicates that SSO is in effect only for transactions using SSL. If this is the case for you, ensure that either at the IHS server or even before that at the load balancer level any request that is made using plain HTTP is redirected to HTTPS; otherwise, SSO will not be active in transactions made in clear text (for example, non-SSL).

The field that follows, **Domain name**, specifies a portion of a DNS domain entry to which all servers involved in the SSO cluster must belong. It is possible to enter more than one domain name in that filed to allow servers from multiple trusted domains be part of the SSO cluster; names in the field must be separated by semicolons (for example: *yourcompany.com; yourothercompany.com*). Moreover, if in the Domain name field the special value **UseDomainFromURL** is included, the other names in that field are matched not against the DNS domain of the host where the application executes, but rather the DNS domain is taken from the URL included in the request.

The next check box, **Interoperability Mode**, is used to signal to the SSO mechanism in WAS ND7 to include an **old format** of the cookie sent to the browser; in this way SSO would also work with WAS environments prior to version 6.

Finally, the check box **Web inbound security attribute propagation**, an optional parameter, indicates that it is desired that during the login operation at a front-end server, information be added which will then be forwarded to other front-end servers. With such information, it would be possible for a server other than the one where the SSO token was generated to identify the originating server, in case that it is needed or desired to retrieve original serialized authentication information.

Fine-tuning authorization at the HTTP server level

As it was reviewed in *Chapter 3, Configuring User Authentication and Access* it is possible to define users and groups employing the interface provided by the selected user registry. Keep in mind that the content of groups may be users (or more technically correct User IDs) and groups (group IDs) as well.

Infrastructure component: User Registry (aka, LDAP server)

The first external component to the WebSphere environment involved in configuring the IHS server is the **LDAP** server. (In more general terms, the user registry). This server would probably already exist in your organization as part of the IT infrastructure. It is used to provide information about users and groups they belong.

This type of approach requires that security policy rules be enforced at the application deployment level or during the packaging of the EAR. Recall how in *Chapters 5, Securing Web Applications* and *6, Securing Enterprise Java Beans Applications* there was a need to map groups to access roles. Consequently, a scalable solution to manage security policies would be needed. For an organization (such as department within a larger corporation) with a small deployment of J2EE applications the methodology used in *Chapters 5* and *6* may be just fine. However, for large corporations with a common infrastructure designed to serve different types of IT solutions there would be a significant number of deployed J2EE applications, the method used in those chapters could be prone to human error or may be completely impractical.

Infrastructure component: Centralized Access Manager

The second external component, which is part of the enterprise IT infrastructure, used to fine-tune the IHS server, is a centralized **Access Manager** (or simply an AM), which *must be compatible* with the user registry selected (LDAP being the most popular).

Furthermore, most large corporations would already be using a type of centralized AM solution serving different types of IT user applications (for example, Lotus Notes applications) and service applications (for example, ERP systems); and not only WebSphere EAR applications or Web applications. Moreover, it would be likely that in such type of corporation there would include some sort of IT security team managing the security policies and how LDAP is to be organized.

Why use an external access management solution

Therefore, embracing a practice in which using an external security policy/access manager that is part of the enterprise infrastructure is a more general solution. Contrary to what Orson Wells stated:

> *"We're born alone, we live alone, we die alone. Only through our love and friendship can we create the illusion for the moment that we're not alone"*

In the WebSphere world there are no illusions, *we're not alone*. As such, it is very likely that an enterprise may have adopted an access manager as its solution for all types of IT applications. Moreover, there may be an IT group dedicated to manage this type of infrastructure. It follows that it is beneficial and probably necessary for the WebSphere environment to tap into that infrastructure-level solution

In view of what has been presented, the benefits of using a, possibly existing, centralized AM solution are as follows:

- Policies involved in authorization are kept centralized, making it easier to perform audits.

- In the same way, the centralization of this information makes it easier to perform troubleshooting of applications.

- One of the most evident reasons for using an external AM is that the SSO solution can include members that don't support the LTPA technology (that is, non-IBM products. So an external AM standardized SSO at the IT corporate level, if so desired.

How it works

In general, the technique most often used to integrate Web servers with an external centralized AM infrastructure, is to use a **Web Agent**. The agent will execute inside of the IHS process as a module. Depending on the AM implementation, the Web Agent module may spawn an external process that is tightly coupled to the **httpd** process. The way in which a centralized AM solution works in the IHS sphere is, at a high-level, shown in the following figure:

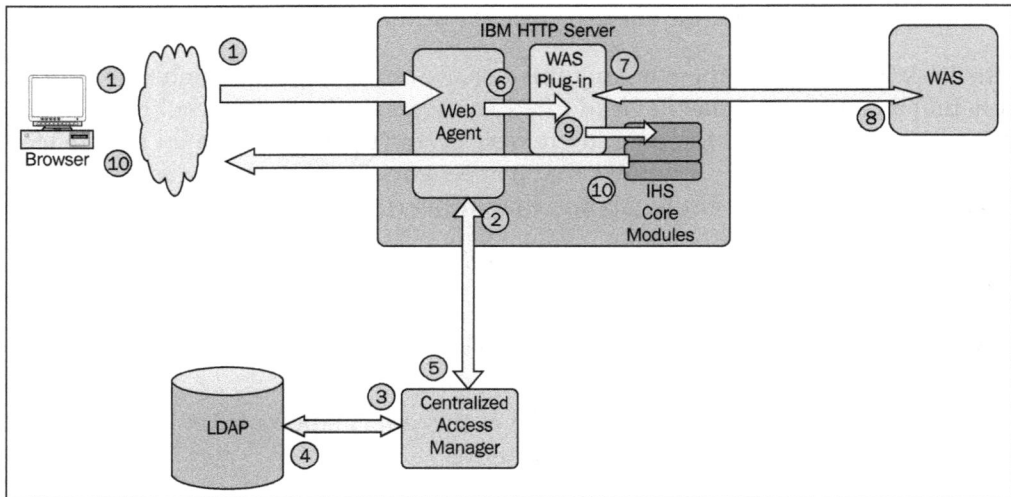

In the diagram, the assumption is that the user has already authenticated with the application and the diagram is showing the normal data flow for a request made to the enterprise application:

1. A user, employing a browser that is represented in the diagram by the dark teal desktop computer, requests a URL from an enterprise application. The request would possible travel through routers, firewalls, and load balancers (represented by the gray cloud shape in the diagram) before reaching the IHS web server.

2. When the request reaches the IHS TCP port, the web agent module intercepts the request. It analyzes if the URI is protected by a security policy rule, if so it requests information about the user making the request from the centralized AM.

3. The centralized AM requests information about the principal making the request.

4. The directory server forwards group information about the principal to the centralized AM.

5. The centralized AM obtains group information about the requester and determines, using the defined set of security policy rules, if she has authorization for the resource (that is, URI) requested. Therefore, the centralized AM forwards to the Web Agent whether access is granted or not.

6. If access is granted for the request, the Web Agent forwards it to the next module within IHS, that is the WebSphere Plug-in.

7. The WAS Plug-in analyzes the URI to find out to which port of the WebSphere Application Server and using what protocol the request should be forwarded, if any. Once the route has been identified, the WebSphere Plug-in forwards the request to the appropriate enterprise application (that is, host and port).

8. The selected WebSphere Application Server hosting the enterprise application would then process the requested resource and will return the result back to the WebSphere Plug-in.

9. The WAS Plug-in forwards the response to the IHS server, indicating that it has been processed.

10. Finally, the IHS core module(s) receives the response from the Plug-in and sends it to the requestor.

Probably after reviewing the dataflow just described an obvious question would rise. How does an external AM may affect the performance of my application? The way this dilemma is solved varies by product. However, it would suffice to mention that the use of caching techniques at the Web Agent level in addition to other technical tricks, I mean solutions, would answer any concern regarding possible poor performance.

What tool to use

The obvious question now is what tool to use for this purpose. IBM offers the product Tivoli Access Manager WebSeal Plug-in for Web Servers. However, there is another product that has proven to be more popular and this chapter will describe its infrastructure in relation to a WebSphere Application Server ND v7 environment. For those readers that use WebSeal, you can refer to the IBM documentation provided with the product and follow along the description and procedures that follow.

The third-party product is the SiteMinder WebAgent formerly known as Netegrity SiteMinder WebAgent (now rebranded as CA eTrust SiteMinder) in conjunction with the SiteMinder Policy Server.

> Due to this rebranding, it is sometimes difficult to find SiteMinder documentation using online search engines. In order to find documentation about using SiteMinder that is still valid and that was created prior to the CA acquisition, a query such as the following could be useful (tested in Google): **(Netegrity | CA) ("Web Agent" | WebAgent) +SiteMinder eTrust**

If we take the *generic* diagram from the previous section, omitting the data flow, and then we instantiate the Centralized Access Manager with the SiteMinder infrastructure, we obtain the *branded* diagram shown as follows. The main additions and modifications are as follows:

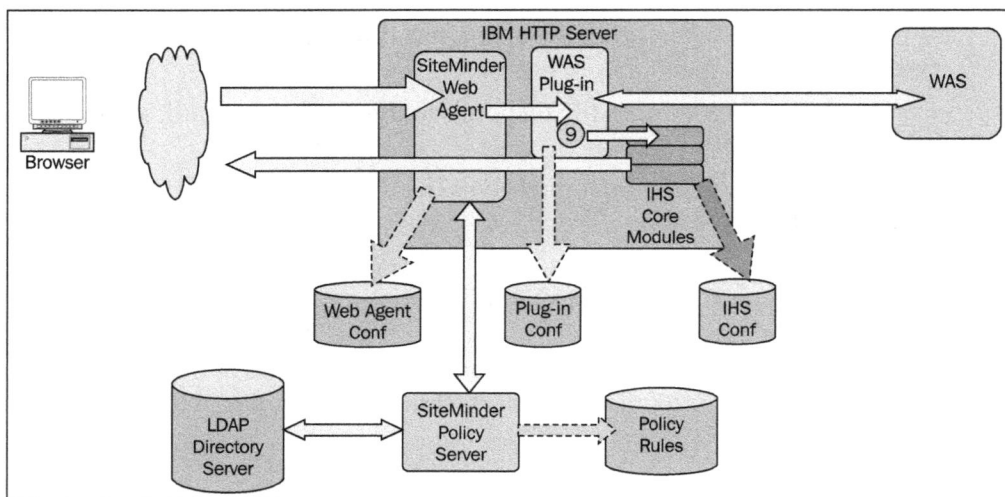

The branded **SiteMinder Web Agent** has replaced the generic *Web Agent* component. In addition, the branded diagram includes a local configuration file that directs the behavior of the SiteMinder Web Agent. Furthermore, the SiteMinder Policy Server has replaced the Centralized AM. In order to show how each component can be tailored to the requirements of the application and its security, the branded diagram shows the various configuration files that tune in the behavior of the WebSphere Plug-in as well as that of the IBM HTTP Server.

It is now possible to show what the dataflow for a request is and how it is handled by the infrastructure. The following diagram presents a simplified dataflow in a branded environment:

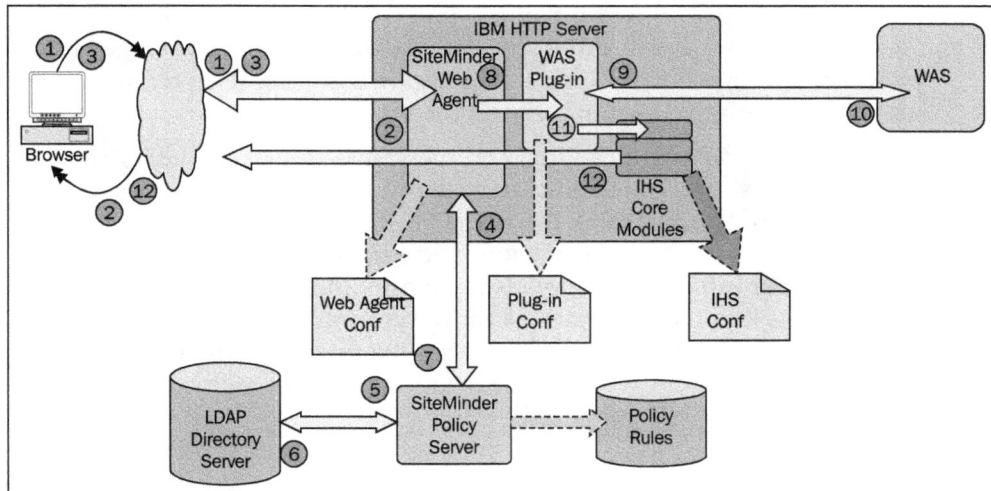

1. As in the case of the generic transaction data flow described in the previous section, a user (U1), employing a browser that is represented in the diagram by the dark teal desktop computer, requests a URL (resource) from an enterprise application (EA1). The request would possible travel through routers, firewalls, and load balancers (represented by the gray cloud shape in the diagram) before reaching the IHS web server.

2. In our branded case, when the request reaches the IHS TCP port, the **SiteMinder WebAgent (SMW)** module intercepts the request. It analyzes if the URI is protected by a security policy rule, and if so it challenges U1 for credentials.

3. U1 receives the challenge for credentials. This challenge could be made in the form of a basic authentication dialog box or a login form page or even a redirection to an external authentication application (XA2) that is external to the intended target application EA1 where the user can enter his credentials and send them to the application EA1.

4. Once the credentials are received, SMW intercepts the transaction flow and it determines that the credentials need to be validated. Therefore, SM1 sends the credentials to the SiteMinder Policy Server (SPS) to validate the data sent by U1.

5. At this point, SPS receives the inquiry to verify U1 credentials. In order to do so, SPS requests a user search from the **LDAP Directory Server (LDS)**.

6. LDS receives the request to verify that U1 exists in the user directory. LDS performs a search and sends the results back to SPS. In this example, it will be assumed that U1 exists to demonstrate the normal flow for a request.

7. Once that LDS has confirmed that U1 exists in the user directory, SPS creates a session token to be sent along with a response to U1. At this stage, it sends SMW a confirmation that U1's credentials are correct and therefore validated. The confirmation includes the session token.

8. With the credentials confirmation and the session token available, SMW is ready to convert the request into an authorized request. This is accomplished by adding a cookie, SMSESSION, to the headers of the HTTP request. The SMSESSION cookie contains in encrypted format, all the information that the SiteMinder infrastructure needs to identify the user plus information that indicates that U1 is authorized for the current session. Once the HTTP headers have been modified, SMW passes the request to the WebSphere **Plug-in** (**PLG**) module, which is the next module to continue processing the request within the IHS engine.

Troubleshooting tip: Using the SMSESSION cookie

When troubleshooting an application that is front-ended by an HTTP server integrated to the SiteMinder infrastructure using a Web Agent, using the presence or absence of the SMSESSION cookie in the headers of the HTTP request and response will help pin down where the issue may be. For instance in a scenario where an application is being developed or tested, consider that a user requests a URL that is protected by rules in the Policy Server and the application (in this particular case referring to the whole infrastructure that supports the enterprise application) returns the URL requested w/o requesting for credentials. An administrator could look at the headers for the request, by either indicating the IHS server to include header information in its log files or by using a tool at the browser level that shows that information. If the request headers do not include the SMSESSION cookie, it could be an indication that there may be a missing policy rule to protect the URI. Therefore, the Web Agent would not intercept the request and would pass it to the next IHS module. If there is an SMSESSION cookie, it is an indication that the browser has been used in a prior access to the application or to an application sharing the same SSO.

---

9. From this point, the data flow is similar to the case described in the previous section. PLG then analyzes the URL to find out whether or not it is handled by the WebSphere application. If so, PLG would select a route to which port of the WebSphere Application Server and using what protocol the request should be forwarded, if any. Once the route has been identified, PLG forwards the request to the appropriate enterprise application component (WebSphere Application Server and Container) according to the information provided through the `plugin-cfg.xml` file.

10. Once the request is received, the selected WebSphere Application Server hosting the enterprise application would then process the requested resource and would return the result (response) back to PLG. This response would include the SMSESSION cookie that the browser employed by U1 would have to include in any subsequent request.

11. Back at the PLG module in the IHS server, PLG receives the response from the Application server. It then identifies what IHS module is next in the process chain, one that handles responses, and it forwards the response to the identified module.

12. At that point, the IHS module receives the response from PLG. It may or not perform a last analysis and forwards the response back to the browser. After traversing back through firewalls and routers, the response get to the browser, who renders the response code, including headers and content, onto U1 display.

Configuring the HTTP server to use an external access management solution

There are different schools as to what IT team is responsible for the client software (for example, Oracle drivers, SiteMinder Web Agent, and so on) needed by a WAS ND7 installation to interact with other components of the IT corporate infrastructure. In some, the team responsible for the technology server component (for example, DB2 server) would be also responsible for the DB2 client components on the *resource requestor software* (in our case, WAS ND7). In others schools, the client or resource requestor software team would also be responsible for any drivers or clients under the guidance of the resource server team.

In any event, when the SiteMinder Web Agent is installed on the servers where IHS instances are installed, among many things, it customizes the IHS configuration file adding information about the library that implements the Web Agent Apache module, represented by the light blue tall rectangle located inside the IBM HTTP server (maroon rectangle) in the previous diagram. Furthermore, the Web Agent installer also adds a directive to indicate the location of the SiteMinder Web Agent configuration file.

```
# SiteMinder WebAgent
LoadModule sm_module "/opt/netegrity/siteminder/webagent/bin/libmod_sm22.so"
SmInitFile "/opt/netegrity/siteminder/webagent/config/WebAgent.conf"

"httpd_SMWAsample.conf" 936L, 31525C written
wasmaster:/opt/IBM/HTTPServer/conf #
```

The preceding screenshot shows a sample of the Web Agent configuration included in the IHS `httpd.conf` file. One of the directives is the **LoadModule**, an IHS-defined directive. It provides IHS the location of the Web Agent module. The second directive, **SmInitFile**, is defined in the Web Agent module and it indicates to it the location of its configuration file.

> **Troubleshooting tips: Identifying SiteMinder-related errors**
>
> There are a few complications that may take place while integrating IHS to the SiteMinder infrastructure. If at startup you see an error message stating that there is a syntax error related to the keyword **SmInitFile**, it means that the Web Agent module failed to load. If IHS complains about not finding components of the Web Agent module, it is possible that the LD_LIBRARY_PATH does not include the location of the SiteMinder Web Agent library directory. Add this definition in the **envvars** file in the IHS bin directory.

Fine-tuning authorization at the WAS level

The final major topic of this chapter is the trust association interceptor (TAI). In a very simplified way, the TAI component of the WAS ND7 security infrastructure is the equivalent to the Web Agent component for the IHS Server. Both establish a link from the application infrastructure to the security policy-based tier.

When to use TAI

In most cases, in-house custom applications will not rely on TAI on the WAS ND7 side unless there is a business requirement. However, there may be third-party solutions and off-the-shelf products that have been designed with their security centered on TAI. For instance, a third-party solution could be the application that authenticates users implemented as an EA hosted on the WAS environment itself. The SiteMinder J2EE modules rely on TAI to communicate with the SiteMinder Policy Server to establish the identity of authenticate users as well as the authorization side of their interactions. On the other hand, an off the shelf product could be a popular IBM application that relies on using TAI for managing personalization, the WebSphere Portal product. In this case, the authentication of users is lead by the IHS and SiteMinder Web Agent; whereas the authorization and other functionalities could be lead by the SiteMinder Application Server Agent for WebSphere.

Configuring SiteMinder ASA for WebSphere (TAI)

There are two phases to configure a SiteMinder-based TAI. The first one takes place when the SiteMinder ASA component is installed on the nodes where the Application Server runs. As part of the installation, SiteMinder adds several libraries to the WAS ND7 base installation (that is, not in the profile area but in the executables area).

The second phase is the actual configuration of the WAS ND7 component. This involves a few steps as follows:

1. Install the SM ASA configuration file:

   Copy the file `smagent.properties` from the SM ASA `conf` directory to the Application Server profile **properties** directory.

2. Enable TAI on the ISC:

   Using a browser connect to the Deployment Manager Console. Follow the breadcrumb **Security | Global Security | Trust association** (under sections **Authentication | Web and SIP security**) The following screenshot may help with locating the **Trust association** link towards the bottom of the shot:

   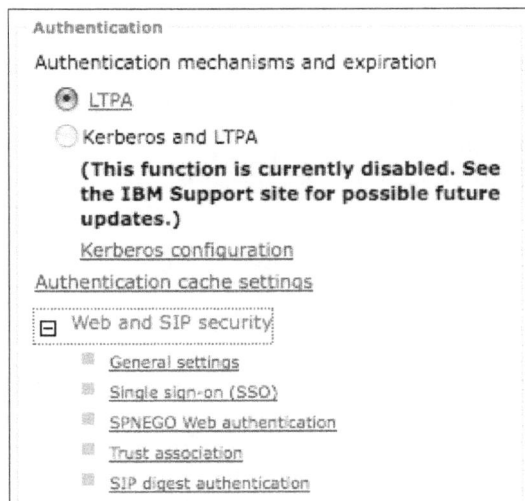

3. **Enable TAI**:

   Check the **Enable trust association** box. Then click the **Apply** button. Click the **Interceptors** link.

4. **Define SiteMinder TAI Java class**:

   On the page that appears, you may see existing TAI classes (by default, out of the box, SPENGO and TAM interceptors are defined). Click the **New** button. In the field **Interceptor class name**, enter the value com.netegrity. siteminder.websphere.auth.SmTrustAssociationInterceptor. In the field **Name**, under **Custom properties**, enter the value /opt/netegrity/ siteminder/smwasatai/AsaAgent-assertion.conf (or the location where SiteMinder ASA TAI was installed). The following screenshot shows the configuration as stated:

5. Click the **Apply** button and save the changes.
6. Restart the environment.

Summary

Besides a quite lengthy definition for enterprise infrastructure architecture, this chapter presented the following major themes:

- The role that LTPA plays in extending the security from a WAS ND7 cell to other WebSphere environments and several other IBM products.

- The concept of SSO, how it works across remote servers, what is required to implement it, and how to configure WAS ND7 for SSO.

- The use of Centralized Authorization Managers, and how they extend the reach of the WAS ND7 infrastructure beyond LTPA. A specific case using the SiteMinder brand of components was analyzed. How to integrate the front-end component IHS with the SiteMinder access management infrastructure using the SiteMinder Web Agent.

- The concept of Trust Association Interceptor. Analyzed the Web Agent complementary SiteMinder Component SMASA for WebSphere. A specific case configuring SMASA for WebSphere was described.

Do you feel like learning another lengthy definition? I didn't think so. OK, I'll give you a break this time. See you on the next page!

9
WebSphere Default Installation Hardening

There is a class of products that when we purchase them they need to be changed in order for them to be useful to us. Consider for an instance that I was travelling to Las Vegas, NV and decided to buy a watch. (Why would I be buying watches in Las Vegas? Well, it beats me; but that is a different story.) It is very likely that I may need to change the time, and perhaps time zone (for some sophisticated watches) to match the time where I live. This change was necessary to make the product useful to me. We also have a class of products that we may want to change to increase their security. Take for instance a GPS. Many of the recent models allow the owner to define a PIN that must be entered for the user to start the device. So only those persons that know the PIN would be able to use it; perhaps deterring thieves from stealing it; or if they do, so they cannot use it or resell it easily. In any event, a watch or a GPS are examples of very simple types of products. A product such as the WebSphere Application Server Network Deployment version 7 (WAS ND v7) is an example of a much more complex product. This chapter deals with the following:

- Engineering the default WAS ND v7 installation by changing its default parameters in order to harden the product's security side
- Customizing the files that hold the WAS ND v7 environment security certificates and signers

Such modifications of default parameters could be grouped in two major categories.

- On one hand, there is the category labeled in this chapter as *'engineering'*. In a nutshell, this term is used for planning and execution activities that modify the product's (in this case, WAS ND7) structural features used in a default (or sometimes also coined as "out-of-the-box") installation. The term *structural* in this context denotes those changes that although possible, may be impractical to carry out.

- On the other hand, there are those changes that, in this chapter, are labeled as *housekeeping* or 'home improvement' type of changes and which can be carried out during or after an installation is completed.

Let's look at the engineering of the installation. The WAS ND7 default installation parameters are a good start. But why settle for good when you can attain the best?" The security installation engineering aspect will concentrate on the features depicted in the following diagram and summarized as follows:

- Customizing the location of key root directories:
  - ° Base product installation
  - ° Application Server profile root directories
  - ° Log file root directories
- Customizing the TCP port range for host ('regular' Application Servers) and administrative (deployment manager and node agents) JVMs.
- Customizing the process execution user and group owners.

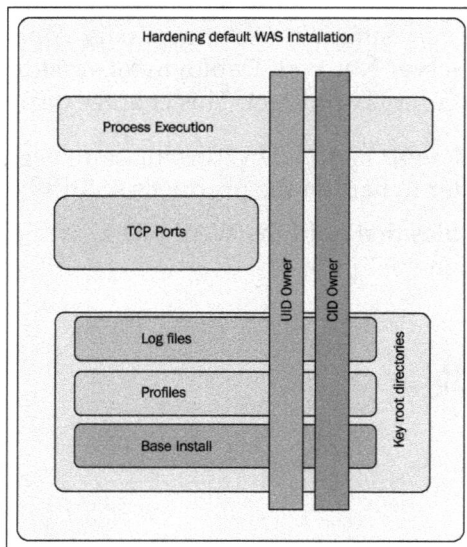

Accordingly with the diagram, the first section of the chapter deals with actions that can be taken before (planning), during (engineering) and after (customizing) the installation process. Among the installation factors that can be planned for are the three main groups shown in the previous diagram.

The first group is the **Key root directories**, which is represented in the diagram as the horizontal rectangle (yellow). It is a good practice to split the location of the base (sometimes referred to as binaries or executable and represented by the thin blue rectangle), files from the configuration files (represented by the thin maroon rectangle), in the case of WAS ND7, the different profiles in the environment. Finally, it is also highly desirable to place the log files not only on a different directory than the configuration files but in a different file system altogether. The ID and group ownership of each of these three groups of root directories will be closely related to the process owner. In other words, the two long rectangles labeled UID (yellow) and GID (light red) Owner rectangles must agree between process execution, top rectangle, and the root directories.

In addition, in terms of the second major group that we referred to as the housekeeping type of changes, the following diagram portrays the concept, which can be summarized as follows.

- Base installation clean-up
    - IHS/Plug-in clutter clean-up
    - WAS clean-up

- Protection of sensitive configuration files
    ◦ Configuration files containing passwords
    ◦ Private key files

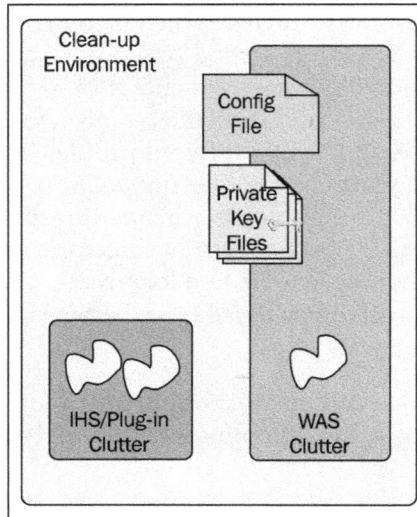

In the previous diagram, the portions of the installation process that should not be present in a production environment installation are represented by the puzzle pieces. Some of the puzzle pieces are located under the IHS installation (orange puzzle); others, under the WebSphere Plug-in (blue puzzle); and yet others under the WAS installation (red puzzle). Finally, the document-shaped rectangles at the top of the diagram represent configuration files (mostly XML files, represented by the yellow document-shaped rectangle) and the key store files (represented by the light blue document-shaped rectangle).

Engineering the how and where of an installation

As stated at the beginning of the chapter, there are some actions that can take place prior to performing the installation of your WAS ND7 environment. It is likely that you already perform all of them or most of them. However, they are included here for those readers for which WAS ND7 is their first experience with a WebSphere environment.

Appreciating the importance of location, location, location!

As in real estate, the location selected for a house (or the product files in our case) is very important. File systems can be a blessing and a curse. They are a blessing in that they help control how our data is organized. They would be a curse if planning is done poorly and the environment runs out of space after your enterprise applications are installed and they have been executing only for a while.

Your corporation may have some established policies and standards that would apply to most third party software packages. If that is your case, your installation should meet those requirements. However, if organizing your directory structure is something that will be carried out as you create your WebSphere environment, then this is a unique opportunity for creating a clean split between executable, configuration, and log files.

> In the following subsections the file systems /executable, /configuration and /logfiles will be used as an example of proposed location based on the content type. WAS ND 7 binaries will be installed under the /executable file system. The WebSphere profiles will be created under the /configuration file system. And finally, the application log files will be stored under the /logfiles file system. It is very likely that your company already has standards for such directory name conventions.

Customizing the executable files location

An example of what could be the root directory for your executables for WAS ND7 could be:

/executable/WebSphere/AppServer

This directory path would be the value assigned to the IBM WAS variable WAS_HOME once the installation is completed. Therefore, the directory /executable would be the root directory for all of the third party products that may be needed in your system. Among them, aside from WebSphere ND7, the directory could include the root directory for your database drivers (or DB client software, if required), monitoring software, and so on. So, if this were the case, the path /executable/oracle could be the root directory for the Oracle database drivers. It is highly desirable to create a file system on the mount point /executable that has enough disk space to hold the various products that you are planning to install.

If you are performing your WAS ND7 installation using the silent method, the parameter installLocation would need to be set to the value given above, for example, /executable/WebSphere/AppServer.

Customizing the configuration files location

It would be under this root directory that your WAS ND7 profiles would reside. It is also highly desirable to create a very clear split between the executable and the profile root directories. If we would follow a similar approach to the one used in the previous sub-section, the root directory for WAS ND7 profiles could be as follows:

/configuration/WASprofiles/<Your_AS_profile>

Similar to the executable directory, it is highly recommended to create a file system on the mount point /configuration that has more than enough disk space to host your current plus future enterprise applications. If at the time of installing your WAS ND7 executable, you create a default or managed profile, in the silent installation method you would need to define the installer property PROF_profilePath as the location stated above, that is, /configuration/WASprofiles/Your_AS_profile.

Customizing the log files location

The last directory structure that it is desirable to customize and split out of the default installation is the log file directory structure. Let's first view the default configuration for the location of these files. The following procedure will help:

1. Using a browser, log in as an administrator user to the Integrated Solutions Console.

2. Open the JVM logs screen of one of your Application servers.

3. The generic path to the page can be found by following the breadcrumb **Servers | WebSphere Application Servers | <Your_AppServer> | Logging and Tracing | JVM logs**. Where the string **<Your_AppServer>** in the breadcrumb above needs to be replaced with an appropriate value. (The value used here is the first Application Server that was created, that is: SecureAppServer01.)

4. Observe the file name for the System.out section.

5. In the following screenshot, it can be observed that the absolute path to the file name field under the section System.out includes a WebSphere variable, the full path being: ${SERVER_LOG_ROOT}/SystemOut.log.

6. Observe the filename for the System.err section
    Similarly, down the same page (as illustrated in the previous screenshot)
    observe the value for filename field under the section System.err . The
    default setting is ${SERVER_LOG_ROOT}/SystemErr.log.

Our goal is twofold. On the one hand, it is desirable (if not a requirement) to change
the location of all of the Application Server's log files to a directory that complies
with your standards. In order to follow our simple scheme, let's assume that it is
desirable to have all of the log files written to the file system on the mount point
/logfiles. The section allocated to the WAS ND7 Application Servers could
be /logfiles/WebSphere and the directory specific to hold the log files for our
Application Server would then be /logfiles/WebSphere/SecureAppServer01.
It seems very simple to just go ahead and on the page shown in the previous
screenshot, in Step 3, replace the value of the WebSphere (environment) variable
SERVER_LOG_ROOT with the value we just defined. However, this may not be the best
approach. Let's see why.

It is likely that a corporate WAS ND7 environment will be made of several Application Servers. Replacing this value on the JVM logs page would imply repeating this procedure on every Application Server. The second side to our initial goal is to minimize effort and therefore, minimize error. How do we go about this? Let's analyze how SERVER_LOG_ROOT is defined.

1. Using the same browser, go to the WebSphere variables screen.

   To get to the page, follow the breadcrumb **Environment | WebSphere variables.**

   At this point, we need to find the definition for SERVER_LOG_ROOT and, if necessary, other variables involved.

2. Set the scope to All Scopes.

   On the **WebSphere Variables** screen, if required, set the scope of the variable search to **All Scopes**.

3. Open search.

   This step is a little bit tricky to explain with words. Therefore, refer to the following screenshot. In order to open the search function, click the **Show filter function** identified in the screenshot by the circle.

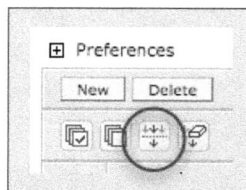

4. Search for SERVER_LOG_ROOT.

   In the area that opens, replace the single asterisk (*) with the string SERVER_LOG_ROOT. Insure that the **Filter** pull-down menu value is set to **Name**. Then click the **Go** button.

   So, what did we get? The result set returned a list of rows in which the definition for SERVER_LOG_ROOT depends on yet another variable, namely LOG_ROOT. Hmm!? What now? It would seem as if this business of changing the location of the log files is getting too complicated and changing the value of the path directly on the Application Server JVM logs screen is simpler. Well, actually it is not so. Check this out.

   In the first place, observe that each definition for SERVER_LOG_ROOT has been made at the Application Server scope. Let's now continue our procedure.

5. Search for variables SERVER_LOG_ROOT and LOG_ROOT.

On the same browser page, change the SERVER_LOG_ROOT search string to *LOG_ROOT. Then perform a search. Your result may be similar to the top of the screenshot:

You can administer the following resources:			
☐	LOG_ROOT	${USER_INSTALL_ROOT}/logs	Node=wasmasterCellManager01
☐	LOG_ROOT	${USER_INSTALL_ROOT}/logs	Node=wasmasterNode01
☐	SERVER_LOG_ROOT	${LOG_ROOT}/server1	Node=wasmasterNode01,Server=server1
☐	SERVER_LOG_ROOT	${LOG_ROOT}/SecureAppServer01	Node=wasmasterNode01,Server=SecureAppServer01
☐	SERVER_LOG_ROOT	${LOG_ROOT}/webmaster	Node=wasmasterNode01,Server=webmaster
☐	SERVER_LOG_ROOT	${LOG_ROOT}/Chap6AppServer	Node=wasmasterNode01,Server=Chap6AppServer
☐	SERVER_LOG_ROOT	${LOG_ROOT}/Chap7AppServer	Node=wasmasterNode01,Server=Chap7AppServer
☐	WAS_SERVER_NAME	server1	Node=wasmasterNode01,Server=server1
☐	WAS_SERVER_NAME	SecureAppServer01	Node=wasmasterNode01,Server=SecureAppServer01

The screenshot above shows that there are two similar definitions for the variable LOG_ROOT. One is defined at the node level and the other at the cell level. In both cases, LOG_ROOT is defined in terms of yet one more variable, USER_INSTALL_ROOT that matches the path to the Application Server profile, but that is not important at the moment. What is important is that there is a choice to make and to make sure that SERVER_LOG_ROOT is also defined. The choice is whether to define LOG_ROOT at both scopes or just at one, the node level. There is no real right or wrong answer, it all depends on what you wish to accomplish. One option that seems like a general solution is to delete the LOG_ROOT variable defined at the node level and define LOG_ROOT at the cell level as /logfiles/WebSphere. Those two changes help us accomplish our twofold goal. There are no more changes needed in this particular environment no matter how many other Application Servers are created afterwards. Therefore, WebSphere will resolve SERVER_LOG_ROOT as /logfiles/WebSphere/SecureAppServer01 for the application server SecureAppServer01.

Camouflaging the entrance points

A really fun part of engineering a WebSphere environment in general and a WAS ND7 in particular is to define the TCP ports that will be used for the dmgr, nodeagent and JVM processes. I could write a dissertation about this topic, but there is no need to worry, I won't. Keep in mind that what we are customizing is how our WAS ND7 infrastructure is going to communicate with other support technologies and to client applications: for example, databases, LDAP, and so on.

Understanding why it's important

There are two reasons why this subject is addressed in this chapter. On the one hand, we have the security factor. It is highly desirable to customize the value assigned to the various TCP ports for each of the JVM processes running. The default values and how they are incremented every time a new JVM is created are widely documented. This fact could provide a backdoor to someone wanting to gain access to unauthorized resources. On the other hand, customizing the TCP ports will help in the areas of organization of the infrastructure, provide adhesion to corporate standards and by using port ranges it makes it easier to administer and protect using firewall rules.

Furthermore, most corporations using WebSphere environments split the overall enterprise IT environment into at least two major and independent infrastructure segments. One is the tier of infrastructure that actually delivers the services for which the IT infrastructure exists in the first place. Many corporations refer to this portion of the overall infrastructure as the production environment. The second piece of the enterprise wide infrastructure could also be split in two or more well defined segments. The most common setting is to have three major infrastructure segments, namely production, quality assurance-load testing, and development environments.

What's more, there are basically two schools of thought as to how to select the range for the needed TCP ports used by the various administrative and application JVMs.

Methodology choices

One school of thought argues to use the same port range for the same application across all infrastructure segments. For instance, if our application server SecureAppServer01 would be assigned the TCP port 10020 for its BOOTSTRAP_ ADDRESS port in the development environment, when the higher infrastructure segments are built they would also use TCP port 10020 for the same use in those segments (for example, test and production). Among the benefits of this approach, the following can be mentioned:

- There is a large capacity for selecting unique ports for all of the JVM's in the environment (for example, 10000-30000 could be made available for this purpose).

- It is easier to move from one infrastructure segment to another for the same application since the ports of the application's URL will be exactly the same.

- Automation by creating scripts to perform a number of tasks such as administrative, auditing, and so on is also simplified.

The other school of thought takes the approach of having unique ports for all of the applications, even across infrastructure segments. What this means is that in this technique, a much narrower range, in comparison with the first method, is allocated for one of the infrastructure segments. For instance, let's assume that for a development infrastructure segment or environment the range 10000-19999 is allocated to be used by the various WebSphere components. In a similar way, the range 20000-29999 is assigned to the next environment and so forth. Therefore, for the same example as in the first technique, in a three-infrastructure segment (which we will refer to as development, test and production), for the SecureAppServer01application server, its port for BOOTSTRAP_ADDRESS will be assigned the value of **10020** in development, **20020** in test and **30020** in production. The next variant is also popular: higher infrastructure segments are assigned the lower TCP ranges (that is, TCP ports for the production environment will be assigned from the pool 10000-19999, for testing from 20000-29999, and for development from 30000-39999).

In any event, the lesson here is to select a methodology for selecting and assigning ports for your application servers and stick to it. It will prove to help you in the administration and auditing of your various infrastructure segments.

Identifying what needs to be configured

The screenshot shown next displays the name of the ports required by the dmgr. Although the screenshot includes twelve ports, if you are not using the IBM DataPower appliance, you can omit the definition for the port DataPowerMgr_ inbound_secure, leaving a total of eleven ports used up by the dmgr process. So you could use a range **nn000 — nn010** of consecutive ports reserved for the Deployment Manager.

Deployment manager > Ports

Specifies the TCP/IP ports this server uses for connections.

⊞ Preferences

[New] [Delete]

You can administer the following resources:

Select	Port Name ⬦	Host ⬦	Port ⬦	Transport Details ⬦
☐	BOOTSTRAP_ADDRESS	wasmaster.siliceoinc.com	9809	No associated transports
☐	CELL_DISCOVERY_ADDRESS	wasmaster.siliceoinc.com	7277	No associated transports
☐	CSIV2_SSL_MUTUALAUTH_LISTENER_ADDRESS	wasmaster.siliceoinc.com	9402	No associated transports
☐	CSIV2_SSL_SERVERAUTH_LISTENER_ADDRESS	wasmaster.siliceoinc.com	9403	No associated transports
☐	DCS_UNICAST_ADDRESS	*	9352	View associated transports
☐	DataPowerMgr_inbound_secure	*	5555	View associated transports
☐	IPC_CONNECTOR_ADDRESS	${LOCALHOST_NAME}	9632	No associated transports
☐	ORB_LISTENER_ADDRESS	wasmaster.siliceoinc.com	9100	No associated transports
☐	SAS_SSL_SERVERAUTH_LISTENER_ADDRESS	wasmaster.siliceoinc.com	9401	No associated transports
☐	SOAP_CONNECTOR_ADDRESS	wasmaster.siliceoinc.com	8879	No associated transports
☐	WC_adminhost	*	9060	View associated transports
☐	WC_adminhost_secure	*	9043	View associated transports

Total 12

The next table displays a summary of all of the ports used by the dmgr, nodeagent, and application servers. It shows the default ports that WAS ND7 will assign to those processes unless you tell it otherwise. From the table, it can be deducted that the number of ports needed by a nodeagent process is eleven. You have a decision to make here. If you are planning to host on the same OS host a deployment manager profile and a federated managed profile, you would need to stack the port ranges. Furthermore, if you are not currently combining deployment manager and node, but there is a possibility that in the future that combination be supported, then it is better to make everything uniform and stack the port ranges. So, the first nodeagent could be assigned the range **nn011 – nn021**. And no, I did not misspeak when I said 'first'. If there is any chance that there may be vertical nodes in your environment, might as well plan for them. So you could reserve the rest of the ports in that 100 count (that is, **nn022 – nn098**) for other nodeagents.

Port names	dmgr	nodeagent	server1	Transport Details
BOOTSTRAP_ADDRESS	9809	2810	2809	No associated transports
CELL_DISCOVERY_ADDRESS	7277			No associated transports
CSIV2_SSL_MUTUALAUTH_LISTENER_ADDRESS	9402	9202	9405	No associated transports
CSIV2_SSL_SERVERAUTH_LISTENER_ADDRESS	9403	9201	9406	No associated transports
DCS_UNICAST_ADDRESS	9352	9354	9353	View associated transports
DataPowerMgr_Inbound_secure	5555			View associated transports
IPC_CONNECTOR_ADDRESS	9632	9626	9633	No associated transports
NODE_DISCOVERY_ADDRESS		7272		No associated transports
NODE_IPV6_MULTICAST_DISCOVERY_ADDRESS		5001		No associated transports
NODE_MULTICAST_DISCOVERY_ADDRESS		5000		No associated transports
ORB_LISTENER_ADDRESS	9100	9101	0	No associated transports
SAS_SSL_SERVERAUTH_LISTENER_ADDRESS	9401	9901	9404	No associated transports
SIB_ENDPOINT_ADDRESS			7276	View associated transports
SIB_ENDPOINT_SECURE_ADDRESS			7286	View associated transports
SIB_MQ_ENDPOINT_ADDRESS			5558	View associated transports
SIB_MQ_ENDPOINT_SECURE_ADDRESS			5578	View associated transports
SIP_DEFAULTHOST			5060	View associated transports
SIP_DEFAULTHOST_SECURE			5061	View associated transports
SOAP_CONNECTOR_ADDRESS	8879	8878	8880	No associated transports
WC_adminhost	9060		9061	View associated transports
WC_adminhost_secure	9043		9044	View associated transports
WC_defaulthost			9080	View associated transports
WC_defaulthost_secure			9443	View associated transports

In a similar way, we can engineer the port ranges for the application servers. From the previous table, it can be deduced that there are 18 ports required for an application server.

Getting started

When starting a brand new installation, the task of assigning ports is not as overwhelming as one would think. The key is to perform silent installations using response files. And, more importantly, when creating profiles, make sure you provide a value to the property `portsFile` giving the path to an external ports file. In the case of federating a node, you can provide to the `addNode.sh` utility the value to the `-portprops` argument that is the path to the ports than should be used by the nodeagent.

If you wish to change the ports of existing profiles, it requires a little more work. Doing this task through the Integrated Solutions Console is not appealing at all. So we must turn to a script-based solution. The method provided by the wsadmin interface is `modifyServerPort` from the object `AdminTask`. The syntax that can be used for existing TCP ports for the method is `AdminTask.modifyServerPort ( '<AppServer>', '[-nodename <NodeName> -endPoint <TCPPortName> -port <NewPort>]' )`. The syntax provided will work for most of the ports. However, there are a few ports that need an extended version of the syntax above. The ports that can use the syntax above are those ports shown in the table above that under the column **Transport Details** the value is set to **No associated transports**. The remaining ports for which the value of the same column is **View associated transports**, require an additional parameter as follows: `AdminTask.modifyServerPort ( '<AppServer>', '[-nodename <NodeName> -endPoint <TCPPortName> -port <NewPort> -modifyShared true]' )`. A script can be written to parse a file where the port assignments are made and then execute the appropriate `modifyServerPort` method call.

If changing the TCP ports of an existing Deployment Manager profile, ensure that the port values in the `<ProfileRootDir>/properties/nodeportdef.props` file match accordingly for all profiles.

Picking a good attorney

It is very likely that almost everybody wants to protect his or her hard-earned income, especially when it comes to saving for retirement. Also, when it comes to somebody's estate, you want the most trustworthy person to handle his or her affairs. In both cases you want the help from the individuals (or perhaps even institutions) most adequate for the task; normally an investor for the former and an executor for the latter. In the WebSphere world, it is also desirable to have the best choice to execute the various WebSphere components processes so your environment runs both smoothly and securely. If you install the product as root, it is most likely that, by default, the profiles created would be configured to be executed as root. In the majority of the cases, this is not desirable since any enterprise application is then running with the privileges of root. At the minimum, it is desired that all the non-administrative JVMs execute as non-root. There may be a couple of options to engineer what is the best setting for process ownership. For both options, however, it is a good practice to leave the executable portion of the installation owned by root, so no file can be altered by mistake or malice.

If all of the JVMs may execute as the same process owner, then the best approach is to have a service type of account to become the process owner for all the WAS ND7 components, that is, administrative and application JVMs. The OS administrator may create an OS account, for example, wasadm, and a corresponding group, for example, was. Thus, after the necessary profiles are created, all of their files should be assigned the ownership of wasadm and was. In this way, all processes must be started as the non-root service account.

However, if there is a requirement that states that groups of applications must execute as their own and unique user and group owner so there is no possibility that communication across applications and their data take place unless the system components are configured to do so, then the scenario is a bit more complex than the first one in which everything is executed as a single non-root owner and group.

> **Best Practice: Use the command chutils to do file owner/group changes**
>
> The use of the command **chutils** is covered in the Information Center article *Verifying and setting file permissions* (available at: `http://publib.boulder.ibm.com/infocenter/wasinfo/v7r0/topic/com.ibm.websphere.installation.nd.doc/info/ae/ae/cins_nonroot_permissions.html`)

Ensuring good housekeeping of an installation

In addition to the engineering aspect of hardening your default installation, there are a couple or three things that can be carried out after the installation is completed. This section will briefly describe them.

Keeping your secrets safe

There are two aspects in terms of your WebSphere secrets that need some attention. The first one is the WAS ND7 environment default passwords for the various stores. The second is insuring that there are no clear text passwords of any type included in the various properties and XML configuration files.

Using key stores and trust stores

Up until WAS ND6.0 all installations came with the same private key. That changed in WAS ND6.1. So in WAS ND7, this key and the other security artifacts associated with it are created at the time of the profile creation. However, the default password for such stores is the same for any installation! If you still have not changed this default password, place a bookmark right here, take this book with you, rush to the data center where your servers are, get on your server's console and change the password. By the way, on your way to the data center make sure you look alarmed and move hastily to your destination, but at the same time you must look confident in what you are doing. Then go to see your supervisor and report that you just saved the company from a potential break in and eliminated a security breach. Maybe she'll be so impressed that she'll offer you a bonus! Make sure to tell her that you learned about it from this book! Hey, you never know, she may order a few more copies! Back to our point, change the default password (WebAS) to something that follows your company standards. The job can be done in several ways. One would be using scripting. The other would be through the **ISC** or **Integrated Solutions Console**.

The following procedure can be used to change the password of all key stores at once.

1. Open a command session to the Deployment Manager host.

2. Optional: if necessary, switch to the ID that is used to administrate WAS.

3. Start the wsadmin interface.

    The following command can be used:

    ```
    wsadmin.sh -lang jython -conntype SOAP -host $(hostname) -port
    <DM_SOAP_PORT>
    ```

wsadmin will ask for credentials. Enter user name and appropriate password. Executing the command in this way prevents the password being exposed had you used the arguments "-user <WASADM> -password <WASPWD>" on the command line.

4. Use the **AdminTask** method changeMultipleKeyStorePasswords.

5. The changeMultipleKeyStorePasswords method of the **AdminTask** object will change the passwords of all key stores and trust stores with a single call. At the prompt, the following command can be entered:

```
wsadmin> AdminTask.changeMultipleKeyStorePasswords
['(-keyStorePassword WebAS -newKeyStorePassword <NewPass>
-newKeyStorePasswordVerify <NewPass>]')
```

A few comments regarding the command that may not be evident from the way it is printed. On the one hand, the command is issued in a single line. In addition, there is no space or breaks between the dash (-) and the property name. On the other hand, when substituting the string <NewPass> with your new password, do not include the angle brackets since they are not part of the method syntax.

6. Save the changes.

7. Terminate the wsadmin session.

The new password is encrypted and stored in XML configuration files. This brings us to our next topic.

Storing passwords in configuration files

WAS ND7 uses several XML files to store encoded passwords. They are mentioned below.

```
<ProfileRootDirectory>/config/cells/<CellName>/security.xml
```

Keeps the passwords for the following properties when defined: Cryptographic token device, Keystore, LDAP user registry bind, LTPA, Truststore and the user registry server. In addition, it also stores the JAAS authentication data.

```
<ProfileRootDirectory>/config/cells//<CellName>/nodes/<NodeName>/
servers/ <AppServer>/resources.xml
```

Keeps the password for the following Application Server level properties when defined: mailStore, mailTransport, MQQueue queue mgr, and WAS40Datasource.

```
<ProfileRootDirectory>/config/cells//<CellName>/nodes/<NodeName>/
servers/ <AppServer>/security.xml
```

Keeps the passwords for the following Application Server level properties when defined: Cryptographic token device, DRS client data replication, Keystore, Session persistence, and Truststore.

By default, when a password is defined through the Integrated Solutions Console or some other type of WAS ND7 interface, WebSphere encodes the passwords. An indication that a password field is encoded is that the content of the field starts with the string {XOR}. When a password has not been defined the only content of the password field will be the identifying string, {XOR}.

Adding passwords to properties files

Each profile contains a properties directory. Under it, there are several files in which various passwords can be defined. One of the most common ones among those files is the soap.client.props properties file, which is used when issuing WAS commands that require authentication, for example, stopManager.sh, and the appropriate credentials are included in that file. In order to enable using this file for the command line, the following properties must be set: com.ibm. SOAP.SecurityEnabled (true), com.ibm.SOAP.loginUserid (for example, wasadm) and com.ibm.SOAP.loginPassword. When you enter the password, ensure that the encoded version of the password is used. The WAS ND7 utility, PropFilePasswordEncoder.sh can be used for this purpose. Using the same file mentioned above, the following procedure can be used to add an encrypted password to a properties file.

1. Open a command session to the Deployment Manager host as administrative user.

2. Change the working directory to the DM profile properties directory.

3. Edit the soap.client.props file as follows:

   Set the value of the property com.ibm.SOAP.SecurityEnabled to true. Add the administrative ID on the line for the property com.ibm.SOAP.loginUserid. Set the value of the property com.ibm.SOAP.loginPassword to the password for the ID just added (in not decoded format). Save the changes.

4. Encode the password using `PropFilePasswordEncoder.sh`.

   Issue the following command:

   `../bin/PropFilePasswordEncoder.sh soap.client.props com.ibm.SOAP.loginPassword`

> The syntax of the `PropFilePasswordEncoder.sh` command is:
> `PropFilePasswordEncoder.sh <PropertyFile> <PropertyName>`

> **Best Practice: Property files and passwords**
>
> Never store clear text (not-decoded) passwords in properties files in particular and in configuration files in general. However, it is still possible to decode passwords that were encoded with the WebSphere supplied utilities. So in addition to encoding passwords in files, to add another layer of security, lock such files so they are only readable by the UID used to execute the WebSphere processes.

Manually adding a password - a bonus tip

A limitation of `PropFilePasswordEncoder.sh` is that it only can be used in properties files; it won't work with XML files. If for some reason you need to manually add a password in one of the XML files the following trick can be used.

1. Create a text file using your favorite editor.

   Create a file named, say, `encpwd.tmp`.

2. Add a line using the format "property=password".

   For instance the following line can be added

   `com.mycompany.rwehvngfn=openpassword`

3. Encode password

   Issue the command:

   `<ProfileRootDir>/bin/PropFilePasswordEncoder.sh encpwd.tmp com.mycompany.rwehvngfn`

That file now has the encoded version of the password that can be added to the target XML file.

Encoding vs. encryption

Encoding passwords with WebSphere supplied utilities implies to rewrite the password in an *obscure* format, so to speak. Such utilities use the Java class com.ibm.ws.security.util.PropFilePasswordEncoder to perform the encoding operation. In IT and Computer Science (CS) encoding is normally used to make information more *usable* rather than more *secure*. Therefore, keep in mind that it is possible to use a supplemental WebSphere-supplied Java class to perform the opposite operation to decode such passwords. Consequently, although it is possible to keep the password from the naked eye, someone with access to such WebSphere classes could potentially decode it. Encryption, on the other hand, uses a cipher (encrypting algorithm) and a key. The strength of the resulting encrypted data depends on the cipher and the length of the key. The only way in which the data can be decrypted to its original value is to use the cipher and the key. Without the key it is practically impossible to decrypt the data. In IT and CS encryption is used to secure information rather than for usability purposes. In WebSphere, there is a way to use encrypted rather than encoded passwords in properties and XML configuration files. Describing such a method is out of the scope of this book. For further details, please refer to the WAS ND v7 information center articles: *Plug point for custom password encryption* (http://publib.boulder.ibm.com/infocenter/wasinfo/v7r0/topic/com.ibm.websphere.nd.doc/info/ae/ae/csec_plugpoint_custpass_encrypt.html) and *Enabling custom password encryption* (http://publib.boulder.ibm.com/infocenter/wasinfo/v7r0/topic/com.ibm.websphere.nd.doc/info/ae/ae/tsec_enable_custpass_encrypt.html)

Summary

In this chapter, you were introduced to two major areas that will help harden a default WAS ND7 installation:

- Engineering the default installation and initial configuration of the WAS ND7 infrastructure components
    - Modifying the file location of the major WAS ND7 components
    - Customizing the TCP port ranges used by the WASND 7 JVMs

- Hardening the security of the WAS ND7 installation components
  - ° Changing the default password of key and trusted stores
  - ° Identifying properties and XML configuration files that contain passwords in order to lock them down
  - o Learn about the existence of an advanced method to secure passwords by using encryption rather than encoding

We have pinned down one more chapter. Decisions; keep working on the next chapter or go out to celebrate. Life is hard!

10
Platform Hardening

When I went to college, during my freshman year, I used to love Physics. Everything, at least it seemed that way back then, looked as though it was very logical. I developed a strategy to commit to rote memory only initial formulas from which others could be derived following a series of logical steps. That strategy, believe it or not, helped me remember more about the subject than having to remember every single formula. Now, when it came to Chemistry, all those methods that I have developed for Physics failed. To me, Chemistry seemed like a large collection of recipes; my poor brain could not find a way to find a logical path from one to the other. Well, when it comes to platform hardening, it is probably closer to my experience with Chemistry than with Physics. In this chapter, you will be exposed to the following:

- Affecting the OS default configuration to increase security
- Identifying boundaries between the OS and WAS to help identify areas to secure
- Hardening areas such as user accounts, service accounts, and kernel modules
- Hardening file system organization and configuration
- Hardening network services

Identifying where to focus

It would be practically impossible for a vendor to create an OS/hardware configuration that would securely and efficiently cover all customers' needs. When at IBM, I heard co-workers sometimes exclaim how *creative* our customers were when it came to finding ways to either use or configure one of our products that we had not thought about. It is probably the same when in your organization systems are configured to better cope with a specific job, that job being a database server or a J2EE application server or what have you.

One of the keys to unlock the art of hardening the default installation of your underlying OS is to identify **borders** between the WAS ND7 environment and the OS/hardware. Finding such borders will make the task a little easier since it will help to narrow the scope of what needs to be analyzed.

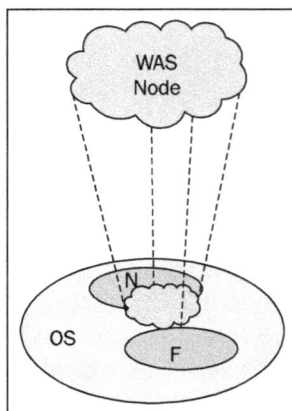

The previous diagram, in a very abstract fashion, depicts the salient borders between a WAS instance and the basic systems within the OS. So, let's take a closer look at the diagram. In the first place, the ovals represent systems and sub-systems that belong to the platform where WAS has been deployed. In addition, systems that are not part of the OS but are hosted by the OS are shown in a shape different than an oval. Therefore, the OS is represented by the large oval labeled **OS** (lavender); and two of its major subsystems that are closely related to security are the file system, represented by the oval labeled **F** (red) and the network system represented by the oval labeled **N** (yellow). In the diagram, one can observe that there is a border between the WAS installation and the file system. In addition, the diagram shows a border between WAS and the network system. Finally, the diagram also shows borders between the OS and WAS.

Consequently, the remaining sections of this chapter focus on the aspects of each of the identified systems that can or should be altered in order to achieve the desired level of security.

Exploring the operating system

Other than the File System and the Network System, there are still additional subsystems and components that can be explored. Thus, selecting what subsystems to explore is not an easy task. It is a well-known fact that accomplishing a task in different types of Unix can sometimes be tricky, especially when dealing with OS specific commands. For instance if we want to know what are the kernel modules that are currently loaded, the command is different for AIX, HP/UX, Linux and Solaris, as shown here:

- AIX: `genkex`
- HP/UX: `kmadmin -s`
- Linux: `lsmod`
- Solaris: `modinfo`

> If you ever wondered how to accomplish a specific familiar task in a different flavor of Unix, there is a nice site that offers the way to perform many administrative tasks using the commands unique to that flavor of Unix. The site is known as the Rosetta Stone for Unix: `http://bhami.com/rosetta.html`.

In terms of a WAS ND7 installation, although this book is not about the actual installation procedure, it is important to highlight that such a procedure will vary depending on the target OS. If you wish to explore your Operating System alternatives, visit the Information Center article "Preparing the operating system for product installation". (`http://publib.boulder.ibm.com/infocenter/wasinfo/v7r0/topic/com.ibm.websphere.installation.nd.doc/info/ae/ae/tins_prepare.html`).

Appreciating OS interfaces

Therefore, identifying which OS subcomponents to analyze is somewhat dependent on the Unix flavor. As such, using our proposed approach of finding the borders between WAS ND7 and the OS, some generic categories will serve as guidelines to further analyze the specific Unix flavor implementation.

Accordingly, this section attempts to analyze changes that may be required on the following four general categories:

- User accounts (UA): OS IDs assigned to individuals (such as administrators)
- Service accounts (SA): OS IDs that are used by the process owner of applications
- Kernel modules (KM): OS custom-enabled core services
- [(x)inetd] services (IS)

These general categories are visually depicted in the diagram that follows, which zooms in a portion of the previous diagram. In the following diagram, a small flag with its corresponding label, which can be mapped to the list above, represents those categories. It is a way to visually represent some possible dependencies between WAS and the general categories. For instance, the diagram shows that WAS ND7 has a dependency on **Service Accounts (SA)**. Therefore, the rest of this section will look into each of these general categories.

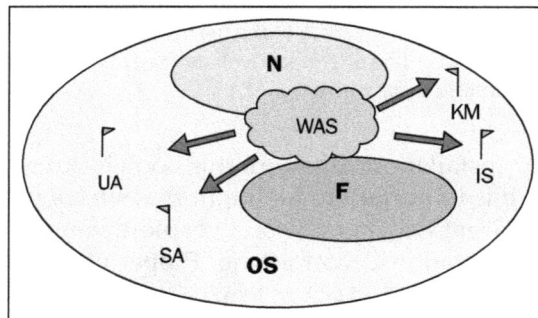

Understanding user accounts

In most corporations there are two schools of thought when it comes to the administration of Unix/Linux Systems. Let's look into each school philosophy.

In one school, there are at least two distinct administrative groups. One is responsible for maintaining the underlying OS and may be referred to as the Unix administrators team. Among their responsibilities, they create accounts, allocate disk space, create file systems, and so on. The second administrative team is responsible for the infrastructure application. In our case, the various components included in WAS ND7, that is, Application Server, Deployment Manager, HTTP Server, and WebSphere Plug-in. This team may be referred to as the WebSphere administrators team or similar names.

Under this school, in production systems, the only user accounts that should be created on the Unix server are those of the Unix and WebSphere administrators. No other user accounts should be created unless there is a secondary (read, support) infrastructure application such as SiteMinder or databases, if such support applications are present in the Unix host.

On the other hand, the second school of thought includes only one team of administrators. They are responsible for both the underlying Unix OS functionality and, in addition, the administration of the infrastructure application and its support applications. So this team creates user accounts, file systems, and maintains and updates both the OS and the infrastructure applications. In other words, this group performs all or most of the tasks that are performed by the two administrative groups in the first school of thought. Therefore, in this case, only the user accounts for the WebSphere administrators should be created. Furthermore, a variant of this scenario is that although there are two teams as in the first case, WebSphere administrators working closely with the Unix administrators team are able to perform some of the functions that are closely related to the infrastructure application (for example, creating user accounts, changing the ownership of directories and files where the infrastructure application is installed, and so on). Most of these tasks would be performed through a tool such as sudo.

Understanding service accounts

Service accounts are those OS accounts that are normally associated with infrastructure applications. They are not used to open interactive sessions with the OS. In other words, when an infrastructure application, such as WAS ND7 or IHS executes, it must run as a particular OS UID. The objective then, is to only give the service account the privileges it needs to execute the infrastructure application and nothing else. In order to accomplish this goal, the following characteristics should be considered.

- **OS group**: As any type of OS account, service accounts must belong to an OS group. It is highly advisable to create a new OS group, which will be the OS UID primary group. Ideally, no other UID should belong to this group.

- **Numeric IDs**: There should be consistency between servers across multiple infrastructure segments when it comes to the numeric ID assigned to user IDs and groups. Therefore, if in a development infrastructure segment the service account ID wasadm is assigned the numeric ID 500, it is highly recommended to use the same ID and numeric ID in the rest of the infrastructure segments. One of several reasons for doing so is that if there is a need to transfer files from one infrastructure segment to another (say, in a *tarball* archive) the chances of the transferred files to be given the incorrect ownership are decreased.

- **Directory access**: Service accounts should only be allowed to read configuration files and execute infrastructure application binaries. In addition, service accounts should only be able to write to log files directories and nowhere else.

Using kernel modules

As mentioned at the beginning of this chapter, it is very unlikely that the default configuration of kernel modules will be 100% suitable to your WebSphere host. Many of the possible module targets may be tied to a service that is not suitable for a server or may involve drivers to hardware that is not present in the system. The following commands can be used to show the modules loaded by the kernel (this list was also shown at the beginning of this section).

- AIX: `genkex`
- HP/UX: `kmadmin -s`
- Linux: `lsmod`
- Solaris: `modinfo`

For additional information on these commands, depending on your Operating System flavor, you can refer to the system's main pages.

One such module that may not be needed for the normal operation of a server and which may introduce some level of security risk is the module that allows USB memory drives to be mounted. (An example of an unwanted operation involving the use of a USB memory drive would be the unauthorized transfer of large amounts of files from the HD to the USB device.) For further information as to how to disable loading of the USB module, consult your OS documentation.

Creating the file system

The use of the term **file systems** may be a little bit broad for what is desired to communicate. However, the benefit of using it is that it is an expression easy to remember. In any event, the objective of this section is to convey the message of paying attention with ownership and permissions of key directories and files. IBM states that the use of Java 2 Security is enough to secure a WebSphere installation; however, there are a few additional tasks that can be carried out increasing the security of OS files and WAS ND7 files.

In terms of actual file systems, it is a good practice to create an exclusive file system for log files. It makes it easier to monitor the growth of the data in such a file system to make sure it does not fill up. If log files reside on the same file system as the WAS ND7 installation, as new enterprise applications are installed, it's not as easy to identify if a spike in disk usage growth is due to a new enterprise upgrade or installation or by a burst in some log file. For more information about recommendations regarding log files directories placing, refer to *Chapter 9, WebSphere Default Installation Hardening*.

In a similar way to log files, it is also a good practice to create a dedicated file system for the WAS ND7 installation and ideally another file system for the WAS ND7 profiles. Again as in the previous case, additional information about the location for the WAS ND7 profiles can be found in *Chapter 9, WebSphere Default Installation Hardening*.

Influencing permission and ownership using process execution

As also mentioned in *Chapter 9, WebSphere Default Installation Hardening*, it is not desirable to execute the WAS ND7 environment as root. There may be instances in which it may not be possible to execute all of the WAS ND7 components as a non-root ID. The various options in which the WAS ND7 environment can be set up for execution are basically the following:

* Run all the WAS environment processes as root
* Execute all the WAS environment processes as the same non-privileged service account
* Run the node agents as root and the Application Servers (JVM's) as one or several non-privileged service accounts

IBM recommends the second option. However, there are organizations, and yours may be one, whose security policies state that enterprise applications must execute as their own service account. So, we need to identify what ownership and permissions need to be put in place depending on the execution mode your WAS ND7 environment may use. However, right off the bat, the first execution mode, that is, running everything as root, will be discarded.

Running single execution mode

In this mode, as the name implies, all components of the WAS ND7 environment will execute as the same non-privileged service account. Under this mode, the prerequisites are:

- There must exist a service account
- There must be its corresponding OS group

Consequently, we will look at three areas of the environment.

Using executables

The first section is the WAS ND7 executables. Everything under `<WAS_Root_Directory>` must have the ownership: `root:<svcgrp>`. The following command can be used to set the ownership as desired:

```
chown -R root:<svcgrp> <WAS_Root_Directory>
```

In addition, the file permissions must be 750 for directories and either 640 or 750 for files. So, on the first hand, for directories, the following command can be used to set the desired permission:

```
find <WAS_Root_Directory> -type d -exec chmod 750 {} \; -print
```

On the other hand, for files, it may seem tricky at the beginning since it is desired that if the user permission is 7, then the group permission must be 5, which means that the file should have executable mode; or if the owner permission is 6, then the group permission must be 4, that is, read mode. Both cases can be summarized as: group permission must be non-writable. The following command will remove the group write bit to only those files that have it set, all the while setting the *other* bits permission to zero:

```
find <WAS_Root_Directory> -type f –exec chmod o-xrw {} \; -perm -g+w
-exec chmod g-w {} \;
```

> Recursive file permission modification, `chmod`, and file ownership modification, `chown`, can be dangerous if applied incorrectly. Always back-up your files before applying recursive operations on files.

Configuring

The next sector of the environment is the WAS ND7 *configuration* (profiles). This situation is just a little bit more complex than the executable area. The challenge here is that the application server processes (JVMs) will have to have access to write onto log directories. The level of complexity depends on whether you have split and engineered the location of the log files directories.

For this configuration section, the same approach as the one followed for the executable area will be used. In terms of file ownership, all files and directories under the `<WAS_Profile_Directory>` must have the ownership `root:<svcgrp>`. The following command can be used:

```
chown -R root:<svcgrp> <WAS_Profile_Directory>
```

The complication that arises in this scenario is that application servers must be able to write on a number of directories. In general, the following top-level directories should not be modified in terms of file permissions:

- logs
- tranlog
- configuration
- installedApps

It is possible that you have moved out of the profile area of the directories that contain the log files. Therefore, the following command could be used to set the permission of the rest of the files to be not writable by group and inaccessible to *other*. It can always be modified in case logs and tranlog are not present:

```
find <WAS_Profile_Directory> -exec chmod o-xrw {} \; \( -name logs -o
-name tranlog -o -name configuration -o -name installedApps -prune \) -o
\( -perm g+w -exec chmod g-w {} \; -print \)
```

In essence, the command is to skip the directories identified above and their children, and then remove the group write permission from those files and directories that have the bit set under the other top directories.

Setting ownerships and permissions on log files

The final region is the log files directories. Of the three WAS ND7 environment regions, this one is the most straight-forward of all. As in the previous sections, it is desirable to set the ownership to `root:<svcgrp>` for all files and directories under `<Log_Files_Directory>`. As a result, the command to be used is practically identical to the equivalent command used in the previous environment sections:

```
chown -R root:<svcgrp> <Log_Files_Directory>
```

The simplification for this situation comes in terms of setting the permissions. The desired permissions are broken down in two groups: directories 770 and files 660. Notice that there should not be any executable files under the log directories. Consequently, the following single command can be used to accomplish setting the desired permissions:

```
find <Log_Files_Directory> \( -type d -exec chmod 770 {} \; \) -o \(
-type f -exec chmod 660 {} \; \) -print
```

Running multiple execution mode

This third method is only valid in a shared environment in which enterprise applications from different groups within an organization must execute. Therefore, the method for executing a WAS ND7 environment is to have the **nodeagent** process run as the **root** ID and the application server processes (**JVMs**) as their own service account where each application server will execute as a different service account from the other application servers.

IBM does not recommend this scenario, as it is not well documented. However, since there may be a business reason for using it, such a scenario cannot be overlooked. A commercial scenario in which this type of setting may be needed would be at an application hosting company. In order to provide an economic advantage to its customers, the hosting company offers a shared environment in which hosted applications leverage on a common WebSphere infrastructure (for example, license, system maintenance, and so on). In order to increase the level of privacy and security for each hosted application, they must run as a different OS service ID so their working area and application files cannot be accessed by other applications (which in turn would be executing with their own OS service ID).

Therefore, in this section the areas in which the administrator must pay close attention to will be highlighted, based on the same WAS ND7 environment segments used in the single execution mode.

The first consideration is what service IDs and service groups to create and how to organize them. For our purposes, let the term **Business Service Account/Group (BSA/G)** be an OS ID assigned to one or a small group of enterprise applications belonging to the same business organizational entity. Such a group of applications will execute in a single JVM or a small number of JVMs on the same host as other groups' applications execute.

In addition, there should be an extra service group to which all service accounts must belong. Let this group be referred to as **Common Service Group (CSG)**. This completes the configuration of the OS user and group IDs.

Thus, the *executable* segment of the WAS ND7 installation must be configured to be owned by root:<CSG>. The permissions for files and directories are the same as in the single execution mode, that is, 750. This guarantees that only those processes that belong to the CSG OS group will be able to access the executable area.

Furthermore, the *configuration* section of the WAS ND7 installation is trickier to configure since certain areas need to be made available to all application servers such as the properties directory, and similar directories should have the ownership root:<CSG>, a 750 directory permission, and a file permission of either 750 or 640. Be that as it may, there are other directories that should be available only to a specific BSG OS group and no one else. Among some of the directories that would need to be configured for specific BSG access are those under the installedApps directory; specifically the directories under:

<WAS_Profile_Directory>/installedApps/<Cell_Name>/

which are the root of each of the enterprise applications expanded EARs. For each of those enterprise application directories, the ownership should be root:<BSG>, where each BSG must match its corresponding EAR. Moreover, the permission should be 750 for directories and either 750 or 640 for files.

What's more, the top-level directory configuration may need to be accessed by all JVMs. Therefore, the ownership of all of the files under it should be root:<CSG>. Initially, the file and directory permissions should not be changed. However, some JVMs may need write permission and that will be evident from the log files. Adjust permissions accordingly. Alternatively, the permissions for all directories under <WAS_Profile_Directory>/configuration could be set to 770.

As for the third section of the WAS ND7 installation, the log directories, it is not any more difficult than the single execution mode. The only difference is that each of the JVM log directories must be owned by the corresponding root:<BSG> and the directory permission should be 770.

If for some reason you are dealing with a very complex configuration environment and are running out of time to deliver the WAS ND7 infrastructure, there is still another approach. I do not particularly care for it, but it will get you out of the hole while you buy time to engineer a more sound solution. In this solution, I hate to call it that, you will have to create multiple profiles on the same OS host. Each profile will be dedicated to a particular BSA:BSG. Each profile, therefore, would need to be configured as if it were a single execution scenario. Ugly, I know, but will help you achieve the solution required by the business. As the late PG Wodehouse, through his character Bertie Wooster stated it: *We're not put into this world for pleasure alone.*

Safeguarding the network system

The network system or simply networking is an area that has improved security over the years. It is also the area that is exploited the most since through it, potential attackers could gain access to unauthorized resources from a remote location. However, there are a few points that should be highlighted. Whenever possible, do not enable any of the following services/protocols and 'siblings'.

Connectivity services: There are several protocols (communication services) that were popular in the early days of the Internet. Those protocols are very weak in terms of security as they are 'clear text' protocols; that is, user IDs and passwords are transmitted without encryption. Among them, the following are the most common:

- FTP
- telnet
- TFTP
- rlogin

File sharing services: Another area in which production servers may be compromised is that of file sharing. The two most popular are shown next. They are application level protocols that lack the use of encryption, thus open to be a point of exploit of a system.

- nfs
- smb

Many corporations struggle with the decision of what technology to use when a technical solution requires file sharing. In WAS ND7 environments, the use of shared file systems could be avoided. However, if an unavoidable requirement calls for file sharing, there are other more secure alternatives such as AFS and its derivative, DFS.

Miscellaneous services: There are a couple of services/protocols that have been used for multiple purposes. In a WAS ND7 environment, there is no need for them and they should be at least disabled, or better yet uninstalled if they reside on your production systems. The most common of them in this area are the following two:

- rpc-based services
- nis services

For additional network services specific to your platform, the Center for Internet Security website is a great resource (`http://cisecurity.org/`). Specifically, look for the corresponding Security Configuration Benchmark for your specific OS.

In the event that any of the aforementioned services or protocols must be enabled due to a business reason and not a technical solution, the following trick could be used to mask your WAS ND7 network configuration and usage.

In the first place, ensure that the weak service or protocol can be bound to a specific IP address and not use a wildcard '*' configuration. This is the prerequisite for this trick. In addition, create an IP alias (or if you can afford it, add an extra network card to your system). Only one of the IP addresses will be returned by the command `hostname`. Let's call the IP associated with the result of the hostname command, the principal IP. The IP alias, which must resolve to a different host name than that returned by hostname, will be denoted as a secondary IP. Moreover, the procedure is to configure the weak service so it binds to the principal IP. All of the TCP/UDP ports required for the WAS ND7 environment and any of its support technologies running on the same host must be configured to bind to the secondary IP address. In that way, if the weak protocol is discovered, no other services are offered through that IP and it would make it harder to find a relation between the principal and the secondary IPs through the weak protocol.

In order to wrap up this section and the chapter, let's look at two categories of network security possibilities.

Establishing network connections

WAS ND7 is fully dependent on network connectivity, that is, the capability to establish communication channels to both the front-end and the back-end of the infrastructure architecture.

If the native protocol used by the WAS ND7 environment offers the use of encryption, make sure it is enabled. If, on the other hand, the native protocol does not offer encryption but it accepts the use of SSL communication, make sure to use it. This will require the exchange of SSL certificates and update the key stores and trust stores accordingly. Lastly, should the target protocol not offer either data encryption or support for SSL, then it may be necessary to use SSH tunneling between the WAS ND7 host and the remote host, such as a database server.

Using any of the three methods mentioned can help you comply with any business requirement that calls for a secure channel for data transmission.

Communicating from process to process

The second category is that of inter process communication; that is, communication channels between processes executing on the same OS host. In order to secure the channel, the preferred method, if the processes involved are flexible enough, is to configure the processes to bind to the OS host private IP address, 127.0.0.1. Using this port prevents the OS to expose the data communication flowing between the processes.

If one of the processes to be involved in the communication does not allow to bind to the OS host private IP address, then the same approaches that were used between network connections can be used between process-to-process communication.

Again, if there is a business requirement that calls for an encrypted (or secured) transfer of data between processes running in the same OS host, you can deliver that type of solution.

Summary

By this point, you have been introduced to the art of platform hardening. As one works with various WAS ND environments and discovers creative ways of how enterprise applications operate, one will be gaining experience in this somehow obscure art. Specifically, you have been exposed to the following:

- Identifying OS areas that may need further attention to make them more secure.

- Breaking down complex OS to a few main categories that can then be worked on to increase the security of your WAS ND7 environment.

- Techniques to use to your advantage regarding user and service accounts, elimination of kernel modules, and so on.

- One of the major OS areas that have a high relationship with a WAS ND7 installation is that of log files; you've reviewed some organizational techniques as well as appropriate configuration of ownership and permissions.

- The other major OS area, that of network services, is also very closely related to how the WAS ND7 environment operates. This chapter presented techniques to increase the security of the network layer.

11
Security Tuning and Troubleshooting

Writing about WebSphere Application Server security tuning and troubleshooting could take a full chapter. But wait! We have already allotted a chapter ... oh yeah ... let's rephrase that. Each topic could use up at least a full chapter, and perhaps a book. No wonder there are practitioners out there who specialize in said areas. Therefore, in this chapter some of the salient aspects of each area will be covered. Furthermore, at the end, a summary of additional security related tips is provided.

So, in this chapter you will learn about:

- Tuning general security, CSIv2 connectivity and authentication related settings
- Troubleshooting general security configuration and runtime exceptions
- Selecting security tips

Tuning WebSphere security

The generic term "tuning security ... " some say, it's an oxymoron. Why so? Well, in many cases, tightening up security is normally reflected in poor performance. So, if a portion of your environment is performing poorly, it may need a review of the security configuration in order to see if loosening it a bit does not compromise the environment itself. This section briefly describes tuning in three major areas:

- General security configuration
- CSIv2 connectivity
- LDAP and Web authentication

Tuning general security

There are several general security aspects of a WebSphere environment that can be tweaked to either loosening or tightening the security level. This tweaking will have an inversely proportional effect on performance of the WebSphere system. This section briefly describes some of them.

Tightening security using the administrative connector

The administrative connectors are used for communication of various WAS ND7 components such as the deployment manager, node agents, application servers, and the wsadmin interface. On the one hand, by default the connector for communication between WAS ND7 components located in different physical hosts (remote connector) uses the SOAP protocol. On the other hand, the connector for communication between WAS ND7 components located on the same physical host (local connector) by default uses the IPC protocol.

The recommendation for the **remote connector** is to use the RMI connector. The reason for doing this is because the RMI API uses stateful connections, whereas the SOAP protocol uses stateless communication.

This parameter can be changed on the application servers **Administration services** page. In order to get to an **Administration services** page, one needs to follow a breadcrumb similar to: **Servers | Server Types | Application servers | AppServer_ Name | Administration services**. The resulting page should be similar to the one shown in the following screenshot:

It is always a good idea to perform a benchmark to ensure that performance is not being significantly affected.

Disabling security attribute propagation

Security Attribute Propagation (SAP) is the capability of WAS ND7 to carry principal (the caller) static and dynamic security related information from one server to another in the infrastructure according to your configuration. Static security information may include data normally derived from the user registry. On the other hand, dynamic security information may include information about the principal context such as the identity, IP, and so on.

If enterprise applications are not using this type of propagation, it is recommended to disable SAP in order to avoid its overhead. In SAP, security attributes would need to be serialized using Java serialization to carry out the propagation. Therefore, by disabling this feature, the serialization portion of the process is eliminated.

Disabling SAP is accomplished by adding and setting to false the property com.ibm. CSI.disablePropagationCallerList. The location where this property must be defined is at the global security level. Therefore, follow the breadcrumb **Security | Global security | Custom properties**. On that page you need to click the **New** button and you will be presented with a page similar to the one shown in the following screenshot:

Global security > Custom properties > **New**

Specifies an arbitrary name and value pair of data. The name is a property key and the value is a string value that can be used to set internal system configuration properties.

General Properties

\+ Name

| .ibm.CSI.disablePropagationCallerList | ⬅ com.ibm.CSI.disablePropagationCallerList

\+ Value

| true | ⬅

Description

| Prevents SAP |

[Apply] [OK] [Reset] [Cancel]

⬆

For additional information on Security Attributes Propagation, refer to the WAS ND7 Information Center link:

```
http://publib.boulder.ibm.com/infocenter/wasinfo/
v7r0/topic/com.ibm.websphere.nd.doc/info/ae/ae/csec_
secattributeprop.html
```

Using unrestricted Java Cryptographic Extensions

The JCE have been part of the Java SDK since version 1.4.x. JCE, very succinctly, is the Java technology that offers a scheme and realization for encryption, key generation, and key agreement. In addition, the JCE policy files are the portion of the JCE which determines the strength of the encryption to be supported. Furthermore, due to several country laws, the JCE policy files that are included with the WAS ND7 SDK only enables to perform strong and limited cryptography in a way that can be shipped to any country in the world. For instance, the local policy file limits encryption of various methods to the values shown in the following screenshot:

```
permission javax.crypto.CryptoPermission "DES", 64;
permission javax.crypto.CryptoPermission "DESede", *;
permission javax.crypto.CryptoPermission "RC2", 128,
                            "javax.crypto.spec.RC2ParameterSpec", 128;
permission javax.crypto.CryptoPermission "RC4", 128;
permission javax.crypto.CryptoPermission "RC5", 128,
        "javax.crypto.spec.RC5ParameterSpec", *, 12, *;
permission javax.crypto.CryptoPermission "RSA", 2048;
permission javax.crypto.CryptoPermission *, 128;
```

IBM states that there is a possibility that the restricted policy files may affect performance. Therefore, it is strongly advised to use unrestricted encryption JCE policy files.

> **Warning:** Before you replace the JCE policy libraries with their unrestricted version, it is imperative that you check your local laws regarding encryption.

Should you determine that it is permissible to use unrestricted encryption, the following procedure describes how to obtain and install the Unrestricted JCE policy files. In order to download the JAR files, you must be registered with IBM. Use your company's authentication credentials when they are requested.

Obtaining the Unrestricted JCE policy files

The first stage in the procedure is to obtain from IBM the ZIP file `unrestricted.zip` that contains the Unrestricted JCE policy files.

1. Open the URL `https://www14.software.ibm.com/webapp/iwm/web/reg/pick.do?source=jcesdk&lang=en_US`.

   Using a browser open the Unrestricted JCE files page at `https://www14.software.ibm.com/webapp/iwm/web/reg/pick.do?source=jcesdk&lang=en_US`.

2.   Select the libraries for version 1.4.2+.

     From the choices presented, select **Unrestricted JCE Policy files for SDK for all newer versions. Version 1.4.2+**.

3.   Click the **Continue** button.

4.   Log on with your company's credentials.

     Provide or update information as needed. Check the **I agree** check box. Click the **I confirm** button.

5.   Download the `unrestricted.zip` file.

6.   Click the **Download now** link.

Installing the Unrestricted JCE policy files

Once the policy files have been downloaded, you can proceed to install them.

1.   Log on to the host where WAS ND7 is installed.

     Do this procedure for each WAS ND node (Deployment Manager host and node hosts), that is, every host in which you have installed the WAS ND7 binaries for your environment.

2.   Stop all profiles associated with the binary installation.

3.   Extract the JAR files.

     Create a temporary directory and in it un-archive the content of unrestricted. zip. The content is two JAR files: `local_policy.jar` and `US_export_poli-cy.jar`

4.   Change the working directory to security Java directory.

     Change the working directory to `<WAS_BIN_ROOT>/java/jre/lib/secu-rity`

5.   Backup existing policy files.

     Make a copy of the files: `local_policy.jar` and `US_export_policy.jar` located in the `security` directory.

6.   Install the Unrestricted JCE policy files.

     Copy the policy files obtained in the previous subsection into the `security` directory.

7.   Restart the WAS ND7 environment.

Tuning CSIv2 connectivity

In WAS ND7, the **Common Secure Interoperability Version 2 (CSIv2)** is the authentication protocol used by EJBs. CSIv2 is the security protocol that undertakes the stipulations of CORBA security for interoperability authentication, delegation, and entitlements. Therefore, if your environment is using EJBs, the following tasks can improve performance without compromising security.

Using Active Authentication Protocol: Set it only to CSI

When an enterprise WebSphere environment is made up of WebSphere Application nodes of multiple versions, there may be a need for setting the CSIv2 authentication protocol to both, CSI and SAS (Security Authentication Service). However, in WAS ND7, the SAS has been deprecated for communicating with WAS versions 5 and newer. Therefore, it is highly recommended to set the property com.ibm.CSI. protocol to the value csiv2. When the protocol is set to CSI, WebSphere ND7 eliminates, on both server and client, a call to an interceptor for each request that a client makes.

In order to configure the protocol to CSI, the file <Profile_Root_Directory>/ properties/sas.client.props must be edited by adding the line shown below:

```
com.ibm.CSI.protocol=csiv2
```

Other possible values for this property are:

- **ibm**: Should be used if the clients connecting to the WAS ND7 environment are hosted in a WebSphere Application Server version 4 or earlier setup
- **both:** Should be used if the clients that communicate with the WAS ND7 environment are hosted in WebSphere Application Server installations versions 4 or earlier and versions 5 or newer

In order to make the change effective, the complete WAS ND7 cell needs to be restarted.

Enforcing client certificates using SSL

When a WebSphere client sends secure requests to an enterprise application hosted in a WAS ND7 setup, the requestor can be authenticated either using a user ID and password combination or an SSL certificate. Since the channel is already secure, employing ID and password to validate the communication adds overhead to both client and server. Therefore, it is recommended to select the use of client SSL certificates to perform the authentication of client requests.

The configuration to enforce the use of certificates for authentication can be done at the global security level or at the security domain level. The recommendation is to do it at the global security level and use this setting in all security domains.

The procedure to set the use of certificates over user IDs and passwords at the global security level is as follows

1. Log on to the ISC (Deployment Manager).

2. Follow the breadcrumb **Security | Global security | (Authentication | RMI/IIOP security) CSIv2 inbound communications**.

   Refer to the next screenshot to identify the link to the CSIv2 inbound communications.

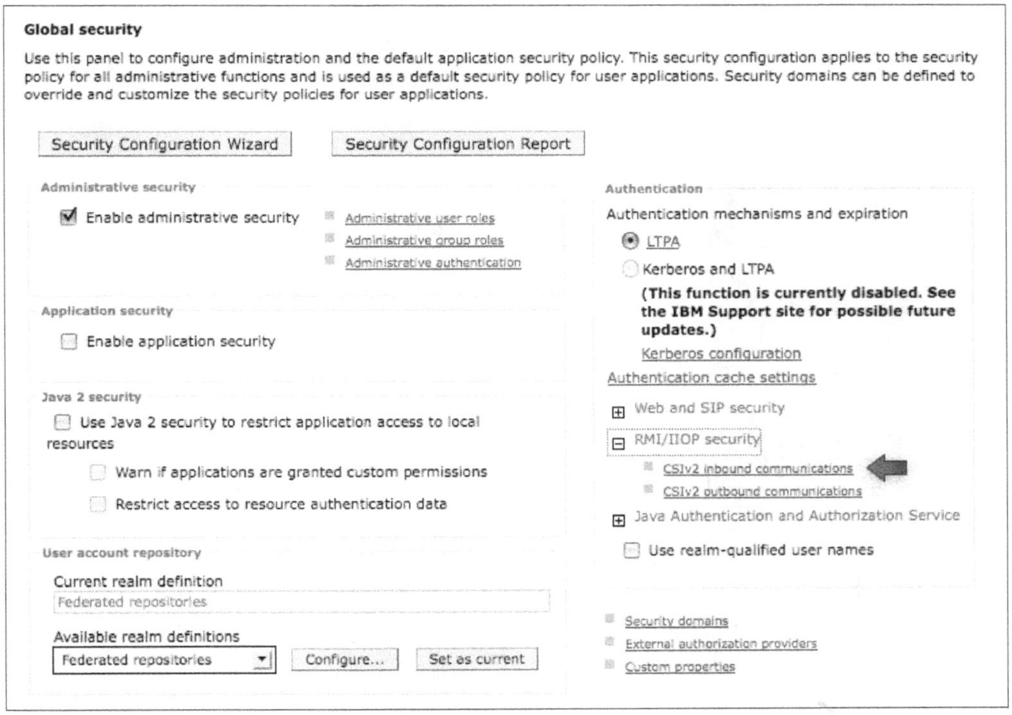

3. Enforce the use of client SSL certificates.

   Set the following parameters as shown in the following screenshot:

   - ° Client certificate authentication (required)
   - ° Transport (SSL-required)
   - ° Message layer authentication (never)

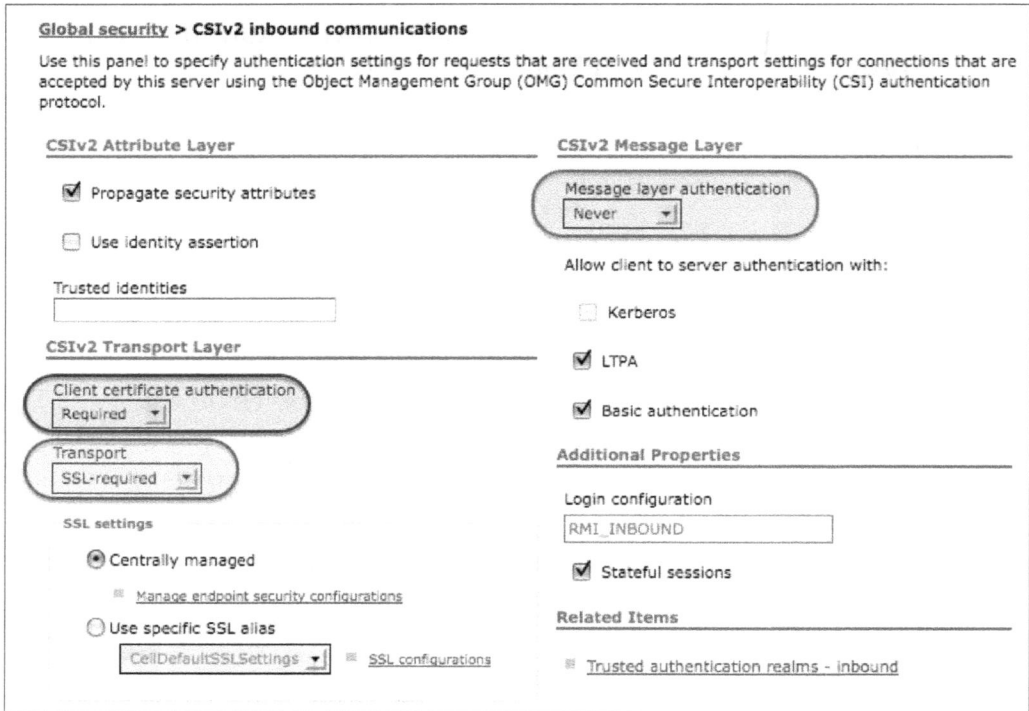

Note, however, that if client fails when the message layer authentication is set to never, it may need to be modified to the supported value.

4. Ensure not to override setting in security domains.

   Finally, for each security domain that is defined in your WAS ND7 environment it is recommended to set the RMI/IIOP security using the global security settings, as shown in the following screenshot:

```
Security Attributes

⊞ Application Security: Customized - Enabled

⊞ Java 2 Security: Customized - Disabled

⊞ User Realm: Customized - defaultWIMFileBasedRealm

⊞ Trust Association: Customized - Disabled

⊞ SPNEGO Web Authentication: Customized - Disabled

⊟ RMI/IIOP Security: Customized

      ⦿ Use global security settings  ⬅
      ○ Customize for this domain
           CSIv2 inbound communications
           CSIv2 outbound communications
```

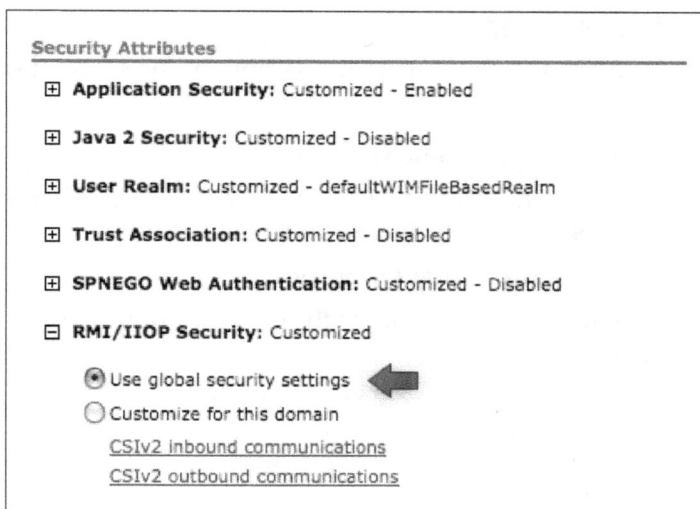

However, if additional customization of the security domain RMI/IIOP is needed, ensure to set the values for CISv2 Transport Layer and CISv2 Message Layer as those shown in step three.

5. Save the changes of configuration. Log off.

Enabling stateful sessions

When using stateful sessions, the first communication between client and server must fully authenticate. If stateful sessions are not enabled, full authentication must take place for each request. Therefore, it is a best practice to enable stateful sessions, in order to eliminate the authentication overhead per request. Under this scenario, the appropriate session credentials are included in each request, which minimizes the authentication process of the requestor.

By default, stateful sessions are enabled, thus this task only calls for ensuring that they have not been modified. On the server side, this setting is available on the CISv2 inbound communications screen in the ISC. On the client side, the setting is found in the `<Profile_Root_Directory>/properties/sas.client.props` file.

Configuring the server

In order to review and change if necessary the setting for the server, use this procedure.

1. Log on to the ISC (Deployment Manager).

2. Follow the breadcrumb **Security | Global security | (Authentication | RMI/IIOP security) CSIv2 inbound communications**.

3. Review the section **Additional Properties**.

    The setting for session should match the configuration shown in the following screenshot:

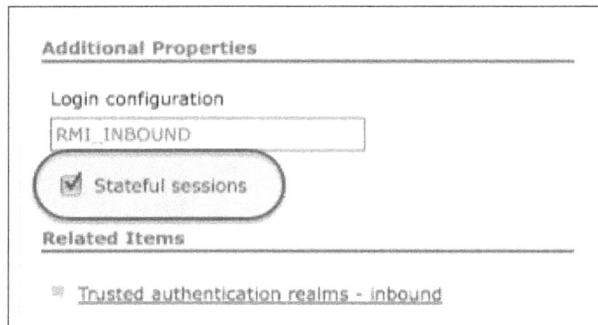

```
Additional Properties

Login configuration
RMI_INBOUND

☑ Stateful sessions

Related Items

▧ Trusted authentication realms - inbound
```

4. Save any changes made.

Configuring the client

The procedure for insuring that the session configuration is set to stateful on the client side is as follows:

```
# ----------------------------------------------------------------------
# CSIv2 Configuration (see InfoCenter for more information on these properties).
#
# This is where you enable SSL client certificate authentication.  Must also
# specify a valid SSL keyStore below with a personal certificate in it.
# ----------------------------------------------------------------------

# Does this client support stateful sessions?
com.ibm.CSI.performStateful=true
```

Tuning user directories and user permissions

In the area of user registry and permissions, there are several opportunities to improve performance by making a few key modifications to the default settings. This section briefly describes some simple changes in the areas of user directories (LDAP) and user authentication.

Configuring LDAP

When selecting an LDAP server as user registry, there is an opportunity to improve performance of the communication between the WAS ND7 administrative constituent and the LDAP server. In order to configure the LDAP, follow the breadcrumb **Security | Global security | (User account repository | Available realm definitions) Standalone LDAP registry** to get to the LDAP configuration. The following screenshot shows the portion of the Global security page that is used to open the LDAP configuration page.

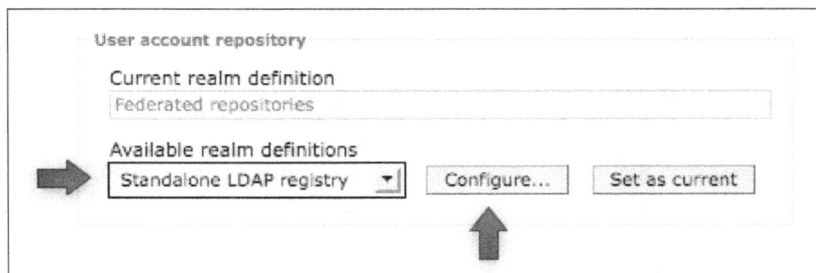

Reusing the established connection

In the normal course of interactions, WAS ND7 security components will communicate with an LDAP server on multiple occasions. For instance, when users log on to enterprise applications hosted in the WAS environment, the security mechanisms will collect the required data from the LDAP server. For this reason, it is important to reduce any overhead that may take place between WAS ND7 and the LDAP server. Selecting to reuse the connection will ensure to keep alive a connection between those entities after the connection has first been established. Selecting this option is particularly important if using the recommended SSL protocol between WAS and LDAP.

Therefore, on the Standalone LDAP registry configuration page ensure that **Reuse connection** is checked as shown in the following screenshot and highlighted by the maroon arrow pointing to the right.

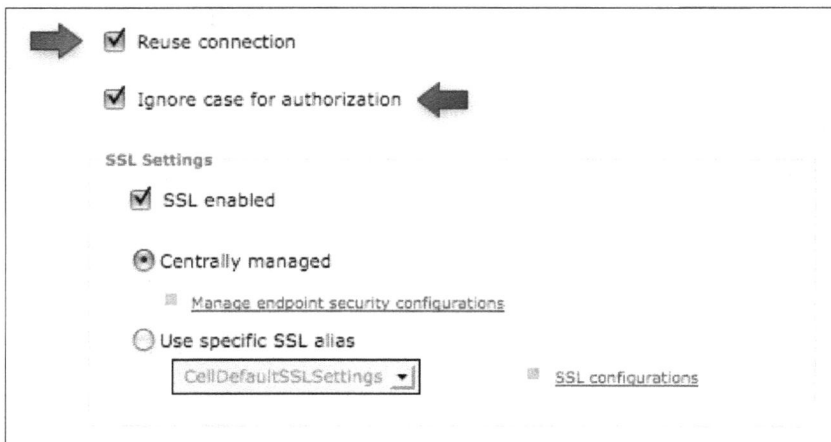

Ignoring case during authorization

Another opportunity to improve performance of the interactions with an LDAP server is to ignore the case when performing LDAP default authentication. Furthermore, this setting may be required by the brand of LDAP server in use in your organization. For instance, one of the popular LDAP brands is the Sun One Directory server (rebranded as Oracle Directory Server) which requires this setting. It is recommended that you verify the requirements of the particular brand of LDAP server used in your environment to help you decide if this setting is supported, in which case it is recommended to do so.

So, in order to turn on ignoring case during LDAP default authentication, refer to the screenshot shown previously. The blue arrow pointing to the left highlights the desired setting, that is, **Ignore case for authorization**.

Tuning user authentication

In the area of user authentication to J2EE applications, there are several opportunities for tuning security parameters that will increase the performance of the user authentication process without compromising security. However, as always is the case when lessening security, care needs to be taken in analyzing a specific organization environment and its needs which are always unique. In this section, two of them, authentication cache timeout, and enabling SSO, will be presented as identified in the following screenshot. The screenshot was taken from the Global Security configuration screen. (Breadcrumb: **Security** | **Global security**.)

Authentication

Authentication mechanisms and expiration

- ⦿ LTPA
- ⦾ Kerberos and LTPA

  (This function is currently disabled. See the IBM Support site for possible future updates.)

  Kerberos configuration

Authentication cache settings ⬅

- ⊟ Web and SIP security
    - General settings
    ➡ Single sign-on (SSO)
    - SPNEGO Web authentication
    - Trust association
    - SIP digest authentication
- ⊞ RMI/IIOP security

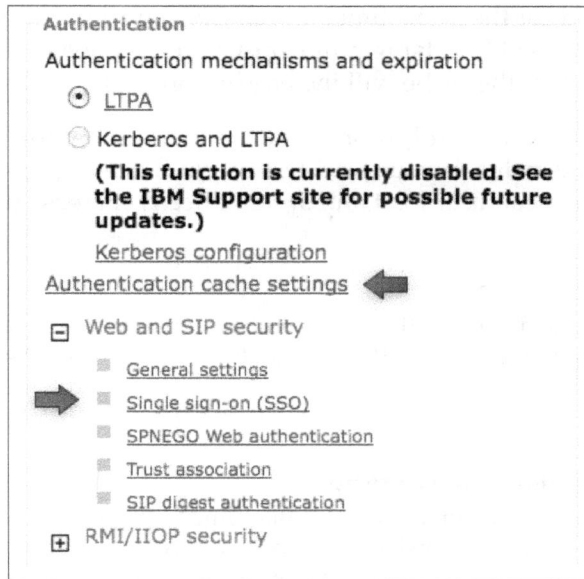

Increasing authentication cache timeout

In WAS ND7 environments, security information related to beans, access to resources and authentication credentials is kept in a cache. In our specific case, operations requiring authentication information first access the authentication cache in order to access the required information. Therefore, the cache helps to accelerate the continuity of such operations. Elements in the authentication cache that have not been accessed for the period indicated by the authentication cache timeout are removed from the cache. When a subsequent operation that requires the authentication information takes place, additional actions to obtain the required information are executed. These actions could involve accessing the user registry and perhaps even a database lookup. Such operations are expensive in terms of performance. Moreover, this type of tuning needs to take into consideration the following facts:

- In a non-secure environment, such as users accessing your application from the Internet, increasing the authentication cache timeout may allow a potential hacker from stealing an authentication token and give the hacker enough time to penetrate the system before the token expiration. This should not be the case if your application is accessed only within your intranet.

- A short period for the timeout will affect performance in that the system would have to request the desired information from back-end and support systems more often.

- A long period for the cache timeout may also affect performance if your application is used by a large number of simultaneous users since the memory used by the cache will increase accordingly.

The default value for the authentication cache timeout is ten minutes. You may wish to consider tuning this value in your load-testing environment by stressing your application under the peak user load and systematically increase the value of the cache timeout.

The selected value of the authentication cache timeout must be less than the value of the LTPA timeout, by default set to 120 minutes.

Infrastructure architecture tip

One thing to keep in mind is that the value for the authentication cache timeout can be modified at the global security level and overridden at the security domain level. What this means is that if your environment has a set of enterprise applications with similar security and user load requirements, they should be placed in the same custom security domain. This simplifies the configuration and maintenance of your environment.

In order to access the global security level authentication cache configuration screen, follow the breadcrumb **Security | Global security | (Authentication [page section]) Authentication cache settings**. On the other hand, to access a security domain authentication cache settings screen follow the breadcrumb **Security | Security domains | Custom_Security_Domain | (Authentication Mechanism Attributes [expand] | Customize for this domain [select] |) Authentication cache settings**, as it is shown in the following screenshot.

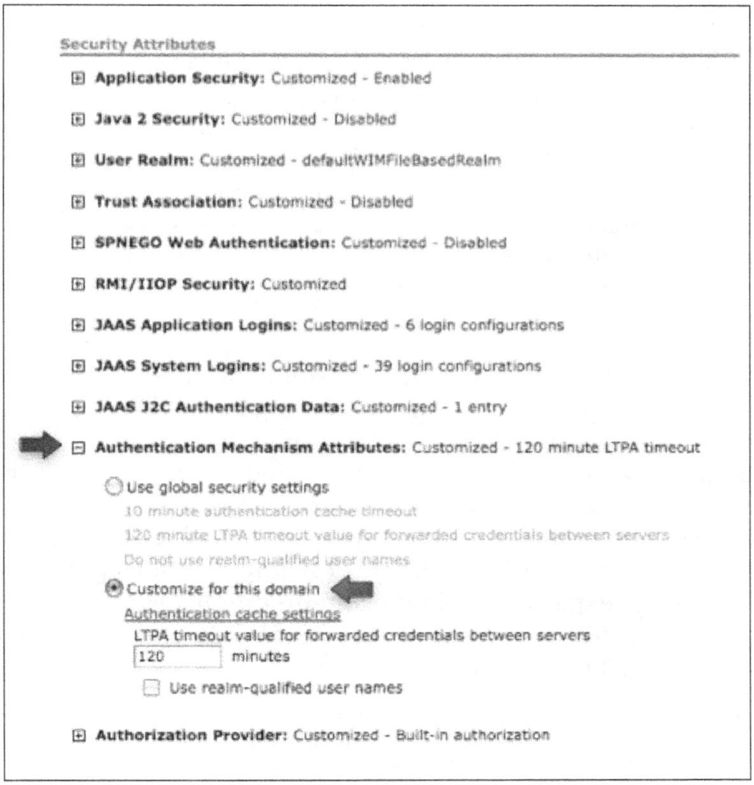

Finally, to tune the value for the timeout, ensure that the Enable authentication cache box is checked. Followed by the desired minutes value, set in the cache timeout field. The following screenshot shows a timeout of 30 minutes.

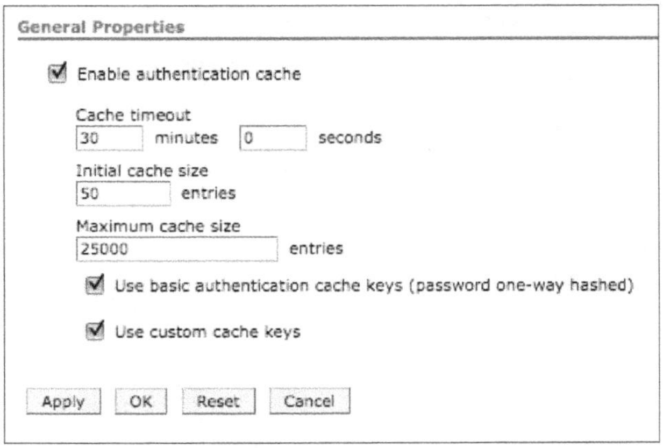

Enabling SSO

It is not uncommon for an organization that employs WebSphere Application Server as its J2EE application server hosting environment to run a number of applications that require the same type of authentication credentials for users. In other words, in order for a user to authenticate against one of such applications, his credentials would be matched to the same user registry that other applications in the environment use. It, therefore, does not make sense on the user experience aspect of the environment to require users to log in individually to each application. On the other side, it is also expensive from the performance point of view, having to re-authenticate users every time they switch applications in the same environment (or domain).

What is needed in this type of setting is the capability to re-use the authentication credentials used in one application when attempting to access another application in the same domain. Therefore, the solution to this scenario is enabling and configuring **Single Sign-On (SSO)**. SSO was covered in detail in *Chapter 2, Securing the Administrative Interface* consequently, if you need a refresher, please refer to the sub-section *Setting the domain name*. In order to access the SSO settings page follow the breadcrumb **Security | Global security | (Authentication [page section] | Web and SIP security [expand] |) Single sign-on (SSO)**. On that page, check the **Enabled** checkbox and enter the name of the SSO domain under the **Domain name** field as shown in the following screenshot:

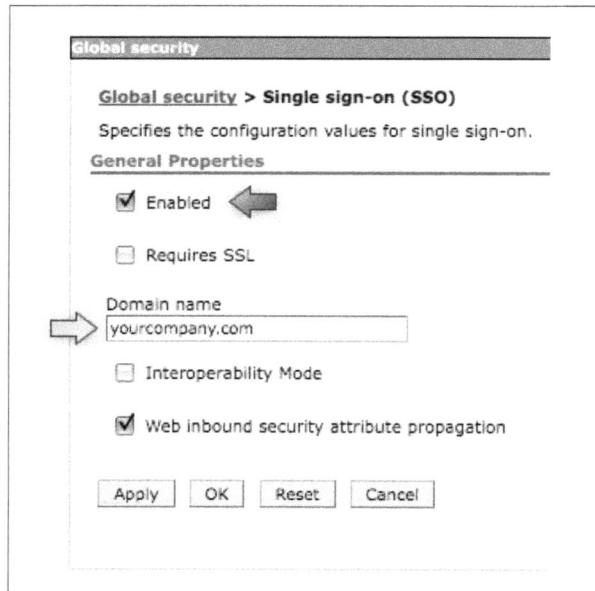

Troubleshooting WebSphere security-related issues

It is not uncommon to run into issues when global security is first enabled in a WebSphere environment. Some of those situations may occur due to performing tasks out of order. Other problematic conditions related to security configuration may take place due to inadvertently omitting one or more steps in a set up process. Moreover, a third category of errors that may happen due to security configuration is caused by using the wrong values to one or more parameters.

This section presents a set of some conditions that may appear in a WebSphere Application Server ND version 7 (WAS ND7) when global security is first enabled. The first subsection covers circumstances that may come about during the configuration phase. Next, a subsection is included that presents circumstances that may happen at runtime.

Troubleshooting general security configuration exceptions

The selected cases in this subsection concerns the situations when various aspects of configuring security are carried out and, as a result, error conditions occur.

Identifying problems with the Deployment Manager—node agent communication blues

Several of the problems that may take place due to either wrong or incomplete security configuration are found in the communication of the administrative layers of the WebSphere environment, i.e., between the deployment manager and the node agent(s).

A couple of the most common situations are shown below, along with recommendations as to how to correct the condition.

Receiving the message HMGR0149E: node agent rejected

The message **HMGR0149E** is the result of the Deployment Manager rejecting a request to connect from the node agent. This type of error and the display of this message normally takes place when security changes in the Deployment Manager were not synchronized with the node in question. An example of log file clip where this message is found can be seen in the following screenshot:

```
[5/19/10 2:14:37:536 EDT] 00000016 DefaultTokenP E   HMGR0149E: An attempt to op
en a connection to core group DefaultCoreGroup has been rejected. The sending pr
ocess has a name of wasmasterCell01\wasmasterNode01\nodeagent and an IP address
of /10.37.129.1. Global security in the local process is Enabled. Global securit
y in the sending process is Enabled. The received token starts with f#@P]E/
^. The exception is com.ibm.websphere.security.auth.WSLoginFailedException: the
realms do not match
        at com.ibm.ws.security.ltpa.LTPAServerObject.realmsMatch(LTPAServerObjec
t.java:2825)
```

One way to fix this problem is by using the **syncNode.sh** command. The syntax for this command is:

```
syncNode.sh dmgr_host [dmgr_port] [-conntype <type>]
            [-stopservers] [-restart] [-quiet] [-nowait]
            [-logfile <filename>] [-replacelog] [-trace]
            [-username <username>] [-password <password>]
            [-localusername <localusername>]
            [-localpassword <localpassword>]
            [-profileName <profile>]
syncNode.sh [-help]
```

Furthermore, a very simple procedure to correct this problem is given next:

1. Stop the affected node agent(s).

2. Execute, on the node agent OS host, the `syncNode.sh` command.

3. Monitor the `SystemOut.log` file for both `dmgr` and `nodeagent` processes.

4. Start the node agent.

For additional information on messages from the high availability manager, refer to the WAS ND7 Information Center link:

http://publib.boulder.ibm.com/infocenter/wasinfo/
v7r0/topic/com.ibm.websphere.messages.doc/com.ibm.
ws.hamanager.nls.HAManagerMessages.html

Receiving the message ADMS0005E: node agent unable to synchronize

This message, **ADMS0005E**, is the result of the node agent attempting to synchronize configuration with the Deployment Manager. It is likely caused when changes in security-related configuration occurred and the node agent were not available. The following screenshot shows an example of this type of error.

```
[6/26/10 22:18:10:459 EDT] 000012ca NodeSync    E    ADMS0005E: The system is u
nable to generate synchronization request: com.ibm.websphere.management.exceptio
n.ConnectorException: ADMC0009E: The system failed to make the SOAP RPC call: in
voke
        at com.ibm.ws.management.connector.soap.SOAPConnectorClient.invokeTempla
teOnce(SOAPConnectorClient.java:825)
```

One way to solve the issue is to shut down the node agent, and then, manually execute the command **syncNode.sh** from the node OS host using a user ID and password that has administrative privileges on the Deployment Manager. For syntax or usage information about this command, kindly refer to the previous example.

In case this action does not solve the problem, follow the next procedure:

1. Stop the node agent(s)
2. Using the ISC, disable global security
3. Restart the Deployment Manager
4. Start the node agent(s)
5. Perform a full synchronization using the ISC
6. Using the ISC, enable global security
7. Synchronize changes with all nodes
8. Stop the node agent(s)
9. Restart the Deployment Manager to activate global security
10. Start the node agent(s)

> For additional information on messages about the administrative synchronization, refer to the WAS ND7 Information Center link:
> http://publib.boulder.ibm.com/infocenter/wasinfo/
> v7r0/topic/com.ibm.websphere.messages.doc/com.ibm.
> ws.management.resources.sync.html

Troubleshooting runtime security exceptions

To close the section on troubleshooting, this subsection presents several cases of error or exception conditions that occur due to security configuration of various WAS ND7 environment components. Such components can be all within WAS or some components could be external, for example, the IHS/WebSphere Plug-in.

Troubleshooting HTTPS communication between WebSphere Plug-in and Application Server

When setting up the HTTPS communication between the WebSphere Plug-in and the WebSphere Application Server there may be instances in which exceptions and errors may occur during the configuration phase. Some of the most common are listed next.

Receiving the message SSL0227E: SSL handshake fails

The message **SSL0227E** is a common one when the main IHS process is attempting to retrieve the SSL certificate indicated by the property **SSLServerCert** located in the `httpd.conf` file. What this message is stating is that the intended SSL certificate cannot be found by its **label** from the key ring indicated by the directive **KeyFile** in the same configuration file.

> If you need a refresher on certificate labels, please review the section *Create self-signed certificate* in *Chapter 4, Front-end Communication Security* that can be found following the breadcrumb: **Securing front-end components communication | Securing the IBM HTTP Server | Create the SSL system components**.

An example of this type of message is shown in the following screenshot. In order to correct this error, there are two possibilities that can be explored.

```
[Sat Jun 12 13:50:36 2010] [notice] IBM_HTTP_Server/7.0.0.7 (Unix) configured --
resuming normal operations
[Sat Jun 12 13:50:36 2010] [notice] Core file limit is 0; core dumps will be not
be written for server crashes
[Sat Jun 12 13:54:31 2010] [crit] [client 10.37.129.1] [81b2f18] [10028] SSL0227
E: SSL Handshake Failed, Specified label could not be found in the key file. [10
.37.129.1:37496 -> 10.37.129.1:8444] [13:54:31.000676025]
[Sat Jun 12 13:54:31 2010] [crit] [client 10.37.129.1] [82ed0f0] [10028] SSL0227
E: SSL Handshake Failed, Specified label could not be found in the key file. [10
.37.129.1:37497 -> 10.37.129.1:8444] [13:54:31.000677097]
```

On the one hand, one needs to insure that the directive **KeyFile** is pointing to the correct key ring file. That is, that the key ring file actually stores the target SSL certificate to be used with this IHS server.

On the other hand, there may be a typographic error in the value of the property **SSLServerCert**. In other words, the label that is mapped to the target SSL certificate was misspelled in the `httpd.conf` file.

In both cases, the command **gsk7capicmd** can be used to list the content of the key ring file. The syntax for listing the contents of a key ring file is:

```
<IHS_ROOT_Directory>/bin/gsk7capicmd -cert -list all -db <Path_To_kdb_
File> -pw <kdb_File_Password>
```

Remember to review Chapter 4 for details on this command.

> For additional information on messages about handshaking issues, refer to the IHS v7 Information Center link:
>
> `http://publib.boulder.ibm.com/infocenter/wasinfo/v7r0/`
> `topic/com.ibm.websphere.ihs.doc/info/ihs/ihs/rihs_`
> `troubhandmsg.html`

Receiving ws_config_parser errors while loading the plug-in configuration file

If the `configParserParse` message of the `ws_config_parser` component is observed in the errors log file of the IBM HTTP Server; the following screenshot is an example of a possible output that may be found in the error logs. There may be a couple of reasons for this type of message to appear in the logs.

One reason for this type of message is that it occurs at the time in which the IHS process is being brought down. The WebSphere Plug-in module is in its cycle to re-parse the `plugin-cfg.xml` file while the IHS process is shutting down, therefore the `ws_config_parser` component does not have enough resources to perform the parsing of the configuration file and throws this message, possibly multiple times in a row. In order to ensure that this is the correct interpretation of the message, it is necessary to find an indicator, such as a 'shutting down' type of message like the one shown in the next screenshot:

The other reason why this message may appear in the logs is very likely that the process owner of the IHS process does not have the correct privileges to read the `plugin-cfg.xml` file. In this case, ensure that the definition for the property **User** in the `httpd.conf` file has enough privileges to read the plug-in configuration file defined for the property `WebSpherePluginConfig` of the `httpd.conf` file.

> For additional information on messages about WebSphere Plug-in issues, refer to the article *Error message definitions for WebSphere Application Server's webserver plugin component.*
>
> http://www-01.ibm.com/support/docview.wss?rs=180&uid=swg21381320

Receiving the message GSK_ERROR_BAD_CERT: No suitable certificate found

The message **GSK_ERROR_BAD_CERT** appears in log files when the WebSphere Plug-in is attempting to establish an SSL connection with the back-end WebSphere Application Server and it does not have a way to validate the SSL certificate sent by the WebSphere Application Server. An example of this type of message is shown in the next screenshot:

```
[Fri Jun 11 23:08:51 2010] 00005568 4174ebb0 - ERROR: lib_stream: openStream: Fa
iled in r_gsk_secure_soc_init: GSK_ERROR_BAD_CERT(gsk rc = 414) PARTNER CERTIFIC
ATE DN=CN=wasmaster.siliceoinc.com,OU=wasmasterCell01,OU=wasmasterCellManager01,
O=IBM,C=US, Serial=11:af:03:25:58:54:bf:50
[Fri Jun 11 23:08:51 2010] 00005568 4174ebb0 - ERROR: ws_common: websphereGetStr
eam: Could not open stream
[Fri Jun 11 23:08:51 2010] 00005568 4174ebb0 - ERROR: ws_common: websphereExecut
e: Failed to create the stream
```

One way to solve this problem is by adding to the IHS key ring file the signer certificate from the WebSphere Application Server. When doing this, care must be taken to correctly select the WebSphere trust store. In other words, the correct scope for your target Application Server needs to be identified so that the appropriate trust store can be accessed.

For instance, if it was desired to obtain the root certificate (aka, signer certificate) used by the Chap7AppServer Application Server, one needs to identify the scope for that application server. Therefore, one should start with the following breadcrumb in the ISC (Deployment Manager console): **Security | SSL certificate and key management | Manage endpoint security configurations**. The following screenshot illustrates a portion of the resulting page:

SSL certificate and key management > **Manage endpoint security configurations**

Displays Secure Sockets Layer (SSL) configurations for selected scopes, such as a cell, node, server, or cluster.

Local Topology

- Inbound
  - wasmasterCell01(CellDefaultSSLSettings)
    - nodes
      - wasmasterCellManager01
      - wasmasterNode01(NodeDefaultSSLSettings)
        - servers
          - Chap7AppServer ⟸
          - Chap6AppServer
          - nodeagent
          - webmaster
          - server1
          - SecureAppServer01

Once the appropriate scope is identified, continue by completing the breadcrumb: **Security | SSL certificate and key management | Manage endpoint security configurations | Chap7AppServer | Key stores and certificates | NodeDefaultTrustStore | Signer certificates**. The following screenshot shows a portion of a resulting page.

SSL certificate and key management > **Manage endpoint security configurations** > **Chap7AppServer** > **Key stores and certificates** > **NodeDefaultTrustStore** > **Signer certificates**

Manages signer certificates in key stores.

Preferences

Add | Delete | Extract | Retrieve from port

Select	Alias	Issued to	Fingerprint (SHA Digest)	Expiration
		You can administer the following resources:		
☐	datapower	OU=Root CA, O="DataPower Technology, Inc.", C=US	A9:BA:A4:B5:BC:26:2F:5D:2A:80:93:CA:BA:F4:31:05:F2:54:14:17	Valid from Jun 11, 2003 to Jun 6, 2023.
☑	root	CN=wasmaster.siliceoinc.com, OU=Root Certificate, OU=wasmasterCell01, OU=wasmasterCellManager01, O=IBM, C=US	C6:E1:EA:F6:20:28:30:08:6E:4A:28:3F:07:51:CB:43:C7:88:C9:D9	Valid from May 17, 2010 to May 13, 2025.

Total 2

You are now in position to extract the Application Server signer SSL certificate. Once this certificate is extracted, it needs to be imported into the IHS key ring file as a root certificate.

> If you need a refresher on certificate labels, please review the sections *Extract the WebSphere CA certificate* and *Add WAS self-signed certificate to the Plug-in* in Chapter 4 that can be found following the breadcrumb: **Securing front-end components communication | Securing the IBM HTTP Server | Configure IHS for SSL.**

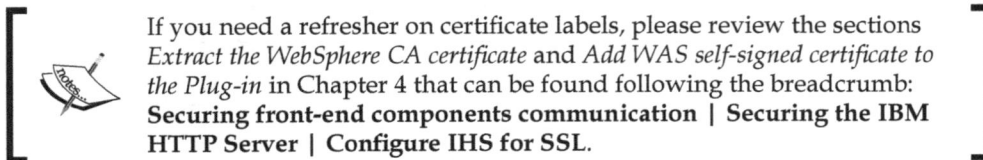

Receiving the message GSK_KEYFILE_IO_ERROR: No access to key file

The message GSK_KEYFILE_IO_ERROR is normally found in log files when the IHS process cannot access the IHS key ring file indicated by the directive **KeyFile**. One common reason is file permissions. It is very likely that the IHS process owner does not have the appropriate access file permissions to the key ring file or one of the parent directories. An example of this type of message is shown in the following screenshot:

```
[Tue Jun 15 23:46:49 2010] 0000170c 4174ebb0 - DETAIL: ws_common: websphereShoul
dHandleRequest: No route found
[Wed Jun 16 00:00:55 2010] 0000176c 4154dbb0 - ERROR: lib_security: logSSLError:
 str_security (gsk error 102):   GSK_KEYFILE_IO_ERROR
[Wed Jun 16 00:00:55 2010] 0000176c 4154dbb0 - ERROR: lib_security: initializeSe
curity: Failed to initialize GSK environment
[Wed Jun 16 00:00:55 2010] 0000176c 4154dbb0 - ERROR: ws_transport: transportIni
tializeSecurity: Failed to initialize security
[Wed Jun 16 00:00:55 2010] 0000176c 4154dbb0 - ERROR: ws_server: serverAddTransp
ort: Failed to initialize security
[Wed Jun 16 00:00:55 2010] 0000176c 4154dbb0 - ERROR: ws_server: serverAddTransp
ort: HTTPS Transport is skipped
```

In order to find out the file permission of the target key ring file, the following shell commands could be used:

```
CurFileOrDir=$(grep ^KeyFile <IHS_Root_directory>/conf/httpd.conf |
awk '{print $2}')
while [[CurFileOrDir " != "" ]]; do
        /bin/ls $LS_OPTIONS -ld $CurFileOrDir;
        CurFileOrDir=${CurFileOrDir%/*};
done
```

The first line extracts the value of the KeyFile directive. The next line is a `while` loop that makes sure that the variable defined in line one is not empty. If it is empty, the loop ends. The first line inside the loop does a full listing of the current file or directory. This type of listing will show the file permissions. The second line in the loop trims off the last portion of the full path, shrinking the path by one, and assigns the resulting value to the initial variable used in the while loop.

> For additional information on messages about GSKit issues, refer to the
> following appendix link:
>
> http://publib.boulder.ibm.com/tividd/td/ITAME/SC32-
> 0845-00/en_US/HTML/am39_error_ref08.htm

Receiving the message WSVR0009E / ORBX0390E: JVM does not start due to org.omg.CORBA. INTERNAL error

The message WSVR0009E is a generic error message that indicates that a start-up error has occurred and the cause is unknown. However, one needs to look for additional information on the same line that can shed a light as to what the possible cause of the problem may be. An example of this type of error is shown in the following screenshot. As additional information, a node agent generated the log file from where this snippet was extracted.

```
[6/27/10 4:26:57:451 EDT] 00000000 ORBRas          E com.ibm.ws.orbimpl.transport.
WSTransport createServerSocket P=214983:O=0:CT ORBX0390E: Cannot create listener
 thread. Exception=[ java.net.BindException: Address already in use - received w
hile attempting to open server socket on port 9101 ].
[6/27/10 4:26:57:453 EDT] 00000000 WsServerImpl    E   WSVR0009E: Error occurred d
uring startup
com.ibm.ws.exception.RuntimeError: org.omg.CORBA.INTERNAL: CREATE_LISTENER_FAILE
D_4  vmcid: 0x49421000  minor code: 56  completed: No
        at com.ibm.ws.runtime.component.ORBImpl.start(ORBImpl.java:427)
```

In the first place, it is observed that following the WSVR0009E message, an indicator is provided, that is, the class org.omg.CORBA.INTERNAL returned an error of the type CREATE_LISTENER_FAILED_4. In addition, before the WSVR0009E message an ORBX0390E message is included in the log file. The additional information this first message provides is that the node agent was unable to bind to one of its ports since that port was already in use by another process.

Therefore, we know that another process, unknown to us up to this point, is using one of the ports required by the node agent. We have the option of either assigning a different port to the node agent or find out what process is currently using the port. Depending on the process, one may wish to disable it or if it is a required process at that point we may have to revisit our port assignment strategy and correct the problem by selecting a different port or a different port range for the node agent.

So, how then can we go about identifying the active process using up the TCP port in question? There is a Unix command that can be used to find out what process is using the conflicting port. It is the **lsof** command (list open files). Without any arguments, the command will list all the open files in the Unix system. (Remember that in Unix any resource—file, Unix pipe, TCP ports, and so on—are taken as files.) There are a few variants for this command, so depending on your flavor of Unix, you may need to tune the syntax given next. In order to find out the process ID of the process currently using the TCP port in question, use the following call for the **lsof** command:

```
lsof -P -i:<PORT>
```

The capital -P indicates to the command not to convert the port numbers into names (that is, names derived from the /etc/services file). The lowercase I flag tells lsof to use its value as an internet address pattern. In our case, we only wish to indicate the port portion of it, which is signified by the preceding colon. A sample output is shown in the following screenshot.

```
user@host conf ][
user@host conf ][ sudo lsof -P -i:9402
COMMAND   PID USER   FD    TYPE DEVICE SIZE NODE NAME
java     7581 root  291u  IPv6  30678      TCP *:9402 (LISTEN)
user@host conf ][
```

The screenshot shows, in this example, that a java process with the PID of 7581 is using the TCP port 9402. With this information, using the commands **ps** and **grep**, one can find out what exact java process we are dealing with (or any other process for that matter).

In versions of WAS ND earlier than 7.0.0.7 the node agent restart action would launch two node agents and this type of error would appear in the logs. If you currently are experiencing this error, make sure that your WAS ND version is at least 7.0.0.7.

> For additional information on messages in the series **WSVR00**, refer to the following information center link
>
> http://publib.boulder.ibm.com/infocenter/wasinfo/
> v7r0/topic/com.ibm.websphere.messages.doc/com.ibm.
> ws.runtime.runtime.html

Concluding WebSphere security-related tips

We conclude this chapter by listing several tips that may come in handy as you continue your work with WAS ND7, specifically in the area of security. The tips included next are in no particular order.

Using wildcards in virtual hosts: never do it!

Many times, when creating virtual hosts, some administrators do not bother to fine-tune the default configuration for the hostname, focusing only on the port. When one clicks on the **New** button to create a new alias, one sees a page that contains the portion shown in the following screenshot:

Never use the alias pair: host name "*"; port "80".

Ensuring best practice: set tracing from wide to specific search pattern

When turning on tracing in order to troubleshoot any type of problem in general and security in particular, one needs to keep in mind that WebSphere logging and tracing parses the trace string from left to right. This means that the trace string element at the left can be overridden by another element at its right. It is, therefore, best to place the more generic trace strings at the beginning and the most specific trace strings at the end.

For instance, if your WAS ND7 environment was using a custom J2C principal mapping module (cf. http://www14.software.ibm.com/webapp/wsbroker/redir ect?version=compass&product=was-nd-dist&topic=rsec_pluginj2c) and you wanted to trace its activity to solve an issue, a possible helpful trace string would be similar to the one shown in the following screenshot.

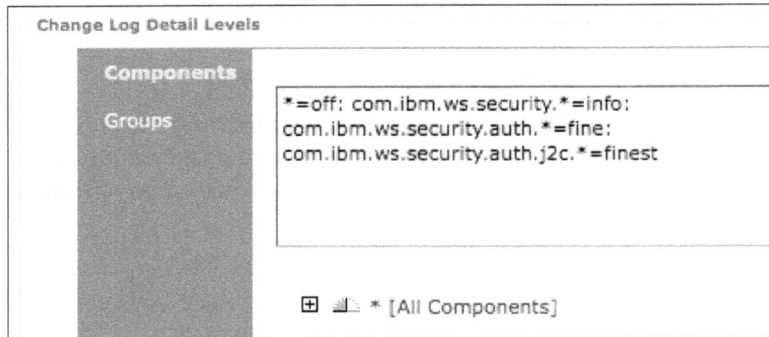

Using a TAI such as SiteMinder: remove existing interceptors

WAS ND7 includes two trust association interceptors by default. If you are planning to use a different type such as the CA/Netegrity SiteMinder TAI it is highly recommended that you remove those configurations from the interceptors list. The following screenshot shows the default interceptors included.

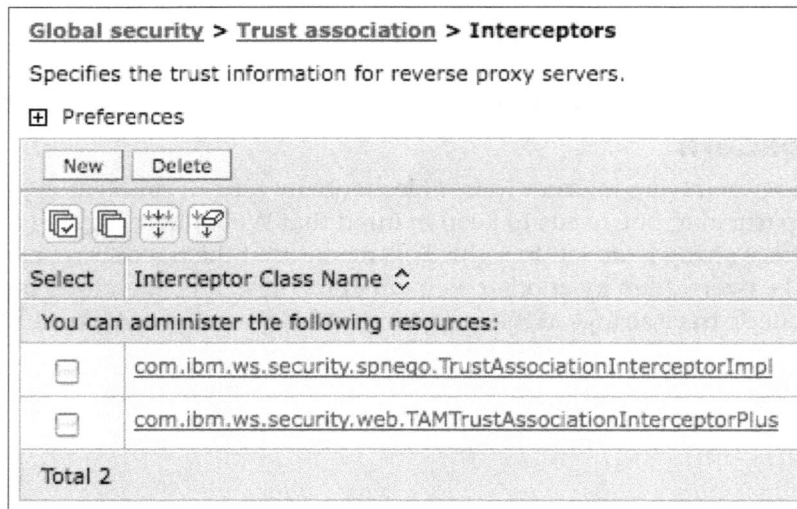

One of the many reasons for removing the interceptors shown in the screenshot above is that when TAI is enabled and a different interceptor is configured and enabled, the SystemOut.log file would include exception messages thrown by these interceptor classes.

Once you have removed these class name definitions you can proceed to create a new definition for SiteMinder. An example of class name that could be used (for version 6.x) is **com.netegrity.siteminder.websphere.auth.SmTrustAssociationInterceptor**. Refer to *Chapter 8, Secure Enterprise Infrastructure Architecture*], under the section "Fine-tuning authorization at the WAS level", for configuration steps.

Summary

With the objective to round up this volume, this chapter ended the journey of learning about WebSphere Application Server Network Deployment version 7 security by offering two important aspects of the field: the aspects of security tuning and security troubleshooting. In a similar way to the subject of security in which sometimes it is left as an afterthought in a WAS ND7 installation, security tuning is often left as an afterthought in WAS ND7 security. Therefore this chapter presented key elements that will help you in improving performance by lessening some aspects of security without compromising the environment. Consequently, after completing this chapter you would have learned about:

- Tuning general security aspects of WAS ND7 such as the administrative connector, security attribute propagation, and Java Cryptographic Extensions
- Tuning particular aspects of the active authentication protocol, improving the use of SSL, and stateful sessions
- Tuning user-related aspects such as LDAP and authentication
- Troubleshooting general security configuration exceptions and security runtime exceptions
- Selecting simple to apply but powerful security related tips

It is the hope of Packt Publishing and the author that this volume not only has proven to provide you essential security information about the WebSphere Application Network Deployment version 7 product but that it its style has been engaging and fun to follow. So long for now and we wish you all the best in your IT career. Until we meet again.

Index

Symbols

45
/configuration 218
[(x)inetd] services (IS) 238

A

Access Manager (AM) 200
ACLs
  application roles based 105
  user registry groups based 103
administrative connectors 252
administrative roles 38, 39
administrative security 75
administrative security configuration steps
  performing 35
administrative security domain
  about 49
  global security domain clone, creating 50, 51
  security domain creating, scripting used 51, 52
  security domains based on global security, configuring 50
administrative security section
  locating 34
administrator view, web application 100
ADMS0005E 269
AIX 240
application groups, enterprise application architecture 102
application JDBC Provider
  creating 63
application memberships, enterprise application architecture

about 103
ACLs, application roles based 105
ACLs, user registry groups based 103
application server
  Enterprise Application (EA), in relation to 188, 189
  protecting 76
application server, security
  about 62
  access to resources, configuring 69, 70
  application JDBC Provider, creating 63
  application server, creating 63
  DataSource, creating 63
  enterprise application, deploying 70
  enterprise application, securing 70, 71
  global security configuring, to use federated user registry 64
  prerequisites 63
  secured enterprise application, accessing 72
  security domain, creating 64
  testing 70
  user authentication, configuring 64
  virtual host, creating 63
  WebSphere environment, assumptions 62
application users, enterprise application architecture 103
authentication 171
authentication cache timeout 263-265
authorization
  fine-tuning, at HTTP server level 199, 200
  fine-tuning, at WAS level 208

B

BOOTSTRAP_ADDRESS port 222, 223
borders 236

both 256
branded infrastructure elements 10
built-in CA certificates
  included in keystores, listing 89, 90
Business Service Account/Group (BSA/G)
  245

C

CA root certificates 84
centralized access manager 200
Certificate Authorities (CA) 84
CommonAssets.war 101
Common Secure Interoperability Version 2.
    See CSIv2 connectivity, WebSphere
    security
Common Service Group (CSG) 245
Connection/Driver Manager method 181
CSIv2 connectivity, WebSphere security
  active authentication protocol 256
  client, configuring 260
  server, configuring 260
  SSL 256, 258, 259
  stateful sessions 259
  tuning 256

D

database channel
  securing, choices 182
data encryption 171
DataSource
  creating 63
Data Source/JDBC provider 181
declarative security 130
DeclareRoles 130
Demilitarized Zone (DMZ) 80
DenyAll 130
deployment descriptor, enterprise applica-
    tion project
  creating 143
deployment manager
  logging in 38
  restarting 37
developer view, web application 100
directory access 240
DWP context root
  defining 144

DWP deployment descriptor
  creating 144
dynamic web application projects, J2EE web
    application
  creating 108, 110
dynamic web applications, J2EE web ap-
    plication
  application role, assigning 114, 115
  application roles, creating 113, 114
  client-server transport type, defining 116
  configuring 110
  content, adding to 118
  initial servlet code, analysis 123
  Java code, completing 123
  Java components, adding 121-123
  log in information, adding 112
  protected URI patterns and methods, defin-
    ing 112
  servlet code, completing 124, 125
  web files, adding 118-120
  web modules, mapping to employees_vh
    116
  welcome files, defining 110-112
dynamic web modules, enterprise applica-
    tion architecture 106

E

EAR version, enterprise application project
    142
EJB application security
  concepts 130
  declarative security 130
  programmatic security 131
EJB interfaces, EJB project
  creating 161
EJB project
  assumptions 139, 140
  creating 161
  prerequisites 140, 141
EJB project, creating
  class definition 163
  declarative security 165
  EJB, creating 163
  EJB interfaces, creating 161
  import statements 163
  initial project, creating 161

WebSphere horizontal cluster, dual-zone architecture used 79, 80, 81
WebSphere horizontal cluster, multi-zone architecture used 81, 82

G

general security, WebSphere security
about 252
administrative connectors 252
Java Cryptographic Extensions (JCE) 254
Security Attribute Propagation (SAP) 253
unrestricted JCE policy files, installing 255
unrestricted JCE policy files, restricting 254
generic infrastructure components 10, 11
getCallerPrincipal() 131
getParamAndForward objective 159
getRemoteUser() 100
global security
about 75
configuring, to use federated user registry 64
GSK_ERROR_BAD_CERT 272, 273
GSK_KEYFILE_IO_ERROR 274

H

HMGR0149E 268
HP/UX 240
hronly.war 101
httpd.conf
modifications 92, 93
HTTP server level
fine-tuning authorization 199, 200

I

ibm 256
IBM HTTP Server
securing 86
IBM HTTP Server, configuring for SSL
about 92
httpd.conf, modifications 92
SSL configuration, validation 95
WAS self-signed certificate, adding to plug-in 94, 95
WebSphere CA certificate, extracting 93, 94
IBM HTTP Server (IHS) web server compo-

nent 10
IBM HTTP Server, securing
about 86
configuring, for SSL 92
environment assumptions 86, 87
SSL configuration, prerequisites 87
SSL system components, creating 88
IHS SSL keystore
creating 88, 89
implementation phase 137-139
infrastructure architecture view 11
initial project, EJB project
creating 161
installLocation 218
internet protocol suite
and LDAP 171, 172
IPortalSelectorSessionBean interface, EJB project
creating 161, 162
isCallerInRole 131

J

J2EE web application, securing
about 106
dynamic web application projects, creating 108-110
dynamic web applications, configuring 110
dynamic web applications, content adding to 118
enterprise application, deploying 126, 127
enterprise application, packaging 125
enterprise application project, creating 106, 108
enterprise applications, configuring 116
enterprise application, testing 127, 128
Java Cryptographic Extension (JCE) Policy files 175
Java Cryptographic Extensions (JCE)
about 254
unrestricted JCE policy files, installing 255
unrestricted JCE policy files, obtaining 254
Java Database Connectivity (JDBC)
about 180
API 181
application layer 181
Connection/Driver Manager method 181

[PACKT] PUBLISHING enterprise
professional expertise distilled

Thank you for buying
IBM WebSphere Application Server v7.0 Security

About Packt Publishing

Packt, pronounced 'packed', published its first book "Mastering phpMyAdmin for Effective MySQL Management" in April 2004 and subsequently continued to specialize in publishing highly focused books on specific technologies and solutions.

Our books and publications share the experiences of your fellow IT professionals in adapting and customizing today's systems, applications, and frameworks. Our solution based books give you the knowledge and power to customize the software and technologies you're using to get the job done. Packt books are more specific and less general than the IT books you have seen in the past. Our unique business model allows us to bring you more focused information, giving you more of what you need to know, and less of what you don't.

Packt is a modern, yet unique publishing company, which focuses on producing quality, cutting-edge books for communities of developers, administrators, and newbies alike. For more information, please visit our website: www.packtpub.com.

About Packt Enterprise

In 2010, Packt launched two new brands, Packt Enterprise and Packt Open Source, in order to continue its focus on specialization. This book is part of the Packt Enterprise brand, home to books published on enterprise software – software created by major vendors, including (but not limited to) IBM, Microsoft and Oracle, often for use in other corporations. Its titles will offer information relevant to a range of users of this software, including administrators, developers, architects, and end users.

Writing for Packt

We welcome all inquiries from people who are interested in authoring. Book proposals should be sent to author@packtpub.com. If your book idea is still at an early stage and you would like to discuss it first before writing a formal book proposal, contact us; one of our commissioning editors will get in touch with you.

We're not just looking for published authors; if you have strong technical skills but no writing experience, our experienced editors can help you develop a writing career, or simply get some additional reward for your expertise.

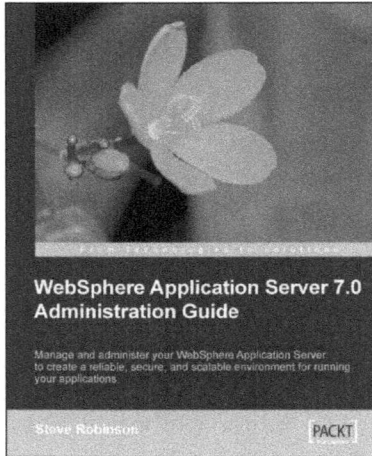

WebSphere Application Server 7.0 Administration Guide

ISBN: 978-1-847197-20-7   Paperback: 344 pages

Manage and administer your WebSphere Application Server to create a reliable, secure, and scalable environment for running your applications

1. Create a reliable, secure, and flexible environment to build and run WebSphere applications efficiently

2. Learn WebSphere security, performance tuning, and debugging concepts with a variety of real-life examples

3. No previous knowledge of WebSphere is expected

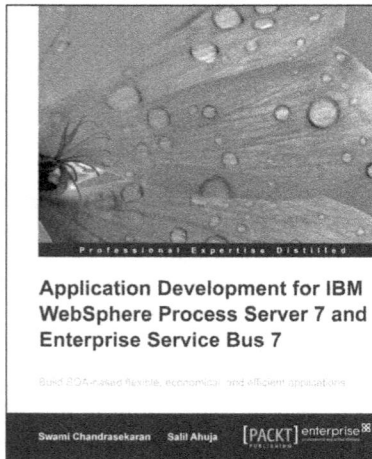

Application Development for IBM WebSphere Process Server 7 and Enterprise Service Bus 7

ISBN: 978-1-847198-28-0   Paperback: 548 pages

Build SOA-based flexible, economical, and efficient applications

1. Develop SOA applications using the WebSphere Process Server (WPS) and WebSphere Enterprise Service Bus (WESB)

2. Analyze business requirements and rationalize your thoughts to see if an SOA approach is appropriate for your project

3. Quickly build an SOA-based Order Management application by using some fundamental concepts and functions of WPS and WESB

Please check **www.PacktPub.com** for information on our titles

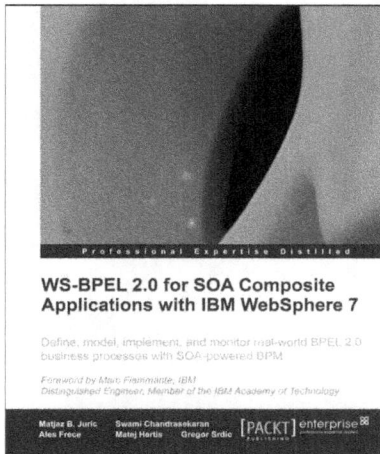

WS-BPEL 2.0 for SOA Composite Applications with IBM WebSphere 7

ISBN: 978-1-849680-46-2   Paperback: 644 pages

Define, model, implement, and monitor real-world BPEL 2.0 business processes with SOA-powered BPM

1. Develop BPEL and SOA composite solutions with IBM's WebSphere SOA platform

2. Automate business processes with WS-BPEL 2.0 and develop SOA composite applications efficiently

3. Detailed explanation of advanced topics, such as security, transactions, human workflow, dynamic processes, fault handling, and more — enabling you to work smarter

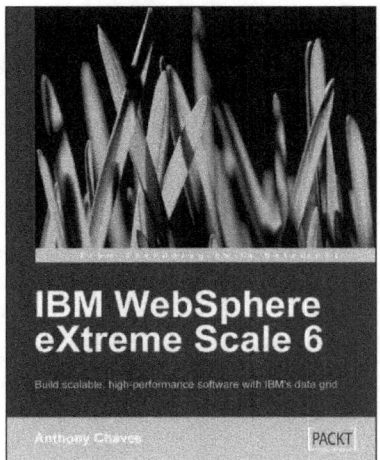

IBM WebSphere eXtreme Scale 6

ISBN: 978-1-847197-44-3   Paperback: 292 pages

Build scalable, high-performance software with IBM's data grid

1. Get hands-on experience with eXtreme Scale APIs, and understand the different approaches to using data grids

2. Introduction to new design patterns for both eXtreme Scale and data grids in general

3. Tutorial-style guide through the major data grid features and libraries

4. Start working with a data grid through code samples and clear walkthroughs

www.ingramcontent.com/pod-product-compliance
Lightning Source LLC
Chambersburg PA
CBHW082108220326
41598CB00066BA/5782